Written and compiled by:
James McCarraher

Foreword by:
John McCoy

Introduction by:
Mo Foster & Mike Hurst

SARUM PUBLISHING

ANGEL AIR

Printed by Antony Rowe Limited of Bumper's Farm Industrial Estate, Chippenham, Wiltshire SN14 6LH.

A catalogue record for this book is available from the British Library.

DEDICATION

This book is respectfully dedicated to all the musicians, singers and song writers who have had their work released through

over the last ten glorious years.

SHIRLEY AND PETER PURNELL'S DEDICATION

We dedicate this book to Nicola and Robert, with love.

We would like to acknowledge and thank all the photographers and artists whose photos and artwork we have used in this book. All have been drawn from relevant Angel Air releases and all credits known are contained in the booklets accompanying those releases with the exception of page 14 and page 272 – David Rose, page 20 – courtesy of L and K Graphics and page 22 – courtesy of Brian Wakerley.

CONTENTS

FOREWORD BY JOHN MCCOY

I met Peter Purnell through my old Gillan compadre, drummer Mick Underwood. We have both had more than our unfair share of dodgy managers, rip-off record labels, and a whole load of unbelievable ways of not getting paid, not least our success with Gillan which ended abruptly in December 1982 leaving us and the rest of the band still unpaid for publishing of our songs, record royalties from the many worldwide hits, merchandising and in fact every which way and then some. So understandably, when Mick passed on Peter's name as a 'straight' guy in the business, I was to say the least, dubious.

A series of polite phone calls between me and Peter followed and as our relationship grew so did the idea of an independent record label where every one of the musicians involved got paid, accounted to, and was involved in the release of their work. The concept was raising a few eyebrows along with mumblings of "it'll never work" etc., etc.

Well, it did work and ten years down the line Angel Air is one of the few independent record companies with a worldwide reputation for honesty and quality in all areas of the business. The first release was a compilation of two of my own albums, for which I had never been accounted for in previous releases during the Eighties. It didn't set the world alight, but sold enough for us to plan future releases having learnt from some of the mistakes we made.

Peter began getting interested in the Gillan situation and slowly began fighting our corner. I had miles of Gillan tapes, mostly outtakes and alternative mixes of the hit albums which I had co-produced and we decided to take the step of releasing these as *The Gillan Tapes* series. That first *Gillan Tapes* release opened the floodgates for artistes in similar situations as me and soon the Angel Air roster was to boast releases by Atomic Rooster, Ian Gillan Band, Mott The Hoople, Saxon, etc., etc. all who had suffered from the music 'biz'. And of course a lot of the releases were of albums and bands that were, because of various problems, true rarities.

Now all these years later, I've signed all my publishing to Peter's CeeDee Music U.K publishing company, and he is my business manager. I only wish we'd met twenty years earlier!

I'm currently working on my Anthology double CD for an anniversary release, and Peter is as interested and caring as he was with that very first release. How many record companies can you ring and speak to the Managing Director on a daily basis? I can't count the number of musicians that have said to me, after becoming involved with Angel Air, "I've never had a royalty statement before!"

I should also mention Peter's wife Shirley who has worked tirelessly trying to keep up with her workaholic husband!

I am now proud of what Angel Air has achieved, and the part I've played in that success, and also proud to call Peter Purnell a true friend.

I love music, but hate the music business and what it does to the people who provide the music - Angel Air.....as things should be.....long may it continue!

John McCoy - October 2006

John McCoy – surviving 'the biz'.

INTRODUCTION BY MO FOSTER

I first met guitarist Ray Fenwick on a recording session at Lansdowne Studios in 1971. We kept in touch and then, about five years ago, he told me about this amazing new record label that he'd stumbled upon called Angel Air.

The label was the brainchild of a chap called Peter Purnell – a successful businessman, Rolling Stones fan, and Magistrate one day a week - who had a passion for music, and who started work every day at the very unmusicianly hour of 7 a.m.

Now, my first record contract many years ago offered the band 3% of 90% of retail – split between five musicians! Peter was offering a 50/50 split on any profits. This had to be good, and I have since placed over twenty albums with the label ("Get the tapes out of the boxes!" as Ray would say to me).

Another plus is that the CDs were always available – especially with the advent of online sales - unlike some major record companies who deleted their product almost immediately after release.

And being able to release music that I had recorded maybe forty years ago gave me the comforting feeling that my career had bookends. There were no loose threads.

Peter had a great vision. Long may Angel Air prosper.

Mo Foster – Author of *17 Watts* (Sanctuary Publishing).
October 2006 www.mofoster.com

Mo in his studio.

INTRODUCTION BY MIKE HURST

I first heard about about Angel Air when my old friend and guitarist, Ray Fenwick, suggested I get in touch with them and see if they were interested in putting out some of my old material.

Thus, I met Peter and Shirley Purnell in the unlikely surroundings of Station Road West, Stowmarket, the music capital of Suffolk!

Peter seemed so unassuming and non-record industry, but I quickly discovered he was that most elusive of 1990s music characters; a real record man. He is also extremely 'hands on', going with a gut instinct and respecting old timers like me and many others. You know, when you have been in the business for over 40 years, to get the chance to have your old, scratchy, sometimes 'iffy' tracks finally released in CD format, not to mention DVDs, you are thrilled. Peter makes that possible, and has done for the past ten years. Angel Air has released six albums of mine and countless others by greater luminaries than myself.

We owe a lot to Peter and Shirley, and let's face it, how many record companies can you phone, to be told that the boss, in this case Peter, is in court for the day? No, not as the accused, but as a JP!

Peter and Angel Air are straight-up with their artists and will be around I assure you in another ten years. Thanks Peter and Shirley, for all your work and love for the music.

Mike Hurst – and all your other artists.
March 2007

VOICES IN THE WILDERNESS

Any musician or song writer who has dared to dip a toe into the murky waters of the music business will be able to share a story or two about the 'sharks' that can be found swimming just beneath the surface.

These individuals can take many forms - record companies (both corporate and independent), managers, promoters et al. True, it would be wholly incorrect for me to tar everyone with the same brush, but the industry has a track record of attracting a particular sort of character.

In the Fifties, it was common for certain record companies to pay their leading stars with a brand new car. Whilst on the surface, this appears to be generosity personified, it in fact meant that the bulk of the royalties went into the back pockets of the label.

In the Sixties and Seventies, musicians were often given disproportionately low 'wages' or 'subs', whilst the bulk of the income was siphoned off elsewhere, often to off-shore accounts. When Jimi Hendrix died, he had just £8 in his current account, yet he was one of the biggest artists on both sides of the Atlantic.

The story of Les McKeown's disappearing wealth has also been well publicised. In the Seventies, The Bay City Rollers were the biggest 'boy band' in the U.K. However, he (and the other band members) was left in financial straits.

The Sex Pistols were left in a similar position, with ex-band members having to convince the Inland Revenue that they had genuinely made absolutely nothing during their meteoric rise to fame (a situation which has now been rectified).

Noel Redding reportedly spent decades chasing monies from his days with Jimi Hendrix, with little tangible result. Anyone visiting his home could testify to the mountains of court papers stacked around the house. It was all so very unfair.

Bands hungry for success were invited to sign the most ludicrous record deals. It was common in the mid-Seventies for an act to be typically offered the deal Mo mentioned in the Introduction, or more generously, a whole 3% of 90% of retail sales at home and half that figure abroad – i.e. 2 ½% in all overseas territories. This regularly meant that any advances given by a record label to record an album amounted to the full sum due to a band. Consequently, however many units of vinyl that were shifted (and labels were often prone to being economical with the truth with figures), it never made enough for a band to collect any further royalty cheques. On the contrary, they regularly found themselves in hock to the label, perpetually working to clear a virtually impossible 'debt'. Add to this equation the high tax burden at the time, and there was little prospect of amassing any wealth, unless you were a powerful act with enough clout and resources to employ a team of lawyers to make sense of the mess.

Thankfully, such abysmal deals are now a thing of the past and wouldn't get past 'The Unfair Contract Terms Act 1977' which came into force in March 1978.

Aside from the record labels, artistes would often fall victim to shrewd managers who were able to take advantage of the naivety, willingness and good nature of their charges. The very people employed to protect their interests, often turned out to be as unscrupulous as some of the record companies. Graham Oliver (Oliver Dawson Saxon) explains the predicament many young musicians found themselves in:-

"Many of us had started out working in the local factories. We had an employee mentality and at the end of the week collected our pay packets. Moving into the music business, our managers kept us on a wage, paying a certain amount each week. They were aware of that worker mentality and took advantage. Yet we were THEIR employers. We should have been paying THEM and not the other way around."

Georg Kajanus, original front man with Sailor, sums up the business beautifully when recalling a fateful meeting with manager Steve O'Rourke:

"Steve just sat there peering at me through his inordinately thick spectacles. Somewhere behind those impenetrable lenses, you could see something resembling a pair of eyes with tiny angry pupils and you just KNEW that he was wondering, 'Why aren't you guys a better return on my investment?'"

Georg Kajanus (December 2006).

The horror stories that have emerged from within the business are endless and those musicians that have sought a haven with Angel Air have amassed their fair share.

Nick Simper of progressive rock band Warhorse recalls the early Seventies and the shoddy treatment they received, declaring that, "We were ripped off something rotten!"

Consortium, another band from the same era, completed a lengthy tour of Scotland without ever being paid.

The Look were focussing on a potentially rosy future. They called around to their independent label for a progress report only to find the offices boarded up with no forwarding address.

John Du Cann (Atomic Rooster, Andromeda, The Attack, Five Day Week Straw People) takes a very philosophical approach to the whole subject of royalties:-

"I am owed so much money by dodgy managers etc. But you can't dwell on it because it eats you up otherwise."

14

John Du Cann (right) with his band, Andromeda.

Often, frustrations were compounded by careless managers despatching bands on ludicrous tours resulting in a mismatch of band and audience, or chasing results in territories where there was little chance of acceptance or success.

Those artistes, who faced the aforementioned difficulties during their heyday, now face a very different kind of problem in their twilight years…one that they could never possibly have anticipated without the aid of a crystal ball or a good psychic!

With the dawning of the compact disc in the Eighties, the re-issues market became the life blood of the music industry. Its very survival depended upon this lucrative market.

Music was licensed around the globe, often without the artiste seeing a penny in royalties (or having any hope of catching up with some very obscure licensees). Albums were regularly re-released with sub-standard recording quality, pitiful artwork and hopeless liner notes (if any), leaving the fans short changed and the reputation of the artiste damaged. To compound the problem, musicians often failed to realise their work had been re-issued until stumbling across it themselves or being notified by loyal fans.

15

Steve Ellis quietly despairs at the number of fake Love Affair albums that have flooded the market, released without any thought or care on cut price budget labels, and more to the point, without his knowledge or consent.

Nick Simper recoils in horror at the first Warhorse re-issues:-

"The covers and packaging were Mickey Mouse in quality. They were awful. It felt dreadful. Producing an album for me is like producing a work of art or a sculpture."

In many respects, Nick has put his finger on the pulse with this statement. To many record companies, their signings were a means to an end…no more than a commodity. In the words of Dave Robinson, boss of Stiff Records, the musicians themselves were just 'pebbles on a beach'.

There was little acknowledgement of the lonely musician practising for days on end mastering his chosen instrument, spending hour after hour composing new material and then rehearsing incessantly with band mates in church halls the length and breadth of the country…and that is BEFORE playing a live show or setting foot in a recording studio. For all their graft, sweat and talent, the artiste rarely had a voice.

So who are Angel Air and what makes them so different?

ANGEL AIR

"Ugh! So YOU are this Peter Purnell who pays money to musicians!"

Angel Air is a record label run by a former 'Captain of Industry', Peter Purnell and his wife, Shirley.

In 1982, Peter found himself at the helm of a major company with an annual turnover of £100m and responsibility for 1,300 staff. The company seemed to specialise in a multitude of different areas including Fuel Distribution, Bacon Processing, Fertilizer Production, and Animal Feed Production to Countryside Stores.

In early 1994, the Board launched a £2m rights issue to its 7,000 shareholders which had not been fully subscribed. Peter took this as a vote of no confidence by the shareholders and left at the end April 1994.

Reflecting on his time with the company, Peter was acutely aware that he had missed out on a lot of the joys of family life. He would often be out of the house before his children were awake and would return long after they were in bed.

Peter decided that whatever he did next, he wanted to be in the driving seat, with control over his time and destiny. The thrill of leading a corporate giant had long gone.

Peter and his wife Shirley had for some time relished the thought of working together. Shirley, a Legal Executive, had a range of skills that complemented Peter's background in business. Indeed, with the children (Nicola and Robert) well into their teens, the timing seemed right for a few life-changing decisions.

In July 1994, Peter and Shirley took the decision to become involved with the music business. Initially, they specialised in offering Mail Order Compact Discs, Music Publishing and Artist Management Services. Within a year, they had obtained over one hundred clients on a 'no win no fee' basis for their Management Services and spent time chasing unpaid royalties and sub-licensing products. Their client base included ex members of Deep Purple, Gillan, Procol Harum and The Spencer Davis Group to name but a few.

They then started work for liquidators of music businesses offering specialist advice on both copyrights and the sale of assets.

Initially, the business was run from the family home near Stowmarket in Suffolk, Eastern England. Stowmarket is a sleepy market town with a population of just ten thousand people. By 1996, they had re-located to their own offices in central Stowmarket, which became the hub of the empire.

At about this time, John McCoy (a client of Peter and Shirley) suggested that they launch a record label and release product themselves. With their imagination fired, Peter and Shirley seized the opportunity with both hands and set up Angel Air Records.

Why Angel Air?

Peter explains:-

"I wanted a label that began with the letter 'A' so we could be first in all the listings. After much deliberation, Shirley came up with the name, 'Angel Air' (the ethereal name for music) and designed a logo. When I attend a music industry event like Midem, it still gives me a buzz to see that Angel Air is listed at the top of all the other labels attending."

The next task was to come up with a series of prefixes for the releases. Peter continues:-

"Thought was given to the matrix/catalogue number sequence for releases and to keep things personal, Audio albums had the 'SJP' prefix (Shirley Joy Purnell) Singles 'RAJP' prefix (Robert Antony James Purnell) and the DVD's when introduced under the Angel Air Waves imprint in 2003 'NJP' prefix (Nicola Jayne Purnell)."

Right from the conception of Angel Air, Peter and Shirley wanted to establish a 'heritage label' to tap into their considerable source of artistes and contacts. They were inspired by such labels as Rhino and Sundazed – both then independent labels where attention to detail was paramount.

Prior to setting up Angel Air, Peter and Shirley had repeatedly found that the majority of their client base had been kept at arms length by the very companies that had grown fat on their talent and success. Consequently, musicians and artistes regularly felt that they had no voice and often were considered no more than a nuisance.

They vowed that Angel Air would be different. From the start, they adopted a business model that the company would share its profits with artistes by title on the understanding that if a title failed to make a profit, then all loss would be carried by the Company.

Furthermore, the artistes would 'have a voice' over their releases and maintain the rights to their product. A 'pay and be paid' philosophy would prevail with all accounts and suppliers being paid on time without any bank borrowings. Today, Angel Air has a well deserved reputation as an 'honest broker' which matters greatly to Peter and Shirley. However, despite this approach, they still came up against a number of obstacles in the early days, as Peter explains:-

"The hardest thing initially was to persuade our international distributors that we would be releasing in excess of twenty titles per year - year in year out thus generating incremental sales. Apart from France and Spain in most cases we are still trading today with the same partners by territory as we started with all those years ago."

The first release was John McCoy's 1983 solo album, *Think Hard*. With added bonus tracks, the album was renamed *Think Hard. Again*.

Thus, on 17th February 1997, the expanded album was launched on to an unsuspecting world, with the prefix 'SJPCD001'.

Shirley and Peter Purnell.

The sleeve (and every release since then) has been designed by Lawrence from L & K Graphics:-

"I had the pleasure of meeting Peter in 1996 when we worked on *Think Hard. Again.* Our working relationship has always been from a distance because we are based in the north east. However, Peter has always been a pleasure to work for and we have had some great laughs on the phone when we 'conflab' about different projects. I enjoy working with the different artistes, awaiting their response to the proofs. It is gratifying when they are pleased with the end results. The most rewarding aspect of the work is when you walk into a music store and see your artwork on the shelves. It is a proud feeling."

When putting a release together, Peter is generally looking for a certain design that reflects the Angel Air brand:-

"From that first release, the look of our products has been very, very important, even down to the shrink wrapped jewel case. Some of our releases have twenty four page CD booklets and the journalists we work with have created some real labours of love based upon their own research and interviews with the artists involved. In addition we often are supplied with an artist's personal scrapbook/photo album to plunder for unseen photos and memorabilia. I feel very humble sometimes with the trust they place in us. We work as closely as possible with the artist at all time and have a reputation for honesty and fairness. Our logo is 'Where The Artist Has A Voice' and that is totally correct as far as our releases are concerned. Without the artist and the customer to purchase the product there is nothing. Business is fun and we share the fun with our artists and keep the day to day operational issues to ourselves. They in turn give us their trust and involvement. Together we are a winning team!"

Lawrence from L & K Graphics.

The next Angel Air release came from another existing client, Ray Fenwick. Ray had an album he had recorded with Mick Grabham as Guitar Orchestra in 1972. Peter met Ray and Mick at a Hotel in Huntingdon, Cambridgeshire and Angel Air's second release was in the bag: *Guitar Orchestra* under prefix SJPCD002.

Ray and Mick had taken some wonderful photos of all of their guitars together and the photograph used on the front cover of this release was also used in the early years on promotional shots and catalogues to summarise what Angel Air was all about - good credible music.

Both Ray Fenwick and John McCoy have continued to be involved with Angel Air through they years, providing exemplary material for release or re-release. Peter is eternally grateful for their input into the label:-

"Without their foresight and commitment, Angel Air would not be where it is today."

Angel Air's reputation began to spread by word of mouth and artistes were soon making contact, offering material for release. For every new contact, came another existing friend, colleague or acquaintance that enabled the label to grow month on month, year on year.

In 2003, the DVD imprint 'Angel Air Waves' was created and a number of artists were filmed in concert to stockpile footage for DVD releases. These included performances by The Troggs, The Spencer Davis Group, Culture Club, Go West, Chicken Shack, The Korgis and Racing Cars. In addition, existing footage was licensed to create further DVD programmes. Despite their status as a 'heritage label', Angel Air has pulled off two top thirty hits in the U.K DVD chart with Culture Club and Go West.

Angel Air's commissioned shows are filmed by Brian Wakerley of Pixelgrafix:

"I was first introduced to Angel Air in 2001 whilst discussing production of a DVD for Oliver Dawson Saxon. They mentioned that their record company (Angel Air) was interested in getting involved with the production of live DVDs.

The timing was perfect and it wasn't long before I had produced DVDs of The Spencer Davis Group, The Troggs and Love Affair. Up to this point I hadn't even met Director Peter Purnell face to face but we had already developed a trust and understanding which is all too rare in this business.

We were all feeling our way a bit at that time, getting better at the productions each time but one morning I received a call from Peter asking if I would like to produce a five camera shoot for Culture Club at the Royal Albert Hall! It was all a bit daunting to say the least, but I appreciated his faith in me and we put together a good programme (not without its problems but worth it in the end). It was during the follow up interviews that I met Peter in person and he was exactly as I expected him to be, straight-forward, honest and a true gentleman.

Each gig we have done since has had its difficulties as well as rewards, but Angel Air's good reputation in the industry remains as solid as ever. Every artist I have come across has only good things to say about Peter Purnell and Angel Air which is a rarity these days in any walk of life but particularly in the turbulent Record Industry."

Since its formation, Angel Air has released around 230 albums, 3 singles and 26 DVD titles. The mission and philosophy of the business remains unchanged with artistes sharing equally in profits on each release.

Brian Wakerley.

Although predominantly a family affair, throughout the existence of Angel Air, Peter and Shirley have been assisted by Christine Couldridge, who plays a significant role in the day to day processing of the business. She has never been afraid to turn her hand to anything and without her, the business would have struggled to run so smoothly.

Like it or not, Peter is known by some of his artistes as 'St. Peter'. At the time of going to print, he was probably unaware of this. John Du Cann was initially convinced that Peter was too good to be true:-
"I thought he must belong to some religious cult or something. He is so black and white when it comes to business, he is straight down the line."
Similar views have been expressed in other quarters, including rumblings from the Mott The Hoople camp, as Dale 'Buffin' Griffin recalls with some amusement:-

"He is so honest and straightforward. Unheard of in the music 'biz'! Overend Watts and I thought him to be deeply religious when we first encountered him."
(Peter is now manager of Mott The Hoople and their ongoing affairs!)

Christine Couldridge.

However, Overend is acutely aware that Peter is no pushover and has seen him at work:-

"Peter is an easy-going, modest, polite, quietly spoken chap - except, that is, to people that attempt to cross him! Peter has a vast and complete knowledge of the music business and how everything works within it. This, combined with an extensive knowledge and understanding of the law, adds up to a terrifying combination for individuals or companies who may underestimate him or try to pull the wool over his eyes. If he thinks that something is unfair or that somebody has been conning one of his artistes he will take on ANYBODY - regardless of their stature within the music 'biz'. He is fearless and undaunted by even the biggest companies - I've seen him do it and succeed. He is like a charming bulldog but once he's sunk his teeth in he just does not let go 'til he gets what he wants! Of course, it's all done quietly, politely and within the law but very, very, very persistently. He will not take 'NO' for an answer!"

Clearly this 'Robin Hood' approach has failed to endear him to everyone.

Peter often attends music fairs and conventions. At one such event he was introduced to a German record company executive, who was clearly unimpressed by the Englishman. Looking Peter up and down with utter disdain, he spat out the words:

"Ugh! So YOU are this Peter Purnell who pays money to musicians!"

The impact Angel Air has had on the lives of many of its artistes cannot be under-estimated. Graham Oliver had a string of albums released by Angel Air, including a solo outing (a tribute to his favourite guitar heroes). Prior to this, despite an astonishingly long and successful career with Saxon, he had never received a single solitary royalty cheque. Peter, who was aware of the significance of the moment, delivered Graham's first cheque in person. He was thrilled:-

"It is fair to say that Peter threw me a lifeline and gave me a voice when there would have been silence."

James Warren, who has two bands signed to Angel Air (The Korgis and Stackridge) has never looked back since the day Val Jennings (Demon Records) introduced him to Peter:

"Peter has proven to be the most pleasant and trustworthy person in the music business. He is consistent and has proven to be the best thing to happen to us in the last ten years."

And in the words of the celebrated guitarist, Ray Fenwick:-

"Angel Air is up there with the best!"

Now you have read about the label, here are the artistes that have made it such a glorious success.

Enjoy!

James McCarraher
www.mccarraher.co.uk

AFFINITY

"The re-issue of Affinity's only album (originally released in 1970) with an added eight bonus tracks is pure class. Jazzy progressive psychedelic rock propelled along by Lynton Naiff's exquisite Hammond playing and Linda Hoyle's stunning vocal work. Solid from start to finish and I can't recommend it enough…Absolutely one of Angel Air's very best releases."

Colin Bryce, *Mohair Sweets* (April 2002)

Affinity were formed in 1968 out of the remnants of a band called Ice (also covered in this book) and its predecessor, the U.S. Jazz Trio.

The line-up consisted of Lynton Naiff (keyboards), Grant Serpell (drums), Mo Foster (bass and double bass) and Mike Jopp (guitar) who were joined by vocalist Linda Hoyle (vocals), a beautiful singer with a belting voice.

Named after an Oscar Peterson album, the group became a familiar site on the jazz circuit and regulars at Ronnie Scotts'. However, the four musicians had to resort to being an instrumental quartet for a brief period when Linda was under doctor's orders to rest her voice.

In 1970, Affinity released their one and only album, titled *Affinity*. It was only the third release from the now famous Vertigo label and is highly collectable.

The band crammed a great number of adventures into their short history, punctuated by mishaps on the road, unreliable vans and lost takings from a European tour. Mo's must-read book, *17 Watts* expands upon these exciting times.

Linda left the band in 1971 and released a solo album (also featured in the Angel Air catalogue). Her replacement, Vivienne McAulifee, recorded a number of demos with her new colleagues before Affinity called it a day and split.

It is down to Mo's reluctance to throw anything out ("Get the tapes out of the boxes Mo!"), that Affinity now have no less than four albums out on Angel Air with a fifth to follow. As well as the original debut album, three other collections have now been released, lifted from live performances and lost demos, many of which (along with other releases on the label) have remarkably been recorded on the most antiquated of sound systems, which Mo still owns.

Reviews for *Affinity*: SJPCD111

"Their sound is great, organ led progressive rock reminiscent of their Vertigo label mates Cressida but occasionally they do venture into jazz rock territory with the use of a brass section á la Chicago, Colosseum, etc., etc.

In Linda Hoyle they had a wonderful vocalist with a powerful rock voice in the Maggie Bell mould and the combination of her vocals and the heavy organ driven sound makes for inspirational listening…"
Steve Ward, *Wondrous Stories* (April 2002)

"Vertigo label collectors unite! Of the bonus material, both sides of the band's super-rare single ('Eli's Coming/United States of Mind') are included (yep, the Three Dog Night song) plus two songs cut for radio sessions and four more intended, in some form, for the band's second album. Of course, that never happened, and *Affinity* remains this remarkable band's sole legacy. It's one to be proud of."
Jo Ann Greene, *Goldmine* (August 2002)

Reviews for *Live Instrumentals*: SJPCD 135

"…nine live tracks recorded in January 1969 and at a time when long sideburns and frizzy hair was de rigueur … and that was just the women! Some jazz standards expertly played and some less familiar, this is a real archive find. The music hasn't dated at all.

There is some great 'Hammonding' from Lynton Naiff and authoritative jazz rock chops from Mike Jopp. Bassist Mo Foster went on to work with Ray Fenwick in Fancy and Jeff Beck amongst others but this release captures a superb band and drips with cool soul jazz that is perhaps now best enjoyed with a good wine, and with the headphones on. Nice."
James Rutherford, *www.getreadytorock.com!* (January 2003)

"While Mo Foster and Grant Serpell kept the rhythm section nailed it allowed guitarist Mike Jopp and organist Lynton Naiff to play melody or go off at a tangent as they desired. Given how powerful their arrangements are it is probably of little surprise to see that Lynton later worked as an arranger for bands as diverse as Gene, Gay Dad and Page/Plant!

Good sleeve notes and photos as well as powerful jazz make this an album that can easily be enjoyed. "

Feedback, (February 2003)

Reviews for *1971-1972*: SJPCD145

"For those who have enjoyed the previous reissues, this collection is closer in spirit to the debut album and actually consists of outtakes and demos for a projected album that never was because the band eventually imploded in 1972. The sound quality is superb, though. Bassist Mo Foster, guitarist Mike Jopp and drummer Grant Serpell went on to join Michael d'Abo on tour and Foster had a subsequent career rubbing shoulders with some of the biggest industry names as a much-in-demand 'sessioner'.

All credit to Peter Purnell at Angel Air, and to Mo Foster, for unearthing this superb archive piece. Investigate, if only for that growling Hammond on a medley of Hendrix and Miles Davis and the sublime instrumental 'Sarah's Wardrobe'! Wonderful stuff."

David Randall, *www.getreadytorock.com* (August 2003)

"What is immediately apparent is that not only is this an enjoyable outing throughout, but that Vivienne had a wonderful voice...If you enjoy good strong songs and great female singing then this is worth seeking out."

Feedback (Nov 2003)

Review for *Origins 65 – 67*: SJPCD167

"...You can almost smell the hairy armpits and unshaven faces of the assembled multitude - and that's not just the band we're talking about. It is a superb period piece and adds a little to our understanding of this rather special jazz-rock band who strangely might achieve more notoriety now - thanks to Angel Air's practised archaeology - than in the good old days.

The genial Mo Foster (to whom we have to thank for helping dust off the tape reels) plays drums whilst a bonus track features the great Linda Hoyle on vocals in 1980. Hey, Mo, how about a reunion?"

David Randall, *www.getreadytorock.com* (May 2004)

With thanks to Mo Foster and Grant Serpell.

See also Mo Foster, Linda Hoyle, Ice, Sailor, Mike d'Abo, RMS, Ray Russell, Survivors, Fancy, RJ Wagsmith Band.

www.mofoster.com

AFTER THE FIRE

"This live set from 2004 features the band on good form, with a welcoming and enthusiastic audience present. The instrumental intro, with some outstanding work from pianist Peter Banks, is an excellent start. Influences from ELP and Genesis mix in well with the straight Seventies rock/pop sound. A couple of bonus tracks and some informative sleeve notes make for the usual Angel Air top notch packaging. Will certainly please fans and a good place to start for others too." ***

www.getreadytorock.com (April 2006)

After The Fire (ATF) were originally formed in late 1971 or early 1972. The band featured Peter Banks (keyboards), John Leach (bass) and Ian Adamson (drums). They lasted for only a short while and disbanded in December 1972. Peter went on to play keyboards for Narnia, playing alongside John Russell.

In 1974, Peter Banks and Ian Leach reformed ATF. They were joined by Andy Piercy on guitar and the following year, Robin Childs joined on bass. The band focused on writing Christian stories and the sound was very progressive in style.

In 1977 Robin left, to be replaced by Nick Battle. Co-founder Ian also departed, to be replaced by the eloquently named Ivor Twidell. Later that year Nick also decided to leave but was persuaded to stay to record the album *Signs of Change.*

Signs of Change (1978) was released on a private label out of frustration with the Christian record labels who insisted that bands pay up front. It was an outstanding album for the time, a little dated now, but well thought through and brilliantly executed. The album had a limited release of just four thousand copies, which now change hands for about £30 per copy.

ATF moved on musically and with Nick's departure, Andy Piercy switched to bass with John Russell joining as the new guitarist.

In 1978, ATF signed for CBS. The album, *Laser Love* followed in October 1979 and charted at number 57 in the U.K album chart. It also spawned two minor hit singles, 'One Rule For You' (number 40) and 'Laser Love' (number 62).

During the preceding August, ATF played The Greenbelt Festival and made a lasting impression on their audience.

Ivor Twidell left the band that October after ill health led to his collapse on stage. He was replaced by Nick Brotherwood.

The band started work on a new album, *80-f,* which was disappointingly turned down by CBS. Brotherwood soon left the band and was replaced by Peter King.

80-f was eventually re-recorded and released. The album sold well in Germany (reached number 69 in the U.K.) and was supported by two singles.

In 1981, ATF toured extensively abroad and raised their profile at home with appearances on *The Old Grey Whistle Test* and *Rock Goes To College.*

The third and final album of the era was *Batteries Not Included*, which registered on the lower reaches of the album chart.

ATF toured America extensively at this time, supporting ELO, Queen and Van Halen over a colossal fifty-one dates.

During the tour, CBS heard the demo tracks ATF had recorded for a new album and requested they return to England and start recording. The band, funded by promoter Harvey Goldsmith, decided to stay on the tour and the tracks remained unreleased.

However, ATF were in serious debt. They were still not making enough money and lacked the public backing they required to carry on. Indeed, the band had been divided about which way to go creatively - along the route of rock or pop.

In December 1982, ATF played their final concert, at the Dominion Theatre in London. It was reportedly one of their best shows.

The final single release by the band was a song by Austrian singer Falco called 'Der Kommissar', which became a massive worldwide hit. Peaking at number 5 on the U.S. Billboard chart, it was fair and just reward for years of hard graft.

CBS asked the band to reform but to no avail.

In 1999, ATF reformed for John Russell's Birthday. It was a one-off gig and another five years passed before he re-launched the band with Peter Banks, following their appearance at an ATF convention. John and Peter were joined by John's son Matthew on drums, Keith Smith on lead vocals and long time fan, Ian Niblo on bass. Sadly, Peter King had died in 1987.

Twenty-five years after their last appearance at the Greenbelt Festival, ATF were invited back. The show was a historical landmark in the history of the band and was filmed. The performance has been released by Angel Air as a CD and DVD. The DVD is supported with a radio interview, unplugged session and slide show.

But the story doesn't end there. In late 2006, Angel Air pulled together a stack of unreleased tracks from the Eighties under the title *AT2F*, thus completing the ATF story. The line-up from this era featured Peter Banks, Andy Piercy, John Russell and Peter King.

Review for *Live At Greenbelt*: SJPCD218

"Now, more than 20 years later, we get to watch this reunion show, which goes through both periods of the band. Well filmed and recorded, the band performs quite well and the crowd is very enthusiastic. It's the kind of show that makes you say to yourself 'I would have liked to have been there'. Well *Live At Greenbelt* makes it almost possible. Recommended indeed!"
Proggnosis (April 2006)

"This is a band having fun in front of a crowd doing the same...The 'plus' part of the CD are two acoustic versions of 'Forged From Faith' and 'Who's Gonna Love You'."
Feedback (July 2006)

With thanks to Joe Hazzard and AFT. www.afterthefire.co.uk.

JAN AKKERMAN

"Jan should need no introduction as the guitarist from Dutch band Focus. He is also one of the most innovative guitarists, ever...His first album in four years, this is experimental, showcasing his guitar skills and range of guitars over some dance rhythms...the guitar work is excellent. Some very interesting tunes and rhythms come from Jan's hands. An interesting and largely enjoyable set. But when Jan goes back and makes a hard rock album I will be very very happy." ***1/2

Joe Geesin, _www.getreadytotock.com_ (June 2004)

Jan Akkerman was born in Amsterdam, just after the end of the Second World War. He picked up a guitar for the first time at the age of five, resisting his mother's wish for him to play the accordion.

As a teenager, Jan played in a number of local bands including The Friendship Sextet, The Shaking Hearts and Johnny And His Cellar Rockers.

Jan recorded his first solo album _Talent for Sale_ in 1968 and undertook session work for a string of Dutch bands and artists, much of which was uncredited.

In 1969, he was asked to play the guitar parts (and Hammond organ) on an album by vocalist Kazimierz (Kaz) Lux. Together with Pierre van der Linden on drums and André Reynen on bass, this recording project turned into the band Brain Box. Their one and only album is now regarded as a Dutch progressive rock classic.

Between 1970 and 1976, Jan was a member of the world renowned band Focus who achieved notable success and scored a top five U.K hit single with 'Sylvia'. During this time, Jan also released two solo albums.

During rehearsals for the Focus U.K tour in 1976, Jan left the band. Two further solo albums followed.

31

In 1978, Jan played with his band at the Montreux Jazz Festival. The performance was released as a live album. He also made a classical album, *Aranjuez*. While many people accused Jan of losing his way, the truth had more to do with his versatility and urge to explore different styles and genres of music. Each new album took him off in a different direction, which often embraced elements of jazz.

In 1981, Jan relocated to Denmark and Sweden, where he performed live with musicians Jon Hiseman (ex-Colosseum) and Stefan Nilsson. In October of the same year, Jan made a bet with a Dutch disc jockey that he could create an entire album within twenty four hours. Jan won the bet! The end result was *Oil In The Family*.

Returning to Holland, he released *Can't Stand Noise* in 1983.

In 1985, Jan contributed to the new Focus album and recorded one of his most celebrated solo efforts, *From The Basement*. He followed this up with *Heartware*, representing one of the most critically acclaimed periods in his career to date.

After a hiatus, in May 1990 Jan released his comeback album, *The Noise of Art*.

However, on a cold August night in 1992, he was involved in a serious car accident. His subsequent recovery took about six months.

The following February, he returned to the stage, undertaking a successful theatre tour. He also released a new album, *Puccini's Café*, which was followed by *Blues Hearts* in 1994. Both albums charted in The Netherlands and featured elements of jazz, funk and blues.

Following a tour in 1995, Jan paid homage to his old band with the album *Focus In Time* - harking back to the renaissance style of the original Focus material.

A double-live set followed and Jan set foot on a British stage for the first time in nearly two decades, playing Euro Wirral Guitar Festival.

In 1999, Jan signed for Roadrunner Records and recorded *Passion*, for which he was nominated for an Edison Award in early 2000. He also undertook his first full U.K tour since 1977 and since then has visited every year.

His latest album *C.U.* has received a release through Angel Air and at the time of going to print, remains the latest release in his long and prolific career.

Reviews for *C.U*: SJPCD180

"...Here is an album that shows why Jan does not have to rekindle music from the past...Jan eases the guitar on top of some funky mixes and dance beats too that makes great listening...an instrumental pleasure... "
Martin Hudson, *Classic Rock Society* (August 2004)

"...If you're inclined to kick back and get all 'loungey', jazzy, dare we say funky, then you'll be more than pleased...All very, er, groovy."
Tim Jones, *Record Collector* (August 2004)
With thanks to Wouter Bessels. www.janakkerman.com

VERDEN ALLEN

"…an interesting mix of eclectic rock and power-pop…Imagine the 'poppier' end of Buggles or Hawkwind, mix in the 'Hoople. And you get a set of strange yet enjoyable pop-rock tracks."

Joe Geesin, *Record Collector* (September 2002)

Terence Allen (renamed 'Verden' by the legendary producer Guy Stevens) was originally from Crynant in South Wales.

As a young man, he received classical piano tuition and passed various piano examinations prior to relocating to Hereford, where he caught up with his uncle, a pub pianist.

Verden was introduced by his uncle to an uninhibited brand of piano playing and was influenced by artists ranging from Jimmy Smith to Liberace. By 1964, he had appeared in his first band, The Inmates, which was followed by The Astrals.

By 1967, Verden found himself as part of The Shakedown Sound but was invited to join The Doc Thomas Group, which featured future members of Mott The Hoople (Mick Ralphs, Peter Overend Watts, Stan Tippins and later, Dale Griffin).

When The Doc Thomas Group had an offer to travel to Italy, Verden opted to stay with The Shakedown Sound, who became Jimmy Cliff's backing band.

In due course, Ralphs succeeded in recruiting Verden into The Doc Thomas Group on a permanent basis. The band changed their name to Silence and with Ian Hunter taking over from Tippins, Mott The Hoople were born. The story is told in more detail later in this book.

Verden had adopted his own style of playing and his Hammond organ sound became his trademark, which very much defined the sound of Mott The Hoople. He was also one of the first rock musicians in the U.K to adopt a Leslie Tone Cabinet (also known as 'The Lesley Rotating Tremolo Speaker System').

Verden stayed with Mott The Hoople until January 1973 when there were political changes within the band. Mick Ralphs also left the band.

In July 1973, Verden released a single with Mooni. However, it was not a commercial success and he decided to turn his back on London and return to the familiar surroundings of Hereford.

The following year, Verden formed a band called The Cheeks with Martin Chambers (drums) and James Honeyman-Scott (guitar). The Cheeks lasted for two years and toured with The Arrows, Hot Chocolate and Trapeze. They also played the Marquee Club and were popular on the college circuit. They recorded just three tracks. Of these, only 'Hypnotized' survives, which has been released as part of Verden's Angel Air album, *Long Time No See*.

In August 1975, Verden found himself working once again with Guy Stevens. Guy had pulled together a band called Little Queenie (featuring Mick Jones, later of The Clash and Big Audio Dynamite). Mick was dropped and the project renamed Violent Luck but it failed to get off the ground. Verden recalls Guy (ever the eccentric) offering to pay for the studio sessions with toy money!

Verden's next foray into music was with the dubiously named Verden Allen's Seven Inches. Again, Verden stamped his mark on the college circuit before signing to the Jet label and releasing a single with Luther Grosvenor (who had replaced Mick Ralphs in Mott The Hoople in 1973).

In 1982, Verden launched his own record label, called Spinit Records. He embarked upon a prolific era, working with the likes of Luthor Grosvenor, Martin Chambers, Norman Jarrett, Overend Watts and Dale Griffin.

Alas, production ground to a halt when the Independent Record Labels Association with whom Verden was working, folded.

Verden continued to gig in and around Hereford and South Wales, joining a band called The Business in 1990.

A line-up and name change saw the band re-emerge as Thunderbuck Ram featuring Geoff Masters (drums), Graham Masters (guitar), Rob Hawkins (bass) and Verden (lead vocals and keyboard). They went on to record *Long Time No See* (1994) which has been re-released by Angel Air with extra tracks under Verden's own name.

Angel Air has released two further Verden albums, *For Each Other* and *Twenty Year Holiday*, each showcasing more recent material.

Reviews for *Long Time No See*: SJPCD036

"...this reissue on Angel Air is to be welcomed...This album is packed with good songs and the arrangements and production are tight...There are some strong rockers on this album, as well as some slower "power" ballads...Of the bonus tracks, 'Hypnotized' dates from 1975 and is the only surviving recording of The Cheeks (Verden's 1974-1976 band with James Honeyman-Scott and Martin Chambers; they both went on to form The Pretenders)...

This CD is an essential purchase not just for Mott The Hoople fans but for all fans of good rock music."

Adrian Perkins, *Outsider*

"...a very enjoyable album containing as it does a good mixture of rockers and ballads."

Keith Smith, *Two Miles From Heaven* (May 1999)

Reviews for *For Each Other*: SJPCD040

"...his undoubted keyboard skills, notably organ work, are well to the fore...The songs themselves are generally well-written and enjoyable MOR rock...The best 'A New Way' and 'Loving You' will find themselves on Mott-related and other compilations shortly..."

David Pearson, *Wondrous Stories* (November 1999)

"...the first two tracks 'A New Way' and 'If Only' are like new wave country - beautiful swilling organ dominating them both...'Loving You' has a more determined sound and is a showcase for Verden's funk organ...Star track is 'All Over You' with its cunning coupling of two quite different organ sounds and plaintive vocal!"

Zabadak (October 2000)

Reviews for *20 Year Holiday*: SJPCD110

"A great rock album with, of course, distinct Mott overtones, its ten songs are all recent Allen originals and won't disappoint anybody enthralled by the earlier *Long Time No See* and *For Each Other* albums or even by his long-ago contributions to Mott's own songbook."

Jo-Ann Greene, *Goldmine* (September 2002)

"...the kind of adult contemporary rock record that needs to be heard. His confident brand of mid-tempo organ and piano driven tunes are of the brand that only requires a few listens to carve a niche in your musical memory."

Jeff Monks, *Mohair Sweets* (November 2002)

See also Mott The Hoople, Silence/ Doc Thomas Group.

ANDROMEDA

"...one of the most fascinating achievements of the progressive era."
Fists In Pockets (Poland) (April/May 2000)

One of the greatest but lesser known bands to emerge from the progressive rock era was Andromeda.

Andromeda was formed by John Du Cann when he was still gigging with a band called The Attack.

He eventually quit The Attack and devoted his time to Andromeda's special brand of psychedelic and progressive rock, aided and abetted by his flatmate Mick Hawksworth (bass) and Jack Collins (drums - later to be replaced by Ian McLane).

Andromeda was an exciting and creative band that soon found a niche on the live circuit. After a few false starts, they signed a record deal, licensing their songs to RCA who released one album and a single. Disappointingly, the record company failed to get behind the band commercially, despite their music receiving a rapturous reception from the music press – including a double page spread in Rolling Stone Magazine. Both original releases are now reasonably scarce. Expect to pay no less than £100 for a good copy of their debut album, *Andromeda* (1969) and in excess of £15 for their single, 'Go Your Way' (also 1969).

Despite inadequate sales, Andromeda continued to gig for a while, but failed to generate any further record company interest. Du Cann, who was hungry for success, took up an offer to join Atomic Rooster and the band folded.

John Du Cann has worked with Angel Air to produce two Andromeda albums. The first, a double CD release, takes in the original album and a swathe of demos and live recordings.

The second showcases the original Andromeda album as the band intended it to be heard.

Nearly forty years on from the formation of the band, justice has at long last been done to the Andromeda back catalogue and interest has once again been rekindled in one of the strongest and most criminally overlooked bands of the era.

Reviews for *Definitive Collection*: SJPCD053

"Some of the guitar is so cool and laid back you could close your eyes and dream of all the good music you've missed over the years. Well there's no need with record companies like Angel Air around, so willing to put their necks on the block and reproduce so much good rock that was all too often destined for dusty shelves.
If you enjoy that late Sixties early Seventies rock you'll not go wrong here..."
Martin Hudson, *Wondrous Stories*, (February 2000)

"1969 was a pivotal year for rock, with psychedelia trailing off, progressive rock gathering speed and classical music - mainly via The Nice - also making its presence felt. Cult trio Andromeda, regulars on John Peel's radio show, were at the apex of all three styles with their only LP...turned into one of the great 'lost' albums of the Sixties."
Colin Shearman, Q, (March 2000)

Reviews for *Originals*: SJPCD187

"Although some people are going to seek this CD out just because of the rarity value, it should be sought out because this is actually a strong collection of songs in its own right...They run through Hendrix-inspired romps to things far more delicate, even bringing in layered harmony vocals as if they were The Moody Blues...a great collection of songs that fans of the era would do well to seek out."
Feedback (November 2005)

"...the holy grail for their fans...There's fun to be had, too, in spotting instrumental quotes such as the Holst-via-Zappa riff on the fade of bitty Return to Sanity..."
Record Collector (March 2006)

With thanks to John Du Cann, Rich Wilson and Claes Johansen.
See also The Attack, John Du Cann, Atomic Rooster and Five Day Week Straw People.

JAY ASTON

"Jay's voice is crisp and captivating especially on the foot-tapping 'Stay With Me'...A varied and versatile album that showcases Jay's distinctive vocals."

Peter French, *Hartlepool Mail* (April 2003)

Rubbing shoulders on the Angel Air label alongside such hairy luminaries as John Du Cann, John McCoy (Mammoth/Gillan), John Fiddler (Medicine Head/British Lions) and Mo Foster (Affinity and just about everything else) is the beautiful Jay Aston.

Jay shot to fame as the youngest member of Bucks Fizz. The group won the Eurovision Song Contest in 1981 and went on to achieve critical acclaim with phenomenal success in the U.K., Europe, Australia and Japan.

In so doing, she chalked up four gold albums, three platinum albums, three number one singles and fifteen consecutive chart singles.

During her career, Jay has received a brace of awards including an Ivor Novello.

Jay is a well respected and much sought after composer, having collaborated with a string of major recording artists including Marcella Detroit (Shakespear's Sister), Dire Straits, Richard Feldman, Underworld, Leftfield, Rupert Hine, Tim Holmes (Chemical Brothers) and Death In Vegas. Collaborations with a number of DJ's have produced club successes including 'Serial Killer', a white label which had a big impact on the club scene and 'Everlasting Love' from her *Alive and Well* album, released on Angel Air and reviewed below:

Reviews for *Alive and Well*: SJPCD137

"Jay…acquits herself well on what is very much a pop album with more than one eye on either the charts or the dance floor."
Feedback (January 2003)

"…far removed from the plastic pop of Buck's Fizz, being closer, in its appropriation of dance grooves, biting rock and introspective lyrics, to the work of Dido and Nelly Furtado. One of the most surprising, and enjoyable, albums of the year so far."
Choice Magazine (May 2003)

With thanks to Jay Aston. www.jay-aston.co.uk.

ATOMIC ROOSTER

"Sweeping Hammond organ, hard rocking guitar and blistering drum beats combine to make the most memorable music."

Hartlepool Mail, 31 December 2001

Once in a while a three piece band will come along which will beg the question…'how the hell are they creating such an enormous sound?'

The Pirates managed it with Mick Green's incredible guitar technique, the Jam were explosive…then there was the deliciously named Atomic Rooster.

Atomic Rooster was founded by Vincent Crane (keyboards) and Carl Palmer (drums). Both Crane and Palmer had been members of The Crazy World Of Arthur Brown but had decided to go their own way. They were joined by Nick Graham on bass.

The trio named the band after a member of the American group Rhinoceros and created a magical sound which fell somewhere between psychedelia, jazz rock and hard rock.

The group was further strengthened in 1970 by the addition of guitarist John Du

Cann from the band Andromeda, whose first task was to overdub his guitar on the debut album (*Atomic Rooster* (1970)) for the American release. However, the departure of Nick Graham reduced the band back to a three piece again. Crane decided not to replace him, instead opting to play the bass line on the Hammond keyboard, a feat unheard of at the time.

So began the creation of the most extraordinary sound, driven by Crane's furious pounding organ, interwoven with Du Cann's guitar and held together by Palmer's hammering drums.

The departure of Carl Palmer to join Emerson Lake and Palmer saw Rick Parnell (son of jazz maestro Jack Parnell) temporarily fill the drum stool before Paul Hammond became a permanent replacement.

A second album was recorded, *Death Walks Behind You* (1970) which hit the U.K. top ten, whilst the single 'Tomorrow Night' climbed to number 7 in the U.K. singles chart. The song caused a lot of ill feeling within the band. To this day, John Du Cann asserts his moral claim to the song, but Vincent Crane put his name to it.

A third album was recorded, *In Hearing of Atomic Rooster* (1971) which became a top five hit, complemented by the hit single, 'Devil's Answer' which reached number 2.

Strangely, everything fell apart just as the band were at their commercial peak. Crane sacked Du Cann and Hammond followed him in protest.

Atomic Rooster ploughed on with Chris Farlowe on lead vocals. Indeed, a variety of musicians came and went before the band called it a day and split up. They never rekindled the sound or success of the Crane/Du Cann/Hammond years, arguably the definitive line-up.

John and Paul went on to form Bullet, later to be renamed Hard Stuff. John also spent some time with Thin Lizzy and recorded a solo album.

In 1979, interest in Atomic Rooster was rekindled with the dawning of The New Wave of British Heavy Metal. John, Vince and Paul reformed Atomic Rooster much to the delight of a new generation of fans.

Between 1979 and 1982 the band toured and recorded incessantly. The live gigs were as astonishing as they were first time around with Vince pounding his 350lb Hammond across the stage, Paul beating the life out of his drums and John's fingers bleeding from the effort of creating the famous 'Rooster' sound. At the end of a show, they would collapse exhausted back stage, barely having the energy to fulfil an encore.

Angel Air has pulled together no less than six Atomic Rooster albums. Two compilations showcase the band's finest studio work, a third release boasts a host of rarities, there are two live outings and finally, the 1980 comeback album completes the set.

Sadly, Paul and Vince are no longer with us. Vince, a depressive, took his own life. Paul died of an overdose.

A strange co-incidence with the album *Death Walks Behind You* still leaves John feeling uncomfortable whenever he opens the sleeve, as he explains:

"The sleeve to the album is a gatefold. It shows the three of us in a grave yard.

Vince and Paul are on the right and to the left of the centrefold is me. We are separated by the crease in the cover although it is the same photo. But on their side are loads of graves and crosses. In fact, they are both wearing crosses too. I am on the left and the background is plain. That, coupled with the title to the album always manages to spook me whenever I look at it."

Reviews for *The First Ten Explosive Years*: SJPCD038

"Put together by guitarist and Rooster original John Du Cann, this oddly-titled sixteen-song 'definitive' covers the gamut of prog/hard rock that he espoused with ex-Arthur Brown organ whizz Vince Crane and buddies between '70 and '72, and then 1979-82...Squawkin'!"

Tim Jones, "Record Collector" (March 1999)

"One of the most enjoyable discs that has dropped through the mail slot this year...one of the best examples of the progressive rock/heavy metal hybrid...be assured that the listener is taken on 75+ minute joy ride...which could just as easily have been titled *The Best Of Atomic Rooster*...As with all Angel Air releases this too comes with extensive liner notes and rare photos of the band."

"*On The Record*" Music America magazine

Reviews for *Live And Raw 70/71*: SJPCD060

"Tracks 1 to 4 were recorded live in London in 1970 and are believed to be the only known live recordings in existence featuring the original line-up of John Du Cann, Vincent Crane and Carl Palmer. These songs alone make this album an indispensable piece of rock history...The disc is accompanied by an excellent booklet with extensive sleeve notes by John Du Cann."

Steve Ward, *Wondrous Stories* (April 2000)

"Those nice people at Angel Air Records have released ...*Live And Raw 70/71*...which contains eight previously unreleased live tracks from two concerts. The quality of the recording is dodgy in places...but this is a collector's album...a piece of history...treat it with the respect it deserves!"

Frank Blades, *Rockhaven*

Review for *Rarities*: SJPCD069

"Angel Air are absolute experts in the field of unearthing a wealth of unheard music. This time they have put together 19 previously unreleased tracks from 1970 through to 1981 - including 3 USA radio ads!...With a combination of previously unreleased tracks (7 in total) including the last ever recording - 'Moonrise' - and demos or different mixes (9 of those), this album shows the power that was Atomic Rooster...Even in a raw, demo or live state, the power is there to hear.

With an excellent 12 page sleeve booklet and rare photos, this is the usual quality package from Angel Air that Rooster fans will want to have."

David Pearson,*Wondrous Stories* (November 2000)

Reviews for *The First 10 Explosive Years Volume 2*: SJPCD086

"Purveyors of classic organ driven rock, Atomic Rooster have been well served by Angel Air's excellent reissue programme...This CD culls together 18 remastered tracks from the period 1972-1982...and is generally a fine testament to a wonderfully inventive band...

For the very best of Atomic Rooster you can invest confidently in any of the band original albums, but releases such as this are fine samplers of the great British progressive rock bands."

Steve Ward, *Wondrous Stories* (Sep 2001)

"...musically this album shows how powerful a unit they could be with the Hammond organ and drums driving Du Cann further on both guitar and vocals..."

Feedback, (November 2001)

Reviews for *Live At The Marquee 1980*: SJPCD104

"I would imagine live this band were good value and well worth seeing. The power of the performances comes through loud and clear on the CD. The whole package is well presented with informative sleeve notes...One for Atomic Rooster fans and those who enjoy the Seventies hard rock sound. "

Jason Ritchie, *get ready to ROCK!* (November 2002)

"...the sheer wall of sonic guitar oblivion and organ-grinding power on show is a superb sound. Old hits ('Tomorrow Night' and 'Death Walks Behind You') sit well next to then-newer songs such as 'Do You Know Who's Looking For You', which has become a classic in the interim...this is an archival gem - another Angel Air treasure."

Record Collector (January 2003)

Review for *Atomic Rooster*: SJPCD188

"You wouldn't normally put money on prog legends mixing it up with the NWoBHM, but this 1980 reformation and EMI signing is a return to form and it did a pretty good job.

"First time on CD, it is well packaged with some bonus tracks. No excuses to overlook it this time round." ****

Joe Geesin, *www.getreadytorock.com* (October 2005)

"...if you're unfamiliar with this stunning release, do yourself a favour, slip on this CD, crank up the volume and let the Rooster crow."

Hartlepool Mail (March 2006)

THE ATTACK

"...there was a lot more to this guitar-dominated band than most chart-minded groups of the time. An inventive foursome who impress with their variety and versatility."

Hartlepool Mail (April 2001)

The Attack was an exciting act signed to the Decca label and managed by Don Arden. The original line-up comprised Richard Shirman, Gerry Henderson, Bob Hodges, Davy O'List and Alan Whitehead although the ever-changing list of personnel ensured that the band rarely remained static.

Their first single, 'Try It' (from 1967 and now valued in the region of £50 for a mint copy), boasted a popular anglicised garage sound but failed to chart. Nevertheless, it represented a promising start for a band that showed enormous potential.

The early departure of guitarist Davy O'List presented a problem which was solved when he was replaced by John Du Cann. Looking for their big break, they recorded 'Hi Ho Silver Lining' as a single. The song was destined to be a smash hit...until Jeff Beck released his own version. Was there foul play afoot or was it a coincidence?

The Attack followed up 'Hi Ho Silver Lining' with the even more commercial 'Created by Clive'...on the same day that The Syn released their own version. Both versions purportedly cancelled each other out commercially and both failed to chart. Who ever said lightning never strikes twice?

A line-up change saw Jim Avery recruited on guitar with John Du Cann taking over the song writing. John took the band in a more melodic and psychedelic direction. However, despite this change the next single, 'Neville Thumbcatch' also failed to chart.

A further line-up change saw Roger Deane join on bass and Keith Hodge on drums.

In the interim, the band had been given studio time by Decca to make an album (provisionally titled *Roman Gods Of War*) but following the failure of the latest single, their record deal was terminated.

The Attack remained a hard working and hard gigging outfit, playing shows in the evening, then diving into studios in the early hours to prepare a series of demos. A sizeable body of work was recorded but the band failed to secure a record deal and, amid some acrimony, decided to split up.

Reviews for *Final Daze*: SJPCD080

"The Attack may never have had a hit or much acclaim but in the late Sixties they were playing everywhere and epitomised the whole Swinging London chic - big hair, foppish clothes and make-up. They sounded like The Small Faces (and just about everybody else around at the time, truth be told), had a noisy guitarist and were endearingly cheesy. Seventeen tracks of sheer nostalgia."
Sheffield Telegraph (January 2001)

"I can't think of a better way to spend an hour of listening to music than with The Attack and their incredible guitars, songs and sonics. They may have missed getting the respect they deserved in the Sixties but anyone in tune with these freak beat/psych/pop-art styled bands now knows full well that The Attack are 'the bizness'."
Colin Bryce, *Mohair Sweets* (February 2001)

AUTOMATICS

"An undiscovered gem and if you like the bands of the late Seventies era like the early work of XTC, The Undertones and The Adverts, add this to your CD collection."

Jason Ritchie *get readytorock!* (June 2003).

At the end of the Seventies, there were two bands labouring under the banner of The Automatics. One was London based and the other from Coventry. The latter underwent a name change, ultimately finding success as Specials. This is the story of the former and their mixed fortunes.

The Automatics were formed in 1976 by Dave Philps, who was keen to start a punk band. Ably assisted by his friend, future record producer Steve Lillywhite, they placed a series of adverts in Melody Maker magazine which yielded a string of mixed results.

Wally Hacon (guitar) was the first to join, followed by Gary Tibbs (bass). Rick Goldstein (drums) completed the line-up.

The new band rehearsed incessantly, but as time progressed, Gary was repeatedly noticeable by his absence. Further enquiries revealed that he had in fact joined a new band called The Vibrators (achieving even greater success in due course with Roxy Music and Adam And The Ants).

Gary was replaced by Bobby Collins and the band set about raising their profile. They would regularly set themselves up on the back of a lorry with a generator and turn up outside major gigs, playing to audiences as they emerged from theatres and concert halls. They found that they could usually get through five or six songs before being moved on by the police!

A record deal was secured with Island Records and one single was released, 'When the Tanks Roll Over Poland Again'. The song was well received and reached the number 1 spot on the Alternative Music Chart – a promising start by any standards.

An album was also recorded for Island but the writing was on the wall when the label underwent an internal reorganisation. The release, *Walking with the Radio On*, was effectively cancelled following the revelation that The Automatic's entertainment expenses had exceeded their recording budget by some considerable amount!

Dave Philps' explanation failed to endear him or the band to the label:-

"I looked them right in the eye and told them that it took a lot of very expensive drugs to make the kind of music we were making."

The band was left without a recording contract or manager and eventually dissolved as they pursued other projects.

The Automatic's story may have ended there but renewed interest in Japan, of all places, has seen the band reform and tour again. A second album has also been recorded and released. Now, for the first time, their debut can at long last be bought by fans, courtesy of those nice people at Angel Air.

Reviews for *Walking with the Radio On*: SJPCD140

"This is a gem of a record from 1978 that at last sees the light of day thanks to the rock and roll archaeologist label, Angel Air...

Twenty five years on, there is an energy, a youthful arrogance, and an attitude that has not dimmed since these tracks were recorded..."

Tony Shevlin, *East Anglian Daily Times* (July 2003)

"This is punk with melody, a style that probably became better known as power pop...Released with copious sleeve notes, interviews, photos etc..."

Feedback (Nov 2003)

BAD COMPANY

Mick Ralphs, formerly of Mott The Hoople, formed the super group Bad Company with Paul Rodgers and Simon Kirke of Free. Boz Burrell of King Crimson completed this amazing quartet.

The new band signed to Island Records in the U.K. and Peter Grant's Swan Song for America. Grant proved to be a major influence.

Their debut album, *Bad Company*, was a huge hit, reaching number 3 on the U.K album chart and number 1 in America, going platinum in the process. They also scored a massive hit with the single 'Can't Get Enough'.

Their second album, *Straight Shooter* maintained the momentum and produced the U.K hit singles, 'God Lovin' Gone Bad' (top forty) and 'Feel Like Makin' Love' (top twenty).

In 1975, Mick and his band mates relocated to America to avoid the horrendous taxes being levied at home. They were part of a major exodus of musicians that was happening at the time.

The third album, *Run With The Pack*, continued to consolidate their success which lasted for a staggering ten years. Peter Grant's policy of sending the band on the road every two years kept audiences baying for more…and Bad Company's live shows were well worth catching!

Their albums repeatedly hit the top twenty on both sides of the Atlantic and further single success followed in America until Paul Rodgers left in the early Eighties.

The disbanding of Bad Company can be attributed to a number of factors. Peter Grant had lost interest in his Swan Song signings. He was viewed by many as the glue that held the band together and his absence resulted in the musicians drifting apart. That aside, they were tired and needed a break. *Rough Diamonds* (1981) became the last album of the era.

In 1986, Mick Ralphs and Simon Kirke re-launched Bad Company with Brian Howe filling in for Rodgers. They released a total of seven album over the following decade, including *Fame And Fortune* (1987), *Here Comes Trouble* (1992) and *Company Of Strangers* (1995). By the early Nineties, Mick was the only remaining original member and in 1996 he brought the project to an end.

In 1999, the four original members of the band re-united, recording four tracks which appeared on *The Original Bad Company Anthology*. They also completed an enormously successful tour, rekindling the glory days of the Seventies.

Angel Air released just one Bad Company album, a thumping double album featuring a show from 1976. Disappointingly, *Live From Albuquerque* was withdrawn inside a week for legal reasons. Consequently, there are no reviews to share with you. The remaining copies in circulation change hands for about £150 a time making it by far the rarest and most sought after Angel Air release.

www.mickralphs.co.uk

BEARDED LADY

"They come across as Mott The Hoople without the keyboards. The melodies are good...Johnny has a vocal style which fits in well, and he is certainly sure of himself, and the result is a band that were probably a really good crack to go and see live. "

Feedback (March 2004)

Bearded Lady started life as a band called Elmo's Fire, comprising Fred Sherriff (guitar), Chris Peel (bass), Mickey Irvine (drums) and Dennis Wilcox (vocals). The band soon ran into trouble with the departure of Wilcox, leaving a vacancy for a new front man.

Fred's girlfriend seemed to have the answer. She had previously dated a guitarist by the name of Johnny Warman, who agreed to join the line-up. It turned out that Warman and Sherriff had been to the same school.

The group changed their name to Bearded Lady and debuted at Morpeth Castle Public House...playing to a little old lady with a bright red nose. She left after the first number, muttering, "I'm not fucking coming here again!"

Slowly but surely, Bearded Lady built up a following on the London pub circuit and before long, were firm favourites alongside the likes of Brinsley Schwartz, Ducks Deluxe, Doctor Feelgood and Dire Straits (yes, THAT Dire Straits!).

A record deal soon followed but the label, Youngblood International Records, failed to release anything within the agreed contractual period and the band was dropped. In fact, it was over a year before the one and only Bearded Lady single was released, a song called 'Rock Star' - perhaps a marker for the punk movement.

A change of personnel followed, with Mickey Irvine departing and being replaced on drums by Paul 'The Mouse' Martin. Bearded Lady also toured Germany at about this time.

Paul Martin's tenure behind the drums was short-lived. He went on to join The Helicopters and was replaced by Clive 'Short Bar' Brooks.

Bearded Lady were an entertaining band to watch with Warman building up an affectionately abusive relationship with his audience. They were given a regular slot at the Marquee Club in London but by 1976, the strain of juggling day jobs with their nocturnal activities began to take its toll. It had long been hoped that a major label would come along and snap up the group...but it never happened.

Angel Air's *The Rise And Fall Of Bearded Lady* pulls together eleven tracks from the era, including the aforesaid single, giving the band their first, long overdue album.

Reviews for *The Rise And Fall Of Bearded Lady*: SJPCD153

"*The Rise And Fall*' is a really good Seventies hard rock album, equally good with any release from the same period. 'Rock Star' is the opening track of the album and the band's first single. This song introduced the band to a bigger audience and helped them book venues throughout London...This Angel Air release contains four bonus live tracks from one of their performances in the Marquee – 'The Riot', 'Silver Box', 'Thank You' and 'Kerb Crawler'.

John Stefanis, www.getreadytorock.com (February 2004)

"...generally rocks and bops through eleven songs of such overwhelming period charm that you forget you're listening to music that's been buried in a box for thirty years. *The Rise And Fall* sounds like every great glam album you've been in love with all your life.

Jo-Ann Greene, *Goldmine* (February 2004)

See also Johnny Warman.

MAGGIE BELL

"Five times voted U.K Female Vocalist Of The Year, her choice of material was impeccable. 'Coming On Strong', Free's classic 'Wishing Well' and a 'Soul Medley' are just a few of the delights to revel in on this album [Live At The Rainbow]."

Colin Bell, On the Record

Peter Purnell is thrilled to have Maggie Bell on his label:-

"Maggie is very special to us. Not only was she the first female to be signed to Angel Air, she also had the 100th and 200th releases, landmarks in our history."

During the Seventies, Maggie earned a reputation as one of the greatest singers of her generation, belting out soul and blues numbers with astonishing feeling and power. There was (and still is) no one to really compare with her. This was duly acknowledged by the public who regularly voted her 'Best Female Vocalist' in both Melody Maker and New Musical Express magazines.

Maggie's career began in Glasgow in the early Sixties when she would occasionally sing on stage with Alex Harvey. Alex introduced Maggie to his younger brother Leslie who had his own band, Kinning Park Ramblers. Maggie joined them for a while, performing the latest American soul hits.

By the time she was seventeen, Maggie was singing professionally with a fifteen piece big band at Sauchiehall Street's Locarno Ballroom, before moving over to the rival Dennistoun Palais Band.

In 1966, she made her recording debut with Bobby Kerr under the name Frankie and Johnny. They released two singles, 'I'm Never Gonna Leave You' and 'Climb Every Mountain'.

In 1967, Maggie found herself playing five hours a night, seven nights a week on the continental club circuit as well as touring American air force bases in Germany.

Maggie moved her career forward with the formation of a band called Power, which included her old friend, Leslie Harvey.

Power soon caught the attention of Peter Grant (Led Zeppelin's manager) who signed them up, securing a deal with Polydor Records. Power changed their name to Stone The Crows (on Grant's advice) and under his guiding hand, embarked upon a career which saw them record four albums and extensively tour the university circuit. They also recorded a host of John Peel sessions, which contributed to their enduring popularity on the live circuit.

The end of the group effectively came about in 1972 when Leslie was tragically and fatally electrocuted at Swanage Top Rank Ballroom. The remainder of the group soldiered on for a while longer with Jimmy McCulloch joining on guitar. A performance from this line-up has been released by Angel Air on DVD, capturing a piece of rock history from the era.

Maggie soon found herself constantly in demand, guesting on a number of albums, including Long John Baldry's *It Ain't Easy*, Ellis's *Riding On The Crest Of A Slump* and *Why Not?* She was also credited with 'vocal abrasives' on Rod Stewart's *Every Picture Tells A Story* (as 'Mateus Rose Maggie Bell').

Maggie also appeared on the orchestral version of *Tommy*, The Who's Rock Opera, for which she earned critical acclaim for her portrayal of Tommy's mother.

Maggie's solo career got off to a rocky start when she recorded two albums for the Atlantic label in New York (one produced by Felix Pappalardi of Mountain and the other by Felix Cavaliere of the Young Rascals). Staggeringly, neither album was granted a release, Atlantic claiming that they were not good enough for marketing. Maggie is however convinced that it was record company politics and not the quality of the recordings that were to blame.

A third album was recorded with Atlantic executive and veteran producer Jerry Wexler, which was deemed to have made the grade. The end result, *Queen Of The Night* (1973), received glowing reviews and was deemed a major success.

Maggie spent much of the following year on the road before heading to Ringo Starr's Tittenhurst Park studio, which was built into his home.

Tittenhurst Park had previously belonged to John and Yoko and was the scene of their *Imagine* film (incidentally, another Angel Air signing, Johnny Warman, recorded an album at Tittenhurst).

Jerry Wexler once again took the producer's chair and the end result was released on Peter Grant's Swan Song label. The album, *Suicide Sal* (1975), sold extremely well in America and Germany.

Maggie went on a number of tours of Europe and America and at one stage supported Bad Company. Angel Air has released two live albums of recently unearthed recordings from this period, *Live At The Rainbow 1974* and *Live Boston USA 1975*.

In 1977, Maggie appeared on Eric Burdon's *Survivor* album with Zoot Money, Geoff Whitehorn and Alexis Corner. The following year, she scored a top forty hit single with the theme tune to the popular TV series, *Hazell*.

At the start of the Eighties, Maggie formed Midnight Flyer with Tony Stevens (ex-Foghat). David Dowle was recruited on drums, Anthony Glynne on guitar and John Cook on keyboards (later to be replaced by Chris Parren).

They recorded one album (at Tittenhurst Park again) which was released on Swan Song. Mick Ralphs was in the producer's chair.

Midnight Flyer was a hard-grafting band that toured with Bob Seger And The Silver Bullet Band and AC/DC (twice). Their story is told in more detail later in this book.

Around this time, Maggie scored another chart success with the single 'Hold Me', a tongue-in-cheek duet with B.A. Robertson which reached number 11 on the U.K. singles chart.

Throughout the Eighties, Maggie released a number of singles and appeared on a Hardin and York album – a musical adaptation of *Wind In The Willows*. She also wrote music for film and television. Maggie will forever be a part of modern television history with her gritty rendition of the theme to *Taggart* (a show she actually appeared in).

In 1987, Maggie embarked upon a new solo album, *Crimes of the Heart,* which disappointingly suffered from lack of promotion.

Maggie continued to work throughout the Nineties, appearing in the stage version of *Wind In The Willows*, working with Eddie Hardin on his *Wizards Convention 3* album and more recently, performing 'Jealousy' on the Frankie Miller tribute album.

2006 saw Maggie on the road with Chris Farlowe and The Manfreds, a happy distraction from her brand new project, British Blues Quintet, featuring Zoot Money, Colin Hodgkinson, Miller Anderson and Colin Allen. Maggie confesses that she still loves being on the road and performing live.

Reviews for *Live At the Rainbow*: SJPCD100

"Bell's powerful yet soulful vocals suit the mix of blues, rock, rhythm & blues and pop in which she dabbled very well and this set encapsulates her rightful claim to be judged as one of the U.K.'s top female singers of the times…The closing number, 'Shout', is so fast and passionate that Maggie all but brings the house down. A fantastic archive package."
Record Collector (March 2002)

"Here's one of the finest female voices to come out of the U.K. Stone The Crows promised so much, but that's another story in their cruelly too short existence. This set comes from the personal archive of band member Mo Foster (bass).… There are good

bass lines in Wishing Well as Maggie gives the song her own treatment...the first half of this CD is worth the price alone."
Blues Matters (July 2003) www.bluesmatters.com

Reviews for *Live Boston USA – 1975*: SJPCD128

"It's a great representation of what made Maggie Bell one of, if not THE best British female vocalists of any era with the sheer power of her gritty vocals being ideally suited to her blues-based material...
This is ballsy, no frills blues rock which really punches its weight."
Steve Ward, *Classic Rock Society* (July 2003)

"...To say this album was recorded back in 1975 seems like a misprint to me, I would be happy to go out tomorrow and listen to a concert like this...this is one great live album."
Modern Dance (Issue 45)

Reviews for *Queen of the Night*: SJPCD200

"...this collection displays a woman with an incredible voice who can switch between rock, soul, jazz and blues."
Evening Star (January 2006)

"...the recording is nothing short of precision...*Queen of the Night* is a careful, dedicated workout and a highly colourful release." (7.25/10)
Maelstrom (March 2006)

Reviews for *Suicide Sal*: SJPCD201

"While her debut was recorded with stellar session players, this album sees Bell's touring band supporting her. Consequently, the album has a more liberated feel and more wholehearted contributions, including some delicate organ and guitar playing." (7/10)
Maelstrom, Issue 43

"This critically acclaimed set has now been released in CD form by Angel Air, giving a whole new lease of life to prime cuts such as 'What You Got', 'In My Life' and Free's 'Wishing Well'."
Kevin Bryan, *Stirling Advertiser* (April 2006)

See also Stone The Crows, Midnight Flyer, Hardin and York.

ERIC BELL

"A classic blues album...Bell is undoubtedly an outstanding guitarist, whose smooth playing gives a lilt to his music that hints at traditional Irish music without being it....Recommended to Thin Lizzy completists and lovers of good Blues."

Bernard Law, *Wondrous Stories* (April 2001)

Fans of Thin Lizzy will be familiar with the name Eric Bell.

Eric grew up in Northern Ireland and was turned on to music as a young lad by the sounds of Lonnie Donegan:-

"Lonnie Donegan was the first singer I ever heard who really opened up and sang like he felt, especially on the last verse and chorus. It was so exciting, pure blues and gospel, and a great guitar player with him."

Hearing the Shadows 'Apache' echoing from a transistor radio around the brick houses of Belfast convinced Eric of where his future lay. With the help of his kindly uncle Harold, he bought his first guitar and proceeded through a string of Irish bands, including a stint with Van Morrison in Them.

In 1970, Eric co-founded Thin Lizzy, playing lead guitar with Phil Lynott on bass and Brian Downey on drums. They were a powerful trio, well suited in style to each other and were immensely popular in their native Ireland, eventually picking up an international audience with 'Whiskey In The Jar' (a massive U.K hit in 1973).

Bell was responsible for writing and arranging a prominent amount of material for the band during this early incarnation, but eventually left due to ill health.

Post Thin Lizzy, Eric's career took a string of interesting twists and turns, including a stint with Noel Redding of The Jimi Hendrix Experience.

Eric Bell Live Tonite...Plus brings us up to 1996 and as the title suggests, catches Eric live on stage.

The album is a showcase for his talents as an excellent guitarist and consummate blues player.

The set opens with the John Mayall classic 'The Stumble' (also used by Paul Jones on his radio show) which sets the scene for the performance. Other numbers include 'Baby Please Don't Go' and Bell's own 'Walk On Water'. A live Eric Bell album would not be complete without 'Whiskey In The Jar' and 'The Rocker', both Thin Lizzy favourites.

The album seems to epitomize what Eric is about musically and is a terrific record of his musical talents.

Reviews for *Eric Bell Live Tonite...Plus*: SJPCD084

"Fabulous playing and surprisingly strong singing make this a pleasurable experience...The sleeve notes proudly places Bell in the front rank of Irish guitarists...only a fool would argue with that assertion."
Michael Heatley, *Classic Rock* (May 2001)

"...The feeling is one of smoky bar intimacy, with Bell and his backing duo running through a number of standards to a warm reception...Buddy Guy's 'Hold That Plane' is supremely rendered and a couple of 'Lizzy knocks include nearly ten minutes of fuzz-laden 'Whiskey In the Jar'...Solid."
Record Collector, (June 2001)

BIG BOY PETE

"Brilliant stuff from a fellow who has always stuck to his principals and believes in the music he makes."

www.lancerecords.com (June 2006)

Pete Miller, known to generations simply as 'Big Boy Pete', is one of those chameleons of the music business who cannot be bracketed.

If there has been a trend to set in the popular music scene, then he most likely has been at the forefront of it.

Pete's early career can be traced through The Offbeats and a visually exciting group called The Jaywalkers. He was an integral part of the Swinging Sixties music scene and toured with The Beatles and The Rolling Stones.

As fashions changed, so did Pete. He left The Jaywalkers, went solo and hired himself out as a session man.

During the dawning of the psychedelic era, Pete recorded a song called 'Cold Turkey', which is now regarded as a classic. Copies change hands for in excess of £250.

Towards the end of the Sixties, Pete retreated to his native Norwich and quietly lost himself in his studio, writing over one hundred songs, many of which were re-recorded by established artists.

Pete also found time to compose his own masterpiece, a forty five minute composition called 'World War IV' which remained unreleased until the late Nineties.

In 1973, Pete packed his bags and headed for Hawaii, settling with his girlfriend (who he later married). After a year in the sun, they moved to San Francisco where Pete set up a brand new recording studio.

Over the years, Pete successfully produced and engineered songs for hundreds of artists, earning a formidable reputation and a tidy living. He also set up The Audio Institute Of America, providing an invaluable service to the music industry by training up engineers and sending them out into the big wide world.

Turning to Angel Air's 2006 release of *The Perennial Enigma*, the tracks featured are lifted from Pete's early days in America and represent just a fraction of the four hundred or so master copies he has accumulated over the last thirty years.

Reviews for *The Perennial Enigma*: SJPCD224

"Pete Miller, aka Big Boy Pete, was famed for recording rock'n'roll and psychedelia solo and with other projects (Peter Jay & Jaywalkers et al). This solo album was recorded in the early Seventies and remained unreleased until now.

Handling the guitar and vocals, and featuring both upright and fender bass, it's a good if rather dated pop album. The rock'n'roll, even its rockabilly touches, pop et al all lean to Sixties psychedelic pop...Of interest to fans, especially with the packing featuring extensive notes and a discography." ***

www.getreadytorock.com (April 2006)

"Served with lots of humour and moderate jams, the mischievous songs that are found here appeal in their underground nature, as they are basically four - and eight-track selections culled from Miller's first U.S recordings in the early Seventies; as such they manage to evoke engaging, vintage charm in spite of being rather basic rock songs that mix power psychedelia with reggae and early rock and roll á la Elvis.

The people at Angel Air did a wonderful job supplying us these recordings in authentic sound and with an impressive booklet." (6.5/10)

Maelstrom (June 2006)

With thanks to Pete Miller. www.bigboypete.com; audioinst@earthlink.net

BLUE ÖYSTER CULT

"Cult completists should find this an invaluable addition to their collections."

Kevin Bryan, *Belfast Telegraph* (June 2003)

Mention the name Blue Öyster Cult and one song immediately springs to mind:- 'Don't Fear the Reaper'.

The song has remained a radio play favourite since it was a hit in 1978 and has been included on just about every conceivable rock compilation since then. For some inexplicable reason, they have never been able to follow it up with another U.K. chart success, remaining predominantly an album-orientated band.

But there is more to Blue Öyster Cult than just this one song. They are a bona fide, living, breathing, creative outfit who still tour and record.

In 1999, Angel Air released one of their more bizarre and interesting projects. It harked back to 1992 when Blue Öyster Cult were invited (along with a number of lesser known groups) to record the soundtrack to a Ted Nicolaou film called *Bad Channels* (SJPCD046).

The film received a lukewarm reception from the critics but the hard rocking soundtrack stood up well, in part due to Blue Öyster Cult's impressive film score.

The film, with tongue firmly in cheek, focussed on a group of aliens taking over a radio station and zapping all the 'babes', interspersed with shots of the featured bands performing music from the soundtrack. All light-hearted fun!

This remains the one and only film soundtrack from the label so far.

TOMMY BOLIN

"A showcase for Tommy Bolin's talent as both guitarist and song writer...One for the fans of great guitar and true musical genius."

Adrian Lyth, Wondrous Stories (August 2000)

Angel Air has predominantly been a vehicle for British artists, but there have been one or two notable exceptions.

Tommy Bolin was born in Sioux City, Iowa. Leaving school at sixteen years of age, he headed for Denver, Colorado and joined a band called Zephyr. He appeared on two of their albums before going on tour with the great bluesman, Albert King.

In 1973, Tommy moved to New York and became an integral part of the local jazz-rock scene, performing with Billy Cobham on his solo album, *Spectrum*. He progressed on to The James Gang which he fronted for a year, appearing on two further albums.

However, Tommy's major break came when he took over from Ritchie Blackmore as front man of Deep Purple.

Following the demise of Deep Purple in the mid-Seventies, Tommy set out on a solo career, signing a record deal with Columbia. Amusingly and quite co-incidentally, Bolin found himself being supported by another Angel Air signing whilst performing at the Bottom Line in New York – Sailor! It was, beyond any reasonable doubt, the oddest match American audiences had ever had the privilege of witnessing.

Tragically, Tommy died of a drug overdose on 4th December 1976. It was a wretched loss of a talented young man, who was just twenty-five years of age.

Snapshot is a fabulous selection of tracks lifted from demos and jam sessions, released with the approval of Bolin's estate.

Reviews for *Snapshot*: SJPCD066

"...It's great and Bolin's acoustic demos are often quite excellent as he had a great feel for rhythm and a good voice. In places he's very akin to the best acoustic stuff by Marc Bolan and often similar in the percussive feel of the playing and also the vocal phrasing. Again a good informative sleeve (twelve pages) with a career overview and track by track breakdown..."
Free Appreciation Society (August 2000)

"...This collection has been put together with the care that one expects from Angel Air, and there is an extensive biography as well as information about these songs, and where they come from...each of these songs are either different interpretations of numbers (sometimes acoustic precursors to an electric recording), or in the case of a couple, songs that have never been heard before."
Feedback (August 2000)

BRITISH LIONS

"They purveyed a hard edged yet melodic power pop/soft rock all accompanied by inspirational and very memorable riffs...an album of the finest quality Rock. By 1978 British Lions were no more but this excellent album is a timely reminder of the fact that there was some fine traditional Rock around in the Seventies amidst the gob and the Oi!"

Steve Ward, *Wondrous Stories* (March 2002)

British Lions rose from the ashes of a band called Mott, which in turn was pieced together from the remnants of classic British rockers, Mott The Hoople.

When Mott came to a miserable end, the remaining members (Overend Watts, Morgan Fisher, Dale Griffin and Ray Majors) were broke and jobless. Morgan managed to find some session work and in so doing, crossed paths with John Fiddler, formerly of Medicine Head (featured later in this book). John agreed to front a revitalised and rebranded version of Mott.

Fiddler, a gentle moustachioed hippie, bonded extremely well with his new colleagues and the hard rocking band, British Lions, were born.

Overnight, John transformed his image, shaving off his moustache and adopting possibly the most dubious perm in rock history. The transformation from hippie to 'rock god' was complete!

John took on the mantle of chief song writer and penned a multitude of commercially appealing songs which helped to secure a record deal. New managers were appointed and the future looked rosy.

British Lions went on to record an album worthy of their name - hard rocking, well executed and packed with tremendous melodies.

A series of U.K warm-up gigs saw the band hone their stage act prior to embarking upon an American tour.

They were lined up to support U.F.O and Blue Öyster Cult. With just thirty minutes on stage per night, British Lions 'cranked it up to eleven' and played a series of rip-roaring sets, winning fans and friends along the way.

They were rewarded handsomely when their single, 'Wild In The Streets', broke into the American Hot One Hundred chart.

The tour came to an end after two months on the road but the band knew that to capitalise on this promising start, they HAD to keep touring America. However, their management failed to secure any more tour dates and the band came home to England.

Staggeringly, each band member arrived home to domestic anarchy!

Overend had left his home in the 'capable' hands of his girlfriend. He came home to find it flea-ridden and peppered with cat shit. The place also showed signs of wear from numerous wild parties – his guitars had been smashed and various items stolen. Indeed, every band member without exception was enduring some form of domestic strife to a greater or lesser degree.

This led to the title of the second British Lions release, *Trouble With Women*.

Amazingly, it was rejected by the record company as sounding "too harsh" and the management team hit the panic button, urging the band to downscale their plans. However, the seasoned musicians knew from experience that only a major tour of America would suffice – without it, they had little future. Dale and Overend left in despair and the rest of the band soon followed. It was an appalling way for such a promising and gifted band to end.

Angel Air has picked up British Lions' two albums and a third has been released, pulling together a treasury of unreleased gems. The joy in all of these recordings is the chemistry between the musicians – the band really did roar.

Reviews for *Live and Rare*: SJPCD044

"…The CD sleeve is one of the most comprehensive histories I have seen, with 100% participation from all band members and adds to the sense of 'what might have been' had the record company not (unfairly) pulled their financial support. An excellent audio document of the band and the times."
David Pearson, *Wondrous Stories*, September 1999

"...This was a damn good band and if you're a Mott fan, you'll relate. What we're presented with here is a collection of live cuts of their best tracks...Interesting stuff and enjoyable..."
Sonic Iguana (Issue 4)

Reviews for *British Lions*: SJPCD065

"...They cut a fine, if occasionally workmanlike, album together...with eight previously unreleased tracks bolstering the nine original cuts (including a Peel session, a live performance, and a clutch of demos), *British Lions* emerge a lot stronger than memory likes to make them out..."
Jo-Ann Greene, *Goldmine* (July 2000)

"I haven't played my vinyl copy of *British Lions* for quite some time and I'd forgotten just how good an album it is. From the opening adrenaline surge of 'One More Chance To Run' to the humorous closer 'Eat the Rich'...this album features great songs and great playing and quite possibly is the strongest post MTH album featuring Messrs Watts, Griffin, Fisher and Majors. A lot of that was down to the great songwriting of the new secret ingredient, John Fiddler, of course...."
Two Miles From Heaven Issue 2

Reviews for *Trouble with Women*: SJPCD075

"...although different from their first it is still distinctly 'Lions...At long last, Angel Air have released it on CD, and a welcome release it is too...look beyond the original tracks and you'll find some real gems in the bonus tracks...I like this album and it withstands repeated playing. The bonus tracks are a delight, and prove (if proof were needed) that The British Lions did indeed have enormous potential and their demise robbed the world of a mighty fine band."
Adrian Perkins, (October 2000)

"I can't recommend this release enough, I've been playing it to death for weeks and after not playing it for such a long time, I keep hearing bits I don't recall hearing before...It's almost like hearing it for the first time. If you're undecided as to whether to pick up *Trouble With Women* let me make up your mind for you. Just go out and buy it OK."
Two Miles From Heaven (February 2001)

With thanks to Dale Griffin, John Fiddler, Overend Watts, Morgan Fisher, and Ray Major.
See also Silence/Doc Thomas Group, Mott The Hoople, Mott, Medicine Head, Morgan and Morgan Fisher, Ray Majors, Overend Watts, John Fiddler.

BROKEN HOME

"…very melodic heavy rock, with just enough pop sensibility to make the songs catchy…"

Bernard Law, *Classic Rock Society* (March 2003)

The history of Broken Home can be traced back through Seventies band Mr Big (an Angel Air signing) and its predecessor, Chaulkies Painful Legg. Mr Big had enjoyed brief chart success with the hit, 'Romeo'.

The break up of Mr Big in 1978 had been a cause of major disappointment for the band. However, two of the band members, Dicken (Jeffery Pain) and Pete Crowther decided to have another crack at the music business.

In 1979, they recorded a series demo tracks under the name of Rough Edge, eventually renaming themselves Broken Home.

Broken Home were initially joined by John Burnip on drums (also from Mr Big) but he switched roles and became their manager. His place was filled by Pete Barnacle with Rory Wilson joining on guitar.

Broken Home secured a licensing deal with Warner Brothers (WEA) and in 1980, set about recording their debut album with Robert John 'Mutt' Lange in the producer's chair. The result was polished, classy and horrendously over budget. Three singles were lifted from the album ('Death Of Gog', 'No Chance' and Run Away From Home') but amazingly, none of them charted. It has been suggested that the album cost so much to make that it cut into the promotional budget, with predictable consequences.

The band promoted the album and singles by touring, which included a slot supporting Slade. They also played The Reading Rock Festival, which sadly proved to be their final date as a live act.

Soon after, Rory and Pete left the band. WEA also declined to renew Broken Home's contract, leaving Dicken and Pete in limbo.

An olive branch was offered by Mercury Records in Europe who recognised the potential of the band. They signed Broken Home but disappointingly, the deal excluded the distribution and sale of albums and singles within the U.K.

Dicken and Pete decided to press on as a duo (time was too tight for new auditions) and in 1981, they recorded the album *Life*.

'Oh Yeah' was lifted as the European single and the album was put out on the continent as planned. But Dicken and Pete heard nothing further – no feedback and no word of chart success. With no band or money coming in, Broken Home inevitably fell apart.

However, despite the wall of silence from the European territories, Broken Home had in fact become a great success in Norway, with the album enjoying a five week run on the Norwegian album chart, peaking at number 22.

Dicken laments the lost opportunity to promote the band in the Scandinavian countries and views this as a dreadfully wasted break.

Angel Air has snapped up both Broken Home albums which are now available again in all their glory.

Reviews for *Broken Home*: SJPCD129

"A beautifully crafted record from Dicken of Mr Big...The future Mr Shania Twain - Robert 'Mutt' Lange - produced a great sounding record, which proves the missing link between the work he had done with the likes of the Boomtown Rats, AC/DC, The Outlaws and Graham Parker, and the work he would go on to do with Def Leppard and Bryan Adams...As ever, this Angel Air release comes with a well thought out and well-presented booklet..."
East Anglian Daily Times (March 2003)

"While it may not quite make it as a full-blown 'classic' it certainly stands up as an album that should have been hugely successful, and those who enjoy British Eighties melodic rock ought to seek this out. A very detailed booklet containing stacks of information completes the package...A definite goody."
Feedback (May 2003)

Reviews for *Life*: SJPCD169

"...the over-riding feeling is that there is massive talent here that maybe never realised full potential, whether due to musical climate or musical politics. *Life* lacks 'Mutt' Lange's sheen but nevertheless all the ingredients of Dicken's art are in place. It will come as no surprise to learn that Mr Big supported Queen in 1975 at the peak of that band's Seventies chart success. In many ways, there is a complementary link with the emphasis on catchy, guitar-driven pop rock here evidenced on the title track, 'Wake Up Mr Doctor' and 'Nobody'."
David Randall, www.getreadytorock.com (February 2004)

"...available now for the first time in more than two decades, and positively overflowing with bonus tracks. Eleven songs were drawn from sources as far apart as Mr. Big's 1996 reunion Rainbow Bridge, and mid-1980s Dicken projects Peculiar People and Dicken. All, therefore, bear the vocalist's so characteristic stamp, wrapping up the surprisingly superlative *Life* album with a swagger that makes you want to hear more. Thankfully, Angel Air has it – both Broken Home and Mr. Big's earlier *Seppuku* are both also available through the label's website."
Jo-Anne Greene, *Goldmine* (March 2004)

See also Mr Big.

CARMEN

"An original mix, and the first (1973) album shows a very heavy brand of rock with as much offbeat prog and Spanish leanings...Well packaged, fans of prog and Hispanic music will love..."

Joe Geesin, www.getreadytorock.com (September 2006)

Carmen was without doubt the most flamboyant and original act to emerge from early Seventies America. Bucking the trends of the time, they invented a new brand of music by fusing Flamenco with rock. The results were astonishing, explosive and extremely exciting.

The emergence of the band can be traced back to a Flamenco restaurant on Hollywood's Sunset Boulevard called 'El Cid', which was owned by the parents of David and Angela Allen.

David recalls as a child the early ambitions his parents had for him:-

"I was in my parents' stage act from the age of four; I was going to be a concert guitarist because they knew all the promoters."

The arrival of The Beatles in America re-wrote the rules of popular music and for a while, David's aspirations lay in the mainstream. However, he decided that it would be senseless to abandon his original training so fused Flamenco with his new found love of the electric guitar. Carmen were born!

Carmen's debut performance was in July 1970 in front of an audience of music executives. The general consensus was that the live performance could not be translated adequately to vinyl.

In 1973, using his university savings, David transferred his Carmen project to Britain, hoping for a more broad-minded approach to his phantasmagorical project:-

"Within four months of coming over we were working, by some ridiculous chance, with Tony Visconti and rubbing shoulders with David Bowie and Marc Bolan!"

David pulled together a line-up that included Sister Angela (vocal, Mellotron, Synth' and footwork), Roberto Amarel (vocals, vibraphone, footwork and castanets), John Glascock (bass) and Paul Fenton (drums). Under the guiding hand of producer Tony Visconti, this dedicated band of musicians brought David and Angela's dream to life with the first ever Carmen album, *Fandangos in Space* (1973). Tony's style of production suited the feel of the music and the result was stunning.

The second album, *Dancing On A Cold Wind* (1974) took the whole concept a stage further. The line-up was further expanded and included contributions from Mary Hopkin (vocals) and Tony Visconti (wind instruments) (husband and wife at the time), David Katz (violin) and Chris Karan (percussion).

Carmen hoped to secure a major tour with their most famous fan, David Bowie. However, this failed to materialise. Instead, they supported a number of major bands including Rush and ELO, thanks to exposure on the U.S television show, *Midnight Special*.

In 1975, Carmen toured with Jethro Tull, although this proved to be an inadequate 'marriage'. As a direct consequence, John Glascock was hired by Ian Anderson and became an integral part of the Jethro Tull family tree until his untimely passing in 1979. Angela was also asked to sing backing vocals on the next Jethro Tull album.

A third Carmen album, *The Gypsies*, was recorded in 1975 and released in America. It lacked the polished production of the previous two albums and had a more commercial sound.

The first two Carmen albums were released in 2006 as a double CD package by Angel Air, with bonus tracks. The third album will follow in 2007, completing the story.

For Carmen to succeed at a major level, they needed a big break and a considerable budget to stage their shows properly. Neither happened and in 1975, the group disbanded.

David Allen, creator of the whole concept, continued as a song writer and has since branched into photography, also training as a psychotherapist.

Review for *Fandangos in Space* and *Dancing On A Cold Wind*: SJPCD229

"Imagine the 'Senor Velasco' part of Spock's Beard's 'The Light', combined with some Moody Blues, Procol Harum, David Bowie and touches of Jethro Tull and Gentle Giant. This might give you a bit of an idea of what Carmen sounded like, although, in all fairness, nothing can prepare you for the delights which are these albums."
www.prog-nose.org (October 2006)

www.fandangosinspace.com

See also Mickey Finn's T-Rex for Paul Fenton and Sundance for Mary Hopkin.

CANNED ROCK

"The style changes from progressive rock to pop but otherwise the music is put together well. The second album (*Machines*) is by far a more professional sound and they seemed to have picked up a bit of Uriah Heep (not a bad thing)...it's hard to believe there were only three of them."

Modern Dance #39 (August 2002)

Candy Rock (as they were then known) were formed in the early Seventies out of the original band known as Rainbow (long before the rock super-group). Rainbow had flirted with chart success, their single 'The Way Love Comes and Goes' missing the top forty by a whisker.

Two of the band members, Don Maxwell (bass and vocals) and Pete Buckby (drums, percussion and vocals) broke away from Rainbow and formed Candy Rock with Doug Kennard (keyboards, guitar and vocals).

In 1974, they secured an H.M. Forces tour of Cyprus. By this time, they were generating a reputation for their full sound and great vocals. Pyrotechnics and special effects had also been added to their live set which on one occasion resulted in band members being showered with burning sparks, ruining their stage outfits. It was all very innovative for the time.

A record deal was secured with Phillips and a single released called 'Captain Captain'.

Their new manager, Tony Avern, secured Candy Rock a spot on the ITV television show *New Faces*, which Don, Pete and Doug were initially reluctant to do (for younger readers, this could be viewed as a prototype to *X Factor*).

Nevertheless, they went on the show and won their heat with a highly respectable rendition of 'Bohemian Rhapsody' (Don had viewed this as a challenge when Freddie Mercury once said that it could not be performed live).

Candy Rock went on to reach The Viewers Winners Final and were pipped at the post by a comedian by the name of Jim Davidson!

Changing their name to Canned Rock, they recorded a debut album, mixing original songs and cover versions. This was supported by an appearance on ATV's 'Pub Entertainer Of The Year' show, which they won, in front of a television audience of eight million.

A Christmas single and an intensive round of touring followed. Canned Rock had a full diary and a massive entourage to support them wherever they went. Their live show was also developing, and classical numbers were introduced, including Holst's 'The Planets' ('Mars') and Tchaikovsky's '1812 Overture'!

Canned Rock became renowned for the latter, which they performed on a return visit to *Pub Entertainer Of The Year*. They were truly the kings of the chicken-in-a-basket market and were household names throughout the country.

The release of their second album, *Kinetic Energy,* was staggeringly hampered by the lack of a record deal. So they pressed six thousand copies, released it themselves and even backed it with a self-funded television campaign. All the copies sold.

The following year, they toured Europe and recorded a live album but still failed to break into the mainstream music scene despite untold success and media exposure.

In the early Eighties, the writing was on the wall. Canned Rock had a steady following but failed to win new fans. A final album, a concept piece called *Machines,* failed to gain any record company attention.

The demise of the band was decided for them when Doug was electrocuted on stage at Mannheim U.S. Base. Unlike Leslie Harvey of Stone The Crows (who suffered a similar accident), Doug survived, but it was a close call. His arm was damaged and he could no longer play any of his instruments. Dates were cancelled and the band went home.

Doug went through a period of convalescence and thankfully regained the use of his arm. Canned Rock embarked on a farewell tour, culminating at RAF Brize Norton in 1984. Reflecting upon their time together, Doug is philosophical:-

"We were earning a living but we weren't making a fortune. We were having a good time, so we saw no reason to change."

Kinetic Energy and *Machines* have been released together as a single package by Angel Air.

Review for *Kinetic Energy/Machines*: SJPCD092

"Harking back to vintage 10CC but with a sound that is pure late-1970s, new-wave cleverness, Canned Rock investigate everything from mutant disco…to rockin' classics. If you want to draw further comparisons, period offerings from John Du Cann, The Monks and Yellow Dog all come to mind, layered with a healthy love of Queen."

Jo-Ann Greene, *Goldmine*, January 2002

ROGER CHAPMAN/ROGER CHAPMAN AND THE SHORTLIST

"...finds Roger and his band in excellent form...The quality is excellent...fans and admirers alike will love to have a copy of the release..."

Classic Rock Society (November 2005)

The early days of Roger's career can be traced back to the Sixties and a band called Family.

Family hailed from Leicester and featured Roger Chapman, Charlie Whitney, Ric Grech, Jim King and Rob Townsend.

The band relocated to London and signed for the Liberty label. In the autumn of 1967, Family released their first single, 'Scene Thru The Eye Of A Lens'.

The following year, they recorded their debut album, *Music In A Dolls House*, showcasing a mix of blues, folk, jazz, pop and psychedelia. It made the U.K. top forty.

The band toured with Jethro Tull and Ten Years After before returning to the studio to record their second album, *Family Entertainment*. The album climbed to number 6 in the charts.

In 1969, Ric Grech left the band to join Blind Faith (featuring Eric Clapton and Steve Winwood) and a replacement was found in John Weider. By November, Family had secured their first hit single with 'No Mules Fool'. This was the last Family record to feature Jim King.

Their third album, *A Song For Me* (1970), introduced Poli Palmer (ex-Blossom Toes) as a band member. The album was an enormous success, peaking at number 4 in the U.K. album charts. They also released the E.P. 'Strange Band' which peaked at number 11.

Their fourth album, *Anyway* (1970) was an unusual release with a live side and a studio side which followed its predecessor into the top ten.

In 1971, John Weider left the band and was replaced by John Wetton.

Wetton played and sang on the band's next album, *Fearless* (1971), which missed the top ten. However, the single 'In My Own Time' (not featured on the album) scored their greatest single chart success, reaching number 4.

Family maintained a consistently high output of material and the album *Bandstand*, was released in 1972. The single 'Burlesque' became their final hit single, reaching the top twenty. At about this time, Poli Palmer and John left the band.

Jim Cregan joined on bass and Tony Ashton on keyboards for Family's final album, *It's Only A Movie* (1973). The group undertook a farewell tour culminating in an emotional finale in their home town of Leicester.

Roger Chapman and Charlie Whitney continued their song writing partnership with a new band called Streetwalkers. They had a sound that was hard and raw. They toured Europe and won over a new generation of fans.

Their debut album, *Streetwalkers* (1974) was made at a time when the line-up was unsettled and this apparently shows through. However, with Bobby Tench on board, the sound stabilised through the next three albums, *Downtown Flyers* (1975), *Red Card* (1976) and *Vicious But Fair* (1977). *Red Card* actually reached the U.K. top twenty.

The curtain came down on Streetwalker with a live double album, *Streetwalkers Live*.

Despite successful tours, they failed to crack the American market. With the usual managerial difficulties, the band split and Chapman and Whitney went their separate ways.

In the late Seventies, Roger recorded his first solo album, *Chappo,* and toured the U.K. However, he was now considered unfashionable at home by an audience more interested in punk, new wave and new romanticism.

Ever the hard working musician, Roger received a major break when he found himself on the German television programme, *Rockpalast*. Suddenly, he had an audience of some twenty five million people spread over fourteen countries.

He released a version of the Rolling Stones' 'Let's Spend The Night Together' which was a big hit in Germany.

Capitalising on this remarkable second wind, he released the album *Live In Hamburg* which featured the song 'Shortlist', which was to become the name of his backing band.

Germany and indeed much of Europe (both sides of the Iron Curtain) had a taste for Roger's brand of high octane rock and he found himself playing in front of some colossal audiences, despite being ignored by the music press back at home.

The album *Mail Order Magic* followed in 1980 and *Hyenas Only Laugh For Fun* the following year.

The ideal showcase of this era was the 1982 live double album *He Was, She Was, You Was, We Was*. It was a thundering album and featured such talent as Nick Pentelow (saxophone), Tim Hinkley (keyboards) Geoff Whitehorn (guitar) (ex-Crawler and Maggie Bell), Steve Simpson (guitar and mandolin), Boz Burrell (bass), Stretch (drums) and Poli Palmer (vibes and synths).

This is one of the best live albums of its kind and has been re-released by Angel Air as a double compact disc package.

Three more albums followed *Mango Crazy* (1983), *The Shadow Knows* (1984) and *Zipper* (1985).

An experimental collaboration with the Dutch Bolland Brothers in 1987 was followed by one of Roger's finest albums. *Walking The Cat* (1989) stayed in the German charts for three months. *Hybrid And Lowdown* followed in 1990.

During the early Nineties, Roger continued to tour Germany and increased his presence in the U.K.

In 1996, he released the album *Kiss My Soul*, which featured song writing collaborations with John Wetton, Jim Cregan, Steve Simpson and Mickey Moody.

A Turn Unstoned followed in 1998 which featured musicians from his old band, The Shortlist.

In 2003, Angel Air released Roger Chapman's *Family And Friends* DVD, which featured a career-spanning set filmed live at Newcastle Opera House. The concert featured Steve Simpson, Ian Gibbons (ex-Kinks and Suzy Quattro), Andy (Stewart) Hamilton, Gary Twigg and Henry Spinetti.

Reviews for *He Was...She Was...You Was...We Was*: SJPCD193

"Hard rock and R'n'B played with a lot of energy, features a large band providing a full sound. Alongside two guitarists (Steve Simpson also playing mandolin), drums and bass also get Poli Palmer on vibes/synths, Tim Hinkley on piano and Nic Pentelow on saxophone. And many will recognise bassist Boz Burrell.

Roger Chapman has been around for a long time and released a range and quantity of material. This album is a definite career highlight, from a time when the U.K. was succumbing to new wave. Here in its entirety with extensive liner notes and a bonus track. A very decent package." ****

Joe Geesin, *www.getreadytorock.com* (October 2005)

"The former Family front man and his free blowing band stomp their way through blockbusters like 'Prisoner', 'Soldier' and 'Who Pulled The Night Down' with the power and passion which has become a Chapman trademark over the years."

Kevin Bryan, *Stirling Advertiser*

With thanks to Pete Feenstra www.feenstra.co.uk and Roger Chapman Official Appreciation Society. www.chappo.com

CHICKEN SHACK

The name Stan Webb is synonymous with the blues explosion of the Sixties.

Throughout the second half of the decade, Stan could be found relentlessly touring his band Chicken Shack the length and breadth of the country and in so doing, cultivated a formidable reputation as a not-to-be-missed live act.

His band featured a gifted young lady by the name of Christine Perfect, who is now better known to audiences as Christine McVie.

Chicken Shack produced a string of singles, scoring a top twenty hit with 'I'd Rather Go Blind' and a top thirty hit with 'Tears in the Wind'.

They also produced a number of solid albums which are now regarded as classics, these being *Forty Blue Fingers Freshly Packed And Ready To Serve'* (1968) and *O.K. Ken* (1969).

In 2004, Angel Air seized the opportunity to film Stan Webb's Chicken Shack live in Lyme Regis, creating a valuable and timeless record of Stan and his band in action (NJPDVD620).

The release also includes a formidable interview with Webb, who talks candidly about his career and the people who have shared the limelight with him.

This is a must-buy for fans of the Sixties British blues explosion.

The following is a review by Roger Collins, a long-term fan who was present at the Lyme Regis gig and regularly saw Chicken Shack during the Sixties:-

"The support had finished and it felt time for the main event as the Marine Theatre was filling up. It may have been a warm summer evening but the warmth was as much from the crowd's delight in being there than any strict reading of the temperature. Stan had just walked through the crowd in order to get back-stage. Shortly after, the band came out fluffing up their musical feathers before Stan edged centre stage, guitar slung low as usual

Chicken Shack was there in the British blues scene of the Sixties. Stan played impeccably. He can be flashy but never takes it further than necessary but tonight the camera was on him and he was cooking it a bit, in the hollow ache of 'The Thrill has Gone' and the impending sense of loss in 'I'd Rather Go Blind', in the tenderness of 'You Are The Sweetest Thing' and the sting of 'Hurt'.

The rest of Chicken Shack backed him with similar professionalism and the evening passed all too quickly as it does when things go well."

COLOSSEUM

"...all of Colosseum are more than capable of taking the lead with their own department and strength. A storming performance by one of the U.K.'s finest exports..."

Martin Hudson, *Classic Rock Society*

During their heyday, Colosseum earned a formidable reputation as a live band. They were renowned for their technical expertise and high standards of musicianship. They scored four consecutive top thirty albums, culminating in the celebrated *Colosseum Live* in 1971. This final outing featured John Hiseman (drums), Chris Farlowe (Vocals), Dick Heckstall-Smith (Saxophones), Clem Clempson (Guitars), Dave Greenslade (Keyboards) and Mark Clarke (Bass).

The band disappeared under a punishing work schedule and re-emerged as Colosseum II, featuring John Hiseman, Gary Moore and Don Airey.

Two decades after the demise of the original Colosseum, band members persuaded John Hiseman to pull the band back together for a few dates. John readily agreed and contacted his German agent, who secured thirty shows for the band. John takes up the story:-

"We decided to put a programme of our 'hits' together for the tour and I sent CDs of the old songs to all the boys. We met in my studio and we counted in 'Those About to Die'. It was as though we had been on a short vacation except that somehow we were playing better than ever. Obviously the years between had not been wasted."

The second concert from the reunion tour (Cologne) was filmed for television and has subsequently been licensed and released by Angel Air. The quality of the film is superb, the sound quality excellent and the musicianship and singing, magnificent. The DVD also includes a ninety minute documentary.

To accompany this release, half a dozen tracks have been pulled together for a live compact disc.

Reviews for *Live in Cologne* 1994': SJPCD162

"Yes, there are loads of solos and long instrumental passages, but the music just sounds right - created by people with tremendous skill and mastery of their craft but at the same time not being over-indulgent...A tremendous gig by a band on top form..."
Feedback (Nov 2003)

"...Farlowe is in especially excellent voice, while his band mates seethe with an energy that absolutely belies the two decades or so that hung between this show and the one recorded for the *Live* double in 1971..."
Jo-Ann Greene, *Goldmine*, (December 12, 2003)

www.temple-music.com

See also Greenslade, Survivors.

CONSORTIUM

"Mixing prog and pop, heavy folk in places, it's a decent affair that would have probably sounded out of place at the time... Well packaged, as is usual from Angel Air."

www.getreadytorock.com (February 2006)

'Perseverance' is the key word when describing the history of Consortium. Where many bands trod and subsequently folded, Consortium ploughed a lone furrow, bouncing back from an endless trail of disappointments and personnel changes.

The roots of the band can be traced back to the mid-Sixties and a superb harmony group called Group 66, which comprised Robbie Fair (now Robbie Leggat) (vocals) John Prodbury (drums), Brian Bronson (Rhythm Guitar), Geoff Simpson (lead guitar) and John Barker (bass).

Although the band initially played cover versions, by 1967, Simpson had started writing original material for the group. Re-branded as X-it, they released two singles, both of which failed to chart, though the latter, 'Colour Sergeant Lilywhite', is now regarded as a minor classic. A third single was released, under the name of Robbie Fair, but this also failed to chart.

The band underwent another re-branding, becoming Consortium. Under the watchful eye of producer/bandleader Cyril Stapleton, they pulled off a U.K. top thirty hit in 1969 with 'All The Love In The World' (number 22 with a nine week chart residency).

On the back of the success of the single, they toured relentlessly, also appearing on television and radio. This included a tour of Scotland for which they were never paid.

On the advice of Cyril Stapleton, Consortium continued to churn out singles without actually making an album. Frustratingly, they failed to emulate their previous success.

By 1970, Geoff Simpson had left the band, unwilling to leave his young family for a tour of Italy. He was replaced by Billy Mangham and organist John Caley was also added to the line-up, bringing Consortium up to a six piece outfit.

But the early Seventies proved a directionless time for the band, who were sounding progressively dated. John Barker and Brian Bronson soon left the ranks, along with new boy, Billy Mangham.

Ken Brown (bass) and Brian Parker (lead guitar) joined but before long, changes were afoot once more with the departure of co-founder John Podbury and the keyboardist, John Caley.

Mick Ware was enlisted as the second lead guitarist and John Parker (Brian's Brother) took over the drum stool. This left just the one original member – Robbie Fair (Leggat) from the original Group 66 line-up. However, stability prevailed and the line-up remained constant for the rest of the decade.

The band changed their sound, tuning into the musical tastes of the time, becoming heavier with the twin lead guitars and ditching the baroque instrumentation of the previous decade.

New songs were written (all band members were credited) and by the middle of the decade, they had become stalwarts of the pub circuit as well as supporting a number of major acts of the time, including Judas Priest.

During one particular gig at the Marquee Club, Consortium were approached by an RCA representative who offered the band the opportunity to record an album. Consequently, the group laid down ten tracks in just two days, replicating their live set…but in time honoured tradition, they were let down at the last moment by an over-cautious record company who were wary of the bleak political and economic climate that prevailed at the time. Ken Brown remembers the times well:-

"We were doing okay, sailing along, happy with our work, happy with our playing, happy with our audience reactions. We thought the big time was just around the corner. We were totally, 200% confident that it was there. It was a real blow when we didn't get accepted."

Consortium pulled themselves together and hit the road again, doing what they did best – playing live.

By the end of the Seventies, the band was 'gigged-out'. Exhausted, they ground to a halt.

After thirty years and various attempts to resurrect the one and only Consortium album, *Rebirth* has received a well deserved release on Angel Air. Sadly, in 2001, John Parker (drums) tragically passed away. Fittingly, the album is dedicated to his memory.

Reviews for *Rebirth*: SJPCD216

"After some long years of singles and live performances, the U.K. band Consortium finally sees the light of day for the first time ever of its sole album, *Rebirth*, recorded around 1975...

Like many albums of its time, *Rebirth* stands at the crossroads of psychedelic rock, hard rock and progressive rock. The music can be described as a hybrid between Grand Funk Railroad and Uriah Heep: it's dirty, train-like rumble and down-to-earth lyrics (sometimes to the point of banality as in the case of 'I Want You') resembling the earlier, while its operatic harmonies and grandiose dimensions reminding of the latter...

And so *Rebirth* is about the decades that shaped rock music being reflected through a certain point in time. It is therefore a shame it was not released close to its recording, as it could have established its reputation as a pivotal album. Still, it holds most of its vitality to this day. (8.25/10)"

Maelstrom, Issue 43

"...after thirty-odd years, the album finally - and deservedly - sees the light of day. Solid guitar riffs propel their hard rock sound..."

Record Collector (May 2006)

With thanks to Keith Smith.

CRAWLER

"...as exercises in polished melodic rock, they're certainly well worth investigating."

Kevin Bryan, *Stirling News*

The first thing to say about Crawler is that they were a rare breed. Whilst some bands have one or two song writers, others often 'buy in' material to make up their repertoire. In the case of Crawler, every member was an accomplished song-smith, which meant that the standards were kept high and there was never a shortage of material.

The foundation of the band can be traced back to the late Sixties. Keyboardist John 'Rabbit' Bundrick played in a Texan band called Blackwell which featured bassist Terry Wilson. They released an album in 1970.

John left Blackwell and worked for Johnny Nash (this is told in more detail under the chapter on Rabbit). In the process, he met Paul Kossoff and Simon Kirke, the remnants of the super group Free.

Kirke and Kossoff had recruited bassist Tetsu Yamauchi with a view to launching a new band and they were joined by John, who completed the quartet.

The resulting album, *Kossoff Kirke Tetsu Rabbit* (1971) served John well. When Free eventually reformed, he was invited to join the new line-up, replacing Andy Fraser on keyboards for the album, *Heartbreaker* (1973), before the band split once again.

The *Kossoff Kirke Tetsu Rabbit* album earned John a two album deal with Island Records. To make the albums, he called up his old friend Terry Wilson, who brought with him Tony Braunagel, a drummer who had played in a band called Buttermilk Bottom.

Terry and Tony went on to form part of Island Records' house band until they were recruited by Paul Kossoff who was forming a brand new band called Back Street Crawler. Terry Wilson-Slesser (not to be confused with Terry Wilson) joined on vocals.

To complete the line-up, Kossoff wanted John Bundrick on keyboards, but John's other commitments prevented him from joining. Mike Montgomery filled the role instead.

Back Street Crawler took to the road and made an album, *The Band Plays On* (1975).

By Christmas of that year, they were wooing audiences in America, joined by John on keyboards. However, problems ensued when Paul broke two fingers during a fight with the band's manager. Then, tragedy struck on the 19th March 1976 when he died during a flight from Los Angeles to New York. It is reported that he had suffered heart complications. He was only twenty five years of age.

Atlantic Records released the second Back Street Crawler album, *Second Street* (1976) and then dumped the band when they recruited Geoff Whitehorn as Paul's replacement. Geoff had been a part of Maggie Bell's band and was a talented and seasoned guitarist.

The new line-up gelled musically and socially but without a record deal they floundered – until 1977 when they were picked up by Epic Records.

They shortened their name to Crawler and their debut album, *Crawler* (1977) picked up rave reviews. They also toured with Moon and Boxer which helped them bond as a group. The new band was more soulful than the previous incarnation and boasted more of a sophisticated sound.

The album served them well in America where they toured, playing a mix of old and new material.

Crawler released one further album, *Snake Rattle and Roll* (1978) before John left to join The Who. The band disbanded soon after.

Angel Air has released three new Crawler albums. The first is a recording of the band live in concert at The Agora Club, Ohio in 1978. The musicianship is exemplary. The second is an anthology of demo recordings from 1975 to 1978 and the third is a collection of tracks recorded prior to the band's conception. All are released thanks to the diligence of John Bundrick, who (like Mo Foster) has an aversion to throwing anything away.

Reviews for *Live - Agora Club Ohio 1978*: SJPCD106

"Recorded towards the end of the touring to promote the debut album, the set is radically different to that on the *Snakebite* CD, which really does make the pair indispensable...In all this is a strong set and a very good show...The master tape has been nicely cleaned up...It's a pleasure to see this in the sales racks."
Free Appreciation Society (Issue 93)

"Touches of soul, funk and blues add to the interest and enjoyment of the audience at this club date, which captures well the band's blend of energetic rockin' for fans and novices alike. This set is well worth checking out."
Joe Geesin, *Record Collector* (March 2002)

Reviews for *Demo Anthology 1975 to 1978*: SJPCD124

"Over seventy minutes of excellent unreleased Crawler material, fully remastered and nicely packaged by those awfully nice people at Angel Air, who have been providing us with some wonderful material over the past few years...if you like Crawler then this really is a gift."
Free Appreciation Society, November 2002

"Don't be put off by the fact that this is made up of demo tracks, it really is a good album of blues rock from the mid-Seventies...Excellent guitar from Kossoff's replacement Geoff Whitehorn give this album real bite...These might not be the polished tracks that would be ready for release but this gives them a more natural feel of live recordings with eighteen tracks lasting for around 78 minutes. "
Alistair Flynn, *Classic Rock Society*, Highway To Hell, October 2002

Reviews for *Roots - Chapter 1*: SJPCD143

"Much of the material has a soulful, funky edge to it which became Crawler's trademark and suggests that if completed this would have been a very good album and even in the format in which it appears there is much to recommend it."
Classic Rock Society (August 2003)

"...long-time Crawler fans will recognise at least a handful of songs...an album that might not satisfy all the average Crawler fans' deepest desires for unreleased material...This is only *Chapter One*, after all. "
Jo-Anne Greene, *Goldmine* (Oct 2003)

With thanks to David Clayton. John 'Rabbit' Bundrick: www.thewho-rabbit.com; Terry Wilson: www.teresajames.com; Tony Braunagel: www.tonybraunagel.com.

See also Rabbit, Maggie Bell.

CRYBABYS

"This is good old punk rock 'n' roll at its best and Darrell (Bath) deserves to be a rock 'n' roll star and in many eyes including mine, he already is."

Phil Holbrook, http://members.tripod.com/~phil_holbrook

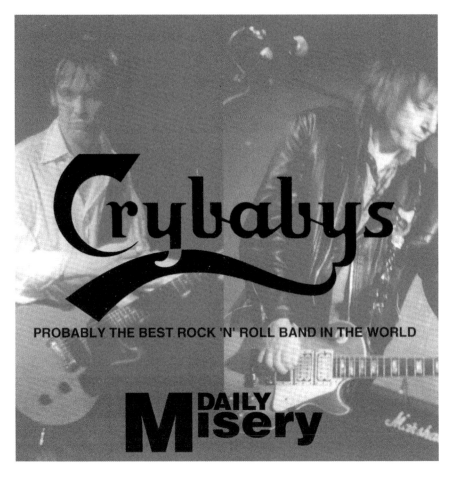

Had it not been for Arturo Bassick (bassist with punk band The Lurkers), Crybabys would probably never have existed.

Crybabys were formed by Honest John Plain and Darrell Bath.
John had cut his teeth in the music business with a number of punk bands since the Seventies, perhaps the most well known being The Boys.
Darrell Bath had emerged on to the same scene, earning his stripes with Bazooka Joe and UK Subs.

Both John and Darrell had been invited by Arturo Bassick to join his band, The Tower Block Rockers. They soon realised that their style of playing mutually complemented each other and in 1990, Crybabys were born. Robbie Rushton was recruited on drums and John Cooper on bass.

In 1991, Crybabys released the first of many albums, *Where Have All the Good Girls Gone?*

A number of singles followed along with a personnel change which saw Vom Ritchie (ex-Doctor and the Medics) replace Robbie on drums.

A second album was recorded for Receiver Records but due to a dispute with the label, was never released at the time.

In 1994, John and Darrell took a new line-up to France to record a third album, *Rock On Sessions*, which was eventually released in 2000.

Crybabys built up a fabulous live reputation over the years, with both John and Darrell maintaining a great stage presence. The high standard of song writing and musicianship ensured that the band went from strength to strength.

In 1996, Crybabys recorded their fourth album, this time relocating to Holland with Vom back behind the drums and Nick Peckham on bass. The end result was *Daily Misery* which has been released by Angel Air.

Reviews for *Daily Misery*: SJPCD120

"...a twelve-track slice of good time rock 'n' roll fun - though like all Crybabys records, it's topped off with a liberal sprinkling of good old-fashioned heartache. And we all know how addictive that tuff can be...*Daily Misery* is also the most punk sounding Crybabys album to date...This album has confounded my expectations at every turn. Well, all but one, thankfully - I thought it was gonna be good, and it is."
Darren Stockford, http://www.scuzz.com/crybabys/company.html

"The twelve tracks served up are pure, classic punk-edged punk rock...This is an album for lovers of straightforward no-nonsense rock...Buy, play, enjoy."
Adrian Lyth, *Classic Rock Society,* Highway To Hell, October 2002

See also Honest John Plain, Medicine Head, John Fiddler.

CULTURE CLUB

"There is no denying the spirit of the man. He simply oozes charisma, and is clearly delighted to be on stage at the Albert Hall…this is a fine representation of what must have been a very special night."

Tony Shevlin, *East Anglian Daily Times* 28.03.03

The origins of Culture Club can be traced back to a band called Sex Gang Children, which featured the talents of Boy George (vocals) and Mikey Craig (bass). The addition of Jon Moss (drums) and Roy Hay (guitar) saw the group undergo a re-branding…and Culture Club were born.

In 1982, Culture Club signed to Virgin Records. Success initially eluded them until the release of their third single, 'Do You Really Want To Hurt Me'. Boy George's cross-dressing and heavy make-up caused puzzlement and consternation when he first appeared on Top Of The Pops, stealing the headlines in the tabloids the following day. His appearance and sharp wit ensured that Culture Club remained headline news throughout their career.

Culture Club's debut album, *Kissing To Be Clever*, capitalised on this success, climbing to number 5 in the U.K charts. The follow up single, 'Time (Clock Of The Heart)' reached number 3. The band's American breakthrough followed in 1983 where they repeated their British success.

The release of their second album, *Colour By Numbers*, affirmed Culture Club's position as the most popular pop group in the world. *Colour By Numbers* spawned 'Karma Chameleon' which became a transatlantic chart topper, selling an astonishing five million copies worldwide. The album was kept off the American number 1 spot for six consecutive weeks by Michael Jackson's *Thriller*.

The band's third album, *Waking Up With The House On Fire* (1984) failed to repeat their earlier success and despite a string of minor hits, it became impossible to recapture some of that old magic.

Angel Air's release of Culture Club's *20th Anniversary Concert* at the Royal Albert Hall is a celebratory affair. Loaded with interviews and extras, the DVD is a fitting record of a band whose history has been described by Boy George as "a living soap opera".

Review for *Live At The Royal Albert Hall - 20th Anniversary Concert*: NJPDVD607

"…sees the band faithfully working through their back catalogue…the selection of bonus features (including footage from the musical Taboo and interviews with the Boy himself) might just clinch it for some fans."
Jon Chambers, *Record Collector* (June 2003)

With thanks to all at www.culture-club.co.uk

See also Sailor (for Phil Pickett, co-author of Karma Chamelon and other Culture Club hits).

MIKE D'ABO

"Lovingly restored from Mo Foster's attic, these tapes are in remarkably good shape and show that d'Abo was a talented song writer, as much as a vocalist and front man...If you like Seventies pop music teetering on soft rock, you will warm to this which is very much of its time. In parts it recalls solo performers like Paul McCartney, Eric Carmen and - wait for it - Gilbert O'Sullivan."

David Randall, www.getreadytorock.com (January 2004)

The name Mike d'Abo has become synonymous with Manfred Mann and the modern counterpart, The Manfreds.

Mike joined Manfred Mann in 1966 as a replacement for Paul Jones. He sang on a brace of hits, including 'The Mighty Quinn' and showed his early credentials as a song writer, penning 'Handbags and Gladrags'.

The break up of Manfred Mann in 1969 saw Mike determined to make his mark in the music business beyond his initial pop career. By 1971, he had sung 'King Herod's Song' on Jesus Christ Superstar and written the soundtrack to the film, 'Girl In My Soup'.

Mike signed up with GEM, a music management company run by Lawrence Myers and Tony Defries, with a view to furthering his career.

GEM recruited bassist Mo Foster from a Melody Maker advert and introduced drummer Henry Spinetti in to the melting pot. Together, the three musicians made a tight little trio. But they were short lived, because Henry was being offered plenty of other work which divided his time.

Mo had a solution to the problem. Only recently, he had been working with Grant Serpell (drums) and Mike Jopp (guitar) as part of the band Affinity. He suggested Mike recruit them to his band. The musicians knew each other, worked well together and were a ready-made unit. Mike had nothing to lose.

This became the classic d'Abo line-up. Together, they recorded the superb *Down at Rachel's Place*. The band toured America and found themselves supporting Jackson Browne, John Prine and Leo Kottke.

Upon their return to England, the band started recording a new album but the sessions were abandoned when Mike was encouraged to change his musical direction and work with American producer Eliot Mazer.

The tapes were quietly salvaged by Mo and stashed away, forgotten until 2003, when they were 'excavated'. As the tapes were looped on to the machine, Mike was transported back over thirty years:-

"As I listened to them once again…one by one, track by track…a mixture of hazy recollections and bittersweet memories came flooding back. At first, I hardly recognised some tracks at all, while other prompted an instant recall on both lyrical and musical content. My reactions also varied somewhat. Whereas certain moments had me purring with delight, others – like the odd dodgy lyric or below-par performance – had me cringing with embarrassment."

The very best of these tracks (and there are many) have been packaged together by Angel Air as *Hidden Gems And Treasured Friends*.

Mike remains an active part of the music business and still tours regularly with The Manfreds.

Reviews for *Hidden Gems And Treasured Friends*: SJPCD156

"The highly listenable contents find Mike searching for a coherent musical direction…some fine live performances have been included as an added bonus, led by the ever memorable 'Handbags and Gladrags'."
Kevin Bryan (March 2004)

"…an exquisitely titled collection of rare and unreleased recordings by Mike d'Abo. Representing an unreleased album d'Abo recorded back in 1973, appended with six songs performed live for a Long Island radio station the previous year, it's an excellent collection."
Jo-Ann Greene, *Goldmine* (February 2004)

See also Sailor (for Grant Serpell).

DAN THE BANJO MAN

"..Hugely entertaining and highly melodic curio."

Classic Rock Society (September 2005)

So far we have encountered such musical gems as Andromeda, Atomic Rooster, Crawler and Colosseum. And now we come to the highly original sound of Dan The Banjo Man!

Dan was a young man by the name of Phil Cordell, who had already scored major chart success under a previous pseudonym, Springwater, in 1971 (see under 'S' for further details).

Phil was a self taught guitarist who had spent the early part of his career with Steve Douglas And The Challengers, playing the clubs of Hamburg, an experience which left very potent memories:-

91

"It was always filthy. There would be a shower room in the venue behind the stage, and they'd put four beds in there for us. But we just got used to it, and I suppose it was just like being in the army."

Following Phil's success as Springwater, he looked for fresh challenges. With the use of a wah wah peddle, he managed to generate a banjo sound from his guitar...and Dan The Banjo Man was born. Phil recorded a whole album of material in the family cellar, using a guitar, metronome and four track tape recorder!

The lead single, a catchy piece called 'Dan The Banjo Man' gave Phil another U.K top thirty hit but in Germany, it took off in a way few would imagine, reaching the number one spot (twice!), endorsing the old saying 'that less is more'.

When it came to re-releasing the album on Angel Air, it was found that no one appeared to own a copy of the original vinyl release from 1974, or indeed the master tapes. Indeed, such was its rarity that a copy was eventually tracked down in South America by Ray Fenwick via an advert on the internet.

Reviews for *Dan The Banjo Man*: SJPCD191

"The Banjo Man juggles styles and moods like an acrobat, refashioning golden oldies with such creativity that one can't help but stand back in amazement, and the originals are just as mouth-watering...A welcome return for a spectacular album that hasn't dated in the least, growing only more magnificent with age."
Jo-Ann Greene, *Goldmine* (November 11, 2005)

"...the whole of the album is all about fuzzed distorted guitars...and it is actually quite listenable...Very Seventies, in fact very very Seventies..."
Feedback (November 2005)

See also Springwater.

DAVE DAVIES

"The crowd are having a great time, as are Dave and the band, and the result is a gig which is pure fun. If you like The Kinks then you will love this, and if not, what do you mean you don't like The Kinks?"

Feedback (November 2005)

Dave Davies is a man who needs little introduction. The opening bars of the Kinks third single (but first hit) 'You Really Got Me', have been Dave's calling card for the last forty plus years.

Born in 1947 to a working class family located in London's Muswell Hill (hence the Kinks nickname of 'The Muswell Hillbillies'), he was introduced to music at a young age by a family that entertained itself with sing-songs around the piano.

At the age of twelve, Dave's mother bought him his first guitar, which he practised incessantly.

Dave went on to form a band with his elder brother Ray, which also featured an old school friend, Pete Quaife. Under the name of The Ravens, they played local dances and church halls. When Mick Avory joined on drums, they became The Kinks.

93

The Kinks went on to become one of the biggest acts of the Sixties, securing a total of nineteen hits between 1964 and 1972 (this included three chart toppers).

Sandwiched in between this phenomenal chart run were two Dave Davies solo hits, 'Death of a Clown' (number 3) and 'Susannah's Still Alive' (number 20), proving Dave's credentials as a solo artist beyond the long shadow cast by his big brother.

The Kinks also produced a consistently strong selection of albums, including *The Kinks Are The Village Green Preservation Society* (1968) and *Arthur Or The Decline And Fall Of The British Empire* (1969). The majority of their albums failed to receive the recognition they deserved at the time of release, but are now revered as quintessential English classics.

The Seventies saw The Kinks head off in all sorts of different directions, both musically and geographically, with Ray and Dave living on opposite sides of the Atlantic.

Ray wrote a number of concept albums for the Kinks with ongoing themes, including *Preservations Acts I and II* (1973 and 1974) and *Schoolboys In Disgrace* (1976). By the end of the decade, through sheer hard graft and perseverance, The Kinks had established themselves in America as a stadium band, a re-invention that was required to ensure their ongoing survival.

In 1979, Dave found time to record the solo album *AFL1 4036*, which sold a highly respectable 150,000 copies. He followed this up with *Glamour* (1981) and *Chosen People* (1983).

The Eighties saw The Kinks riding high in the U.K chart again with 'Come Dancing' (number 12). They also produced a number of albums geared up for the American market which served them well, including the highly successful *State of Confusion* (1983).

The Nineties saw the Kinks produce just one album of entirely new and original material – *Phobia* (1993).

Since then, Dave has picked up on his solo career and released a series of strong albums, including *Bug* (2002), an eclectic studio album and *Transformation* (2003), a live recording showcasing music from the length and breadth of his career.

Reviews for *Bug*: SJPCD179

"*Bug* shows little sign of rust. He comes up with an array of stinging, Seventies-style hard rock riffs and lyrics that rail against the state of the world...the chip on his shoulder has dropped off and the three live bonus tracks...are almost superfluous."
Hugh Fielder, *Classic Rock* (July 2004)

"The collection that firmly asserts Dave's remarkable melodic skills and his popular craftsman approach, unafraid to rock out real venom..."
Beat magazine (July 2004)

Reviews for *Transformation*: SJPCD212

"The Angel Air label deserves a Grammy just for its very existence, having the good sense to put so many influential artists out under their umbrella and giving a twenty page booklet to this project along with the eighteen tracks. The 'You Really Got Me' riff slips in and out of the segues (the full song does get played as the set concludes) on this concert recorded at the Alex Theater in Glendale, CA, for an altruistic cause in 2003. And though Lou Reed is often credited with the dawn of glam rock, keep in mind that it was The Kinks' 'Lola' — which launched two years before Reed's *Transformer* — that really got the thing in motion. *Transformation* is a nice look back at some of those sensibilities, and a good argument for those who consider Dave Davies one of rock's underrated and absolute geniuses."
Joe Viglione, <u>All Music Guide</u>, (October 2005)

"Featuring superb interpretations of classics like 'Death Of A Clown', 'You Really Got Me' and 'Dead End Street' mixed with the best of *Bug*, 'Who's Foolin' Who'...this is the sound of the world's most underrated guitarist at his best...A brilliant album."
Classic Rock Society (November 2005)

With thanks to Keith Smith and Dave Davies.
Dave Davies at <u>www.davedavies.com</u>.

ANDY DAVIS

"...on this beautifully crafted twelve-tracker he demonstrates his wealth of musical talent, from the slow and easy to the traditional as well as the jazzy. This really is a rich offering of styles and sounds."

Hartlepool Mail (March 2006)

You have now reached the first of a 'family' of releases from Angel Air (see also Stackridge, The Korgis and James Warren).

Andy's career began in the early Seventies with Stackridge, a popular West Country group of musicians whose style defied description. They released a succession of strong albums, opened and closed the first Glastonbury Festival and built up a monumental following without ever bothering the commercial mainstream.

In the latter half of the same decade, Andy teamed up with another former Stackridge musician, James Warren and formed The Korgis. The group achieved a worldwide smash hit with 'Everybody's Got To Learn Sometime'. They still record from time to time and are on tour in 2007.

So now to Andy's big solo moment. Drawing upon his experience with the aforementioned bands (as well as working with Tears For Fears, John Lennon, Julian Cope and The Manhattan Transfer), Andy has collected together a selection of timeless songs, which offer a perfect showcase for his talent as both musician and song writer.

The title track, 'Clevedon Pier', harks back to Andy's childhood. He went to school near the Victorian landmark, which suffered substantial storm damage in the Seventies. The opening track, 'Women of Ireland', was used by Tears For Fears as a prelude to each of their shows on the 'Seeds of Love' tour.

The album is predominantly instrumentally orientated and was originally written as part of a New Age series of recordings. Andy and his co-musicians concentrated on producing an album that sounded spontaneous…which they achieved.

Andy's only regret is that the CD did not contain more tracks, but with an extra two bonus compositions, the twelve titles weigh in at a very respectable length.

Reviews for *Clevedon Pier*: SJPCD211

"…the album is gentle and restrained…Once again, Angel Air have produced a fine booklet with two bonus tracks…"
Classic Rock Society (November 2005)

"…it is so laid back it is horizontal - in the right mood then this would be essential…"
Feedback (November 2005)

With thanks to Michael Heatley.
 http/www.andrewcresswelldavis.com/index.html
See also Stackridge, The Korgis and James Warren.

STEVE DAWSON

"Pandemonium Circus is a cranking slab of raw rock 'n' roll."

Jo-Ann Greene, *Goldmine* (May 2002)

Spinal Tap is acknowledged by many to be one of the most amusing, clever and ironic films ever made, spoofing the life of a living, breathing rock band on the road.

From the well meaning 'Dobly' girl through to the undersized and in-effective stage props, it is often so close to the truth, to be uncomfortable. The bass player in Spinal Tap was Derek Smalls, a pipe smoking individual with a drop-handled moustache, who seemed to be the only one between them with half a brain. Smalls was modelled on one of the greatest musicians to emerge from the New Wave of British Heavy Metal – Steve Dawson of Saxon fame.

Prior to making the film, Harry Shearer (who played Smalls) joined Saxon on tour for a few days and spent many hours talking to Steve about his life. Steve shared many rock 'n' roll tales with him, little knowing that Shearer was assembling information for the character of Smalls.

Steve is actually rather pleased with the comparison:-
"I loved it. It's not everyday that someone bases a film character on you and anyway, it made me laugh."

Steve Dawson left Saxon in 1986 after a string of classic albums and hit singles. It seems that both Dawson and band mate Biff Byford were both dominant characters within the band and in time-honoured tradition; there was only room for one big personality.
Steve unhappily found himself on the outside looking in. Despite this, he is forgiving of Biff and bears no malice.

In the three years following his departure, Steve set about writing and recording his own material. These songs have now been gathered together and released by Angel Air as the album *Pandemonium Circus*.
The album serves as a testimony to Steve's excellent musicianship and tremendous talents as a song writer. There is also an inspired version of Cilla Black's Lennon and McCartney-penned 'Step Inside Love', a true rocker!
Material has been gathered for the album from three different sessions and a live set.
Steve can still be found playing live in Oliver Dawson Saxon and is working on a new album with Graham Oliver.

Reviews for *Pandemonium Circus*: SJPCD102

"This is classic Metal with rip-roaring tracks like 'She' mixed with occasional lighter, more Def Leppard-like material such as 'Too Late'. One of the outstanding tracks is the inspired, if on the face of it strange, choice of cover song in the form of the Lennon and McCartney penned Cilla Black hit 'Step Inside Love'. Add to this the fact that the last five tracks are live recordings from one of only two shows played in that period…and you have a great insight into what Steve Dawson is all about. Let pandemonium reign."
Adrian Lyth, *Highway To Hell* (Feb 2002)

"The album kicks off with the incredible 'She' and 'All That I Want'. They are followed nicely by The Beatles cover 'Step Inside Love' that really has been Saxon-ified…This is an album that is frightfully close to a 10/10 mark and anyone who claims Steve Dawson is not sadly missed in today's Saxon deserves a good beating!"
Miggo, (June 2002)

With thanks to Steve Dawson and Rich Wilson. http://www.oliver-dawson-saxon.com
See also Oliver Dawson Saxon, Saxon and Graham Oliver.

DESPERADO

"Heavy, raw rock music, with enough subtlety, excellent melodies and great musicianship...It's incredible that a record company would shelve this...At least the always-exciting Angel Air label is putting the record straight by making this sole Desperado album available at last."

www.prog-nose.org (July 2006)

There is a popular science-based show on British television called *Brainiac*. The host of the programme, Richard Hammond, oversees various scientists who specialise in mixing a cocktail of lethal substances with a view to creating spectacular explosions, punctuated by showers of sparks and blinding flashes of light depending upon the nature of the materials used. The rock 'n' roll equivalent of *Brainiac* is Desperado, a toxic cocktail of talent, featuring legendary guitarist Bernie Tormé and the enigmatic Dee Snider – the results are explosive!

The project came about following the demise of Twisted Sister. Dee was looking for a guitarist to duel with and knew of Bernie by reputation. Catching a recorded snippet of John McCoy's band Mammoth (which featured contributions from Bernie), Dee knew that he had found his man.

Bernie has always proven to be a popular musician, working with Gillan, Ozzy Osbourne and Atomic Rooster as well as fronting his own bands at various times. His pedigree was beyond question, though there was consternation when Dee's manager mistook Bernie's stammer for a bad coke habit!

Bernie brought on board original Iron Maiden drummer Clive Burr. Marc Russell joined on bass, completing the line-up.

Desperado was born!

Dee and Bernie formed a prolific and creative writing partnership, churning out dozens of songs. They signed to Elektra Records, recorded an album and after two years of hard work, performed their debut concert – a 'secret' gig in Birmingham. Then it all went wrong as Dee explains:

"We were signed by this A & R guy called Brian Koppleman; his father was way up in EMI. Brian left Elektra for Giant Records. The management were pissed off so they killed every project he was working on, including us. Totally political. The head of Elektra was not a Metal fan and at one point wanted to dump every Metal act on Elektra. You had Metallica, Motley Crue doing *Doctor Feelgood* - that stuff was funding the label. My management was getting us out of the deal. Left a year later with my songs tied up. The label had spent half a million that they wanted getting picked up, and we had the stigma of being shelved, so we couldn't get signed by anyone else."

The band disintegrated soon after, though Marc and Dee formed a spin off group, Widowmaker. Bernie declined to join due to a punctured lung and the birth of his son.

All the musicians involved are proud of the Desperado album and there is little doubt that the group would have been an enormous success on the Metal scene.

Dee is now back with a reformed Twisted Sister, Bernie is working with John McCoy on the project GMT. Clive Burr has since been struck down with Multiple Sclerosis and sadly can no longer play.

Review for *Ace*: SJPCD154

"Without a doubt, it is a very strong record which should have been released back then, but nevertheless it is a good thing to see it released after all. It does not sound dated at all, because songs like 'Heart Is A Lonely Hunter', 'Calling For You', 'See You At Sunrise', 'Made For Trouble' and 'Ride Thru The Storm' (fantastic!!!) are all very sensational melodic American hard rock songs in the best late Eighties style.

The extensive liner notes and perfect sound quality make this a release worth checking out for sure." (8.5/10)

Strutter'zine *http://www.strutter.8m.com* (August 2006)

With thanks to Joe Geesin.
See also Bernie Tormé, Mammoth, Gillan.
www.retrowrek.com www.bernietorme.com

DOC THOMAS GROUP/THE SILENCE

"This is a superb package featuring an in-depth CD booklet with many rare photographs. Great sound quality and well put together, this CD continues Angel Air's remit to revive and release often forgotten or ignored works from yesteryear."

Terry Craven, *Classic Rock Society*

Who on earth were the Doc Thomas Group or for that matter, The Silence?

The simple answer is that they were the forerunners to Mott The Hoople, Mott and British Lions, all of which are featured in this book.

To find the origin of these bands, we have to travel back in time to 1962. Man had yet to walk on the moon, The Beatles had only just started to change the face of music and England had yet to win the World Cup. But in Ross Grammar School, two musically orientated pupils were having fun forming school bands and generally enjoying themselves. They were Peter Watts and Dale Griffin.

Between 1962 and 1963, Peter was in a band called The Sandstorms before forming The Anchors in 1963, which featured Dale.

The Anchors gave way to The Wild Dog's Hellhounds. Peter's party piece during a show was to pull a rubber bone from a trap door in the stage and to drink out of a bowl marked 'dog'.

Between 1964 and 1965, Peter and Dale progressed on to the Soulents. This was a step up from their previous bands. They owned a van and supported a number of major acts at the time, including The Zombies and The Yardbirds. The Soulents transformed into The Silence who were thrown into disarray when Peter announced that he was turning professional and joined The Buddies, a band that featured Mick Ralphs and later, vocalist Stan Tippins.

The Buddies regularly played in Hamburg, turning in long hours for little (or no) pay and mixing with pimps and prostitutes. They underwent a name change to The Problem, before becoming The Doc Thomas Group, a name they pinched off Dave Mason (later of Traffic) who deputised for Peter on a trip to Germany when the young guitarist was unwell.

Whilst gigging in Germany, the band met a young lad called Rinaldo Ricci, whose father was an Italian agent. As a consequence, they secured a large amount of work in Italy. They also recorded an album.

The group went through a number of personnel changes which also saw Dale Griffin and Mick Ralphs team up with Terry (Verden) Allen in Jimmy Cliff's Shakedown Sound, a name they kept on after the group had split from Cliff, before reverting back to The Doc Thomas Group for further Italian engagements.

Much to the shock of the other band members, Peter stayed behind, falling in love with a beautiful young lady and formulating plans to form an Italian super group, I Giganti.

The plans for the band fell through and in the autumn of 1968, Peter rejoined his band mates (Dale Griffin, Stan Tippins, Terry Allen and Mick Ralphs) who were now playing as Silence. Little did any of them know that Mott The Hoople lay just around the corner.

The Angel Air album, *The Italian Job*, pulls together the original album and a wonderful, historical collection of tracks from these exciting and impoverished times.

Review for *The Italian Job/Shotgun Eyes*: SJPCD020

"Doc who? - You may well ask. From little acorns great oaks grow - as do great rock groups. The two little known 60s outfits featured on this new CD brought together the players that would audition for Island Records in May 1969. One month later they recorded their first album under their new name Mott The Hoople... what we have here is one of the finest R&B albums heard in recent years."

Mike Neal, *Beat Goes On* magazine

See also Mick Ralphs, Overend Watts, Mott, Mott The Hoople, British Lions.

JOHN DU CANN

"Utterly convincing, packing much the same kind of mood and power as the early Ultravox!...the first-ever release for a phenomenal piece of new wave rock and also the first release for a dozen demos, outtakes and oddities recorded by Du Cann and Rooster drummer Paul Hammond around the time of the Rooster reunion."

Jo-Anne Greene, *Goldmine*, (June 1999)

Despite only reaching 'D', this book has already explored three of the high points in the career of guitarist and song writer, John Du Cann.

John started his career with Sixties band The Attack, formed prog/psyche rockers Andromeda and performed as one third of Atomic Rooster with Vincent Crane and Paul Hammond.

Following his departure from Atomic Rooster in the early Seventies, John formed Bullet (renamed Hard Stuff for legal reasons) before joining Thin Lizzy as a replacement for Gary Moore.

John left Thin Lizzy and began writing music for other artistes but, inspired by the punk movement, began writing songs for his own use, compiling a set of demos which in 1976, secured him a deal with Arista Records.

With Francis Rossi in the producer's chair and John McCoy on bass, an entire album was recorded but disappointingly never released. The record label underwent an internal re-organisation and John's considerable efforts were consigned to the archives. It was an illogical step given the amount of money lavished by Arista on the project, even down to the completed artwork.

All seemed to go quiet until 1979 when John recorded a song for a Lee Cooper advert called 'Don't Be A Dummy'. It proved to be a popular track and became a top forty hit. John was rewarded with an appearance on *Top Of The Pops*.

His high profile continued at the end of the decade with the reformation of Atomic Rooster, inspired by a resurgence of interest in the band as a consequence of The New Wave of British Heavy Metal.

Angel Air has given John's album, *The World's Not Big Enough,* a long overdue release, expanded to a massive twenty-seven tracks, including the aforementioned hit single and a wealth of bonus material, including a heap of unreleased demos.

Reviews for *The World's Not Big Enough*: SJPCD043

"...John Du Cann...had an uncanny ability to tap into the spirit of the times: mainstream pop with mid-Sixties group The Attack; psychedelia with late-Sixties Andromeda and then prog rock with Atomic Rooster...recorded in 1977...the album has a pop punk feel...of interest to Atomic Rooster and Status Quo fans."
Colin Shearman, Q, July 1999

"...[*The World's Not Big Enough*] at times seems on the verge of catching the energy of the punk movement that sprang up about that time...A tight rocking album well worthy of attention and it's a pity that it's taken twenty years to see the light of day. Well packaged with informative notes and twelve high quality bonus tracks added to the original fifteen songs, this is another welcome addition to the Angel Air label."
Terry Craven, *Wondrous Stories* (June 1999)

See also Andromeda, The Attack, Atomic Rooster, Five Day Week Straw People.

STEVE ELLIS
(STEVE ELLIS'S LOVE AFFAIR
& LOVE AFFAIR)

"Ellis clearly has a fine voice and the musicianship is first class...the sleeve notes are riveting and include detailed interviews with Ellis, as well as previously-unseen photos."

Rich Wilson, *Record Collector* (April 2001)

Angel Air has served Steve Ellis's back catalogue well, with four very different releases.

Steve was just fifteen or sixteen years of age when he joined a band called The Soul Survivors. They were a popular London act with a residency at the Marquee Club and featured Morgan Fisher on keyboards, Michael George on guitar and Maurice ('Mo') Bacon on drums.

The Soul Survivors were renamed Love Affair and by January 1968, found themselves on top of the Hit Parade with 'Everlasting Love' (the line-up now featured Mike Jackson (bass), Lynton Guest (piano and organ) and Rex Brayley (lead guitar)). Capitalising on their success, they scored further hits with 'Rainbow Valley' (number 5) and 'A Day Without Love' (number 6).

Love Affair attracted an almost unprecedented level of teen hysteria and Steve became a pin-up for thousands of teenage girls.

The band secured two further major hits – 'One Road' (number 16) and 'Bringing Back The Good Times' (number 9). That same year, Steve announced on stage at

Newcastle that he was leaving the band. He had been offered a solo deal that was too good to refuse!

Steve released four strong singles but they failed to emulate previous successes.

He then formed Ellis, a band featuring Zoot Money. They recorded two great albums, *Riding The Crest Of A Slump* (1972) and *Why Not* (1973). The former featured vocal contributions from Maggie Bell.

Steve's next band was Widowmaker (no connection with Dee Snider's Widowmaker), which featured Paul Nichols (Lindisfarne), Huw Lloyd Langton (ex-Hawkwind) and Ariel Bender (ex-Mott The Hoople). They were managed by Don Arden, who had a fearsome reputation in the business. Widowmaker toured America and were a hard working outfit but internal differences led to the band's inevitable demise.

In 1977, Steve returned to the studio to make a new solo album, *The Last Angry Man*. The album featured some familiar faces, including Roger Chapman but it only received a limited release on cassette due to a dispute between the producers.

A couple of solo singles were also released before Steve took the decision to leave the music business. This was in part prompted by the death of his close friend, Keith Moon, which served as a stark reminder to Steve of the perils of the industry.

Steve settled into a routine job as a docker. However in 1981, he suffered a horrendous injury when his feet were crushed by a pair of two-ton forklift blades. Eight years of operations and hospitalisation followed, which included bone grafts.

Steve took up Karate and remarkably regained some semblance of mobility.

In the early Nineties, he took the decision to return to the music business, forming Steve Ellis's Love Affair. Steve took the band on the road and into the studio.

In 1998, he recorded a single called 'Step Inside My Love' with long-term fan, Paul Weller, in aid of the NSPCC.

Angel Air has released three albums and a DVD from different stages in Steve's career. *Love Affair – No Strings* covers the Sixties (with one track from 1999), *The Last Angry Man* gives Steve's 1977 solo album a proper airing (with seven bonus tracks) and we hear Steve in fine voice on *Steve Ellis's Love Affair – Live '95*. The live DVD, *Last Tango In Bradford*, brings Steve's career up to date.

Reviews for *The Last Angry Man*: SJPCD077

"Now then, now then, Angel Air's lost CD sniffer has been successful...The music was way ahead of its time so even now twenty four years on it still has not dated...a magnificent album. "
Modern Dance (November 2001)

"The excellent ten page sleeve notes with this CD tell his story...the second half 'bonus tracks' under the heading 'Basement Days' were recorded with a line-up that never intended to go on the road but laid down some fine tracks...some fine

songs…We enjoyed listening to this much belated release, and must congratulate Angel Air and Steve."
'Byron', *Blues Matters* (Sept 2002)

Reviews for *Live '95*: SJPCD087

"…a night of Motown music, performed superbly…It seems everyone had a fabulous night at the concert and if you buy this you too can enjoy it just when you want."
Modern Dance #39 (August 2002)

"…Steve's blend of soul covers golden oldies such as 'Everlasting Love' and 'Rainbow Valley', serving up a veritable feast of nostalgia."
Stirling News, (February 2003)

With thanks to Steve Ellis. www.stevellis.co.uk   www.fivetrees.com.

See also Roger Chapman, Maggie Bell, Morgan Fisher, Huw Lloyd Langton, Mott The Hoople.

FANCY

"Seasoned with a sizzling sensuality thanks to the sexy vocals of Annie Kavanagh, the songs on this CD…are a mix of covers and originals. An exuberant release - listen out for the steamy 'Touch Me'."

Hartlepool Mail, October 2001

If you were to dig into *The Guinness Book Of Hit Singles And Albums*, the name Fancy would be conspicuous by its absence. However, delve into the American charts and you would find an altogether different story.

Fancy were the brainchild of singer and producer, Mike Hurst.

Mike had an idea (indeed an obsession) to record the Chip Taylor song 'Wild Thing' with a female vocalist, turning the old hit into something sexy and seductive (no offence Reg!)

Mike contacted his old friend Ray Fenwick and together they worked up an arrangement of the song. Mo Foster was brought in on bass, Henry Spinetti on drums and glamorous 'Penthouse Pet', Helen Caunt, on lead vocals. Alan Hawkshaw added the synthesisers, thus completing the session. Everyone then went their separate ways.

Atlantic Records released the single in the U.K. and Holland but it failed to chart. Their subsidiary, Big Tree, released it in America and the song was a colossal top ten hit, peaking at number 7.

Mike was aware that Fancy needed to be more than just a name – as such, the band did not exist, despite being a major success in America. He recruited Les Binks on drums, stuck with Mo and Ray and recruited a fabulous female singer by the name of Annie Kavanagh to complete the definitive line-up.

An album was recorded (*Wild Thing* (1974)) and a new single released. 'Touch Me', written by Ray, hit the American top twenty. The album fared poorly in comparison and the record label soon lost interest.

Fancy recorded a second album for Bell/Arista (*Something to Remember* (1975)) and toured America, playing with the likes of Wishbone Ash and Steppenwolf. By the end of 1975, they were strutting the stage of the Hammersmith Odeon, supporting 10CC.

The band did not progress beyond a second album and those two hit singles remain their commercial highlight.

In a short time, Fancy were transformed from a pop act to a hard rocking band. Both albums are deserving of a fresh listen and have been released together on a '2 for 1' package by Angel Air.

Reviews for *Wild Thing/Something To Remember*: SJPCD094

"Beautifully packaged CD...This is early Seventies rock conceived by Ray Fenwick and Mo Foster, whose career blossomed when they recorded the ever popular track 'Wild Thing' and from then on, things just got better."
Norfolk Suffolk Preview(October 2001)

"More than one hit wonders, Fancy featured three of Britain's top session musicians of the Seventies and were pioneers of British funk. The band's story deserves to be told and this welcome reissue does just that."
Keith Pettipas *www.canehdian.com* (December 2001)

See Mike Hurst, Ray Fenwick, Mo Foster, Affinity, The Ian Gillan Band, Tee Set, RMS, Sundance, Guitar Orchestra, The Spencer Davis Group, Minute By Minute.
www.mofoster.com www.mikehurst.co.uk.

FANDANGO

"... even a cursory listen to Fandango's output places them so far to the forefront of what was gradually coalescing into the New Wave of British Heavy Metal that the group's total obscurity must really hurt. Hopefully, this (as usual) loving and lavish repackaging will at least grant Fandango some historical kudos."

Jo-Ann Greene, *Goldmine*, September 1999

The creation of Fandango can be traced all the way back to the early Seventies and a band called Warhorse (featured later in this book).

Warhorse was the brainchild of Nick Simper, one-time member of Johnny Kidd's Pirates and Deep Purple. The band produced two albums, ground breaking in their day but not a commercial success.

Following the demise of Warhorse, Nick and fellow band member Peter Parks played in a band called Dynamite, which also featured ex-Pirate John Carroll, vocalist James Royal and drummer Mick Richardson. They released just the one single, 'St. Louis', which made a mark in Italy, but by then it was academic because the band had split up.

Nick and Peter turned to session work and song writing for a living, as well as gigging in and around London as part of a band called Flying Fox.

During the late Seventies, Nick formed his next serious recording band, which went under the name of Fandango. Accompanied by Peter Parks, they were joined by drummer Ron Penny and vocalist James Proops. A deal was signed with Shark Records and in 1979 their debut album was released in the U.K and Germany, called *Slipstreaming.*

Financial constraints meant the Fandango remained purely a recording and non-gigging band, but despite this state of affairs the album faired respectably well.

The following year, a second album was recorded, with Mac Poole from Warhorse standing in for Ron Penny on drums. *Future Times* received a release just before Shark Records collapsed.

Fandango re-united briefly on the Paro label to record the single 'Just Another Day' before calling it a day and moving on.

Review for *Slipstreaming/Future Times*: SJPCD041

"To all Deep Purple fans...this is an invaluable release as it provides an inexpensive way to help pad out the collection as this contains both albums and unreleased recordings..."
Feedback, October 1999

With thanks to www.deep-purple.net; www.nicksimper.com

See also Warhorse, Quatermass II.

FAVOURITE SONS

"...the band were obviously at home with their music, despite their apparent youth...Their versions of 'Can't Judge A Book' and 'That Driving Beat' are fine examples of their craft...As a snapshot in time this is an enjoyable - if rather short - album."

Feedback (July 2003)

There have been bands throughout history that have from time to time strived to protect their anonymity, hiding behind pseudonyms and in some cases, make-up or masks. However, the case of The Favourite Sons is far more simple and straight forward...their names have been forgotten!

Not to be confused with a recently formed Scottish band of the same name, our band emerged from the mid-Sixties music scene.

All the musicians involved were no older than seventeen or eighteen years of age. Such was the impression they made on producer Mike Hurst, he took them under his wing and offered to produce an album for them.

The Favourite Sons were a Mod band, heavily influenced by The Who, Birds, Creation and Small Faces.

They recorded a string of cover versions and a couple of Mike's own songs, most of which exuded enthusiasm and youthful energy.

They released one single on Mercury, 'That Driving Beat', but failed to make an impression on the charts.

It is baffling how such a good band could slip into total obscurity but it seems that lack of management and poor promotion were to blame.

Mike Hurst found the unreleased recordings at home and decided that they were well worth a second listen. Peter Purnell at Angel Air agreed and released them as an album.

Whoever they are, The Favourite Sons have left behind a brief but enduring legacy for us all to savour and enjoy.

Review for *That Driving Beat*: SJPCD139

"Even though most of their recorded output consisted of the (more-or-less) usual soul covers, some of the versions delivered by this Mod combo happen to be among the best ones around..."

Most of this half-hour listening is actually best described by the title tune's lyrics: 'listen to the music and when you hear the beat, you can strike the scene and you just gotta move your feet, baby let your hair down and move me all around, cuz when you hear that driving beat you know you gotta go!' ...and in the end, you'll be left with no other choice but to go indeed!"

Goran Obradovic / POPISM radio show; Serbia & Montenegro (May 2005)

With thanks to Jon 'Mojo' Mills, Mike Hurst and Marcus Cawood.
www.mikehurst.co.uk

See also See also Hardin and York, Sundance, Minute By Minute, Summer Wine.

RAY FENWICK

"Now this is important stuff so I want all you musos and anoraks to take notice, 'cause this is for you... Buy this, because if ever there was a musician's musician (and I'm well aware that can be a front for being totally crap in an extremely clever way) it was the very wonderful Ray Fenwick, he of among others, The Spencer Davis Group, Ian Gillan Band (mid-late Seventies) and The Guitar Orchestra."

The Modern Dance Issue 24

Ray's career in music kicked off in the Sixties when he was just fifteen years of age, playing Ska with Rupert And The Red Devils. He went on to replace Steve Howe in freak-beat group, The Syndicats.

Ray's enthusiasm then took him across the North Sea to Holland where he joined an innovative and highly successful band called Tee Set, racking up an enviable run of Dutch hit singles. He capitalised on this with a breakaway group called After Tea.

Ray returned to the British music scene, joining The Spencer Davis Group with whom he served until the mid-Seventies.

In between engagements, he found time to record a solo album, *Keep America Beautiful, Get A Haircut*. The title came from a billboard slogan formulated by American First Lady, 'Lady Bird' Johnson, who had a scheme to clean up the male population of America! The album included many of Ray's friends, including Mick Grabham, Polle Eduard, Dee Murray, Eddie Hardin and Peter York.

That same year, Ray formed Musicians Union Band, releasing a Dutch-only double album. This proved to be an innovative and highly original convergence of British and Dutch musicians from all walks of life, the likes of which has never since been repeated.

Ray and Mick Grabham went on to form The Guitar Orchestra, producing one album. All three of the aforesaid albums have received a much deserved release on Angel Air.

In 1974, Ray co-founded a band called Fancy, who scored huge success in America and are featured in an earlier chapter.

Ray also participated in Roger Glover's *Butterfly Ball* project, playing live at The Royal Albert Hall. In the process he met up with Ian Gillan and joined The Ian Gillan Band, who achieved considerable success in the Far East and modest success on the home front.

Towards the latter half of the decade, Ray joined The South Coast Ska Stars and turned producer for The Teenbeats, scoring a number one hit in Canada.

Throughout the Eighties and Nineties, Ray became an established producer and session musician, building on his hard earned reputation as a favourite in the profession.

Ray still remains an active and creative force in the music business:-

"I am still recording and touring. I have recently toured with Steve Howe from Yes and I am currently recording a solo album. I have my own band called The Ray Fenwick Rhythm And Blues All Stars and I also play with drummer Clem Cattini in the Mike Hurst Rock 'n' Roll Show."

Reviews for *Keep America Beautiful Get A Haircut*: SJPCD013

"Ray Fenwick is another of those super-session men who appear on million-selling records yet are not themselves household names. Originally released in 1971, *Keep America Beautiful, Get A Haircut* was Fenwick's concept, based around his perceptions of the United States at that time.

An all-star line-up joined him for the project, including Mick Grabham, B.J.Cole, Eddie Hardin, Peter York, Dee Nurray, Nigel Olsson and many more. Opener, 'Stateside', berates America's war in Vietnam as a bass-heavy riff reinforces the message. Elsewhere, acoustic guitar plays a large part, with that early 70s earnest delivery much in evidence"

Steve Caseman, *Rock 'N' Reel*

"Ray concentrates more on songs than on guitar histrionics and the album is all the better for it. Some of the songs are blues-tinged, while others are acoustic, but the result is one that will be enjoyed by those who are into thought-out Seventies song-based rock. The reissue comes complete with a Picture CD, good sleeve notes and photos."

Feedback

With thanks to Claes Johannsen and Ray Fenwick. www.rayfenwick.com

See also Tee Set, Minute By Minute, Ray Fenwick, Fancy, Summer Wine, Guitar Orchestra, Ian Gillan Band, Mike Hurst's All Star Band.

JOHN FIDDLER

"It's a superb album that all lovers of good music will enjoy. Some are acoustic while others are electric but at all times John is in total control, and the results are a tonic...an album to savour."

Feedback (June 2000)

This is the second of three major entries in this book for John Fiddler. If you have read this chronologically, you would have come across British Lions, a late Seventies band which John fronted in his post-handlebar moustachioed days.

Prior to this, he achieved tremendous success as one half of the classic Seventies hippie duo, Medicine Head, who are featured later in this book.

So what happened next?

Following the break up of British Lions, John devoted his time to song writing and raising his young family, until he was approached to join a Yardbirds revival. The band metamorphosised into Box Of Frogs, who recorded two albums (*Box Of Frogs* (1984) and *Strange Land* (1986)) before disbanding.

John progressed through a number of other bands throughout the Eighties including Freeway and Western Front.

In 1989, John was approached by The Blues Band to support them on tour. Loving a challenge, he picked up the gauntlet and never looked back. He was a sensation as a solo act.

Recognising a gap in the nostalgia market, in 1991 he pulled together a new version of Medicine Head, performing new songs as well as the old hits to enthusiastic and receptive audiences.

John eventually returned to the studio, recording his first solo album (on an eight track tape player). It took just three weeks to record and mix.

Originally released under the title *The Return of the Buffalo*, it has now been expanded and re-released on Angel Air as *The Big Buffalo*. *The Rough Guide To Rock* describes the album as "an astonishing solo album, capturing all the charge and vision of (Fiddler's) early work."

Reviews for *The Big Buffalo*: SJPCD048

"...this CD is an eclectic mixture of up-tempo rockers, ballads and R 'n' B classics that should prove to be popular with anyone fortunate enough to hear it...There has been much debate within Classic Rock Society circles as to what actually is classic rock and such is the strength of this album that I would be tempted to put it forward as the sheer definition of this genre."

Terry Craven, *Wondrous Stories* (May 2000)

"...The music is modern and very melodic...a fine example of Nineties pop-rock. A far cry from what Fiddler was doing twenty or thirty years ago, but it's done well, and with extra tracks and sleeve notes that are up to Angel Air's usual high standards."

Record Collector (July 2000)

With thanks to Jay Wyatt, Dale Griffin and John Fiddler.
www.johnfiddler.com
See also Medicine Head and British Lions.

THE FIVE DAY WEEK STRAW PEOPLE

Time has been kind to The Five Day Week Straw People. Their one and only album is regarded as a psychedelic classic – a slice of Sixties nostalgia which conjures up images of long hair, short skirts and the sights and smells of swinging London. Even the cover is a work of art.

Unlike the majority of the bands around at this time, The Five Day Week Straw People were a 'manufactured' band. They were formed by John Du Cann, who was endeavouring to break into the big time with The Attack (see earlier in the book). In fact, he was formulating plans for his next band, Andromeda, when he was approached by an independent record label.

The label bosses were keen to increase their portfolio and offered John £25 to produce a psychedelic album to complement their catalogue. Strapped for cash, John rose to the challenge and wrote ten songs, which he and friend Mick Hawksworth arranged over the course of a week. The album was a concept piece charting the weekend adventures of 'the straw people', a phrase John coined to describe people locked into the 9 to 5 working week.

The day of the recording session loomed and John and Mick met up with drummer Jack Collins at the recording studio. The term 'studio' is used loosely, because by day the building served as a nursery school. Consequently, portable recording equipment had to be shipped in for the session once the children had all gone home – there were no sound booths, acoustic walls, or even head phones. The room was large and suffered from reverberation. And whilst the soundman was laying out cables and setting up his levels, the drummer was introduced to the ten songs.

Once everyone was ready to set the tapes rolling, the reality of the situation dawned on John, Mick and Jack. They had just four hours to record the album in its entirety…and they did it!

It was a testament to their professionalism that they pulled off such a major feat, producing an album that was delightfully played and sung, well written and bursting at the seams with charm.

After four hours, everyone packed up and went home and the following day, the school reverberated once again to the sound of children. The Five Day Straw People existed for just those four hours, but the album has endured for forty years. (SJPCD59)

See also Attack, Andromeda, Atomic Rooster and John Du Cann.

MO FOSTER

"One of the best bass players this country has produced..."

Phil Collins

Mo Foster has been at the heart of Angel Air's success from the very early days.

A substantial number of the recordings lovingly compiled and released through Peter and Shirley Purnell's label have been salvaged from his dusty attic. Indeed, his reluctance to throw out historical recordings has been a blessing to the music business and a service to the profession. Consequently, we have a body of work on offer that would otherwise tragically have been lost forever.

Mo has been a bass player and side man to hundreds of major artists since the Sixties. He has enjoyed major chart success on both sides of the Atlantic. Indeed, at the time of going to print, Mo has participated on over three hundred and fifty albums, most recently working with Cliff Richard, Brian Bennett and Brian May on a re-recording of Cliff's first hit, 'Move It'.

His style has embraced anything from pop and rock to jazz, the latter being his true love. His versatility, reliability and technical brilliance ensured that he was rarely out of work.

Tall and bearded with red hair, Mo has spent a lifetime lurking at the back of group photographs, happy to duck the limelight and offer centre stage to friends and colleagues. In his younger days, his wonderful blaze of hair made him easy to spot in a crowd.

After decades as a sideman, Mo seized his big moment and took centre stage. His debut came in 1988 with the release of *Bel Assis*, the original name for Belsize where Mo lives. The album is a beautiful collection of jazz-tinged instrumental pieces recorded with some of the best musicians in the business.

This was followed by *Southern Reunion* (1991), another selection of instrumentals with a more restful and melodic feel.

In 2002, Mo released *Time To Think* on his own Primrose Hill label. An extraordinary album, it was recorded over two days in an Oxford church and featured Ray Russell on guitar. The Observer made it their CD of the week.

Mo's next album, *Live at Blues West 14* (2006) drew upon his experience of playing live at the aforementioned Kensington club. Mo used many an enjoyable session at this venue to cultivate the material which makes up this album.

Bel Assis, Southern Reunion and *Live at Blues West 14* have all been released by Angel Air.

In 2006, Mo released a fifth album, *Belsize Park,* through Leo's Den Music (www.leosden.co.uk). The album is Mo's personal tribute to his late friend, Tony Meehan of the Shadows.

Like all national treasures, Mo should be cherished for future generations.

Reviews for *Bel Assis*: SJPCD151

"If you are ever tempted to believe the old slur about session musicians not being creative artists, just spend half an hour with this and you'll know it's not true. Mo Foster is one of the finest bass guitarists in the world, surrounded here with a band of his peers including saxophonist Stan Sulzman, drummer Simon Phillips, guitarists Gary Moore and Ray Russell. Recorded in 1987, *Bel Assis* is a forgotten minor classic. Clarity of sound and pinpoint accuracy of timing are just the start. The true appeal lies in its simple grace and emotional warmth."
Dave Gelly *Observer.*

"....truly remarkable and exciting, and reminds me in parts of Gustav Holst, too. Leave it to you Englishmen to bring us Americans back to musical quality...."
Carol Kaye

Reviews for *Southern Reunion*: SJPCD163

"If 'Who He' is your first reaction to Mo Foster's name, you've probably already heard the bespectacled bassman's work on dozens of singles and albums.

Foster is rare among British sessioneers in having a solo album register in the Billboard chart but *Bel Assis* did just that, doubtless helped on its way by featuring Gary Moore on its lovely, Beck-esque opener The Light in Your Eyes. Another remarkable thing about Foster's solo outings is that they both differ from the generic 'session man goes solo' efforts by leaning heavily towards his Guitarist compositional side rather than serving as a platform for sheer 'follow that mate' blowing; his vast experience as a solid but sympathetic accompanist is simply awesome to behold. Fans of muso pyrotechnics won't go home disappointed though as Foster clearly relishes the opportunity to let off steam and trade licks with his celeb' mates - as demonstrated by some staggering playing from the likes of Simon Phillips, Snail's Pace Slim, Gary Moore and vibes player Frank Ricotti." ***

Tim Slater, Guitarist Magazine. Aug 1995

"Foster is a first-rate English studio bassist with a gorgeous fretless tone, and he's wise enough to share the melodic spotlight with such accomplished sidemen as guitarist Gary Moore and flutist Ray Warleigh."

Bass Player Magazine. June 1995

Reviews for *Live At Blues West 14*: SJPCD207

"Renowned musician Foster recorded these tracks during the Nineties at The Blues West 14 Club and other similar small clubs, getting that intimate sound. Playing bass, guitar and keyboards (not all at the same time I must add) he is accompanied by Ray Russell, Gary Husband and a host of others.

The music is a gentle and easy mix of blues and jazz, the sort of music you'd listen to over dinner, where it fits in well.

Nothing too taxing, it's hard to just listen to this CD, it's excellent for what it is and the musicianship can't be faulted, but great background music."3/5

Joe Geesin, *www.getreadytorock.com* (June 2006)

With thanks to Neville Farmer and Mo Foster. www.mofoster.com

See also Ray Russell, RMS, Survivors, Fancy, Affinity, Mike d'Abo, RJ Wagsmith Band.

FREEDOM

"Another gem from Angel Air Records sees these two albums get a long overdue re-release...*Through The Years* ...should have set them up as major competition for Led Zeppelin' ...Excellent informative cover notes as always help make this a stunning release."

Terry Craven, *Wondrous Stories* (May 1999)

The Freedom (as they were then known) were formed in 1967 following a well publicised split within the ranks of Procol Harum.

Ray Royer (guitar) and Bobby Harrison (drums) founded the band which offered Bobby the creative freedom to flourish as a musician, song writer and band leader. It is fair to say that had he remained with Procol Harum, he may not have achieved his full potential.

Ray and Bobby recruited Mike Lease on keyboards and Steve Shirley on bass, thereby completing the line-up.

The band recorded their debut album, a soundtrack for the Italian film *Nerosubianco*

123

(Black On White). Disappointingly, it only received a limited release in Italy, much to the frustration of all concerned.

Indeed, Bobby was very unhappy with the way matters were progressing and took the decision to dismiss the band and start again.

Simplifying the name to Freedom, he recruited Roger Saunders and Walter Monaghan. Freedom became a power trio much in the vein of Cream and The Jimi Hendrix Experience, churning out high quality heavy blues rock.

In 1968, the album *Freedom At Last* was unleashed upon the French and German record buying public but for some inexplicable reason did not receive a U.K release. This was again a source of frustration for Bobby.

Nevertheless, the band worked hard and toured relentlessly, including trips to America supporting Jethro Tull and Black Sabbath. Slowly but surely, they built up a following and gained a formidable reputation as a live act.

The two following albums, *Freedom* (1970) and *Through The Years* (1971) received releases in both the U.K. and America, which meant that the band were at last reaching a greater audience.

Around the time of the release of the final album, *Is More Than A Word* (1972), the future of Freedom looked bleak. Roger Saunders had secured a solo deal and the management sacked Walter Monaghan.

Two new members were introduced (Pete Dennis on bass and Steve Jolly on guitar) but Freedom had started drifting towards a sound more generally associated with Procol Harum.

In 1972, disillusioned and disappointed, the band split up.

The whole Freedom back catalogue has now deservedly been re-released on compact disc by Angel Air.

In the 21st Century, Bobby Harrison occasionally takes a version of Freedom on the road as a Christian rock band.

Reviews for *Freedom At Last*: SJPCD175

"This is music from the late Sixties that is influenced by bands such as Cream...For me this is one of the most-played releases that I have had from Angel Air, as it is such an easy album to get into, yet there are so many layers that each time I play it I get even more from it. Plenty of information in the booklet makes this a wonderful release."
Feedback (September 2004)

"...a quality album...An amazing power trio, this is probably the missing link between Sixties bands like Cream and the Jimi Hendrix Experience, and more experimental outfits like Led Zep', Deep Purple and the harder edge that The Who developed. A great gem of an album, released with the impeccable presentation that sets every Angel Air release apart from the crowd. "
Classic Rock Society (September 2004)

Reviews for *Freedom Through The Years*: SJPCD177

"They mix the blues in with more straightforward hard rock...another interesting nugget from Angel Air and one that is worth hearing."
Feedback (November 2004)

"Some listeners will be transported to head banging heaven..."
Trevor Hodgett *Blues in Britain* (November 2004)

Reviews for *Freedom*: SJPCD063

"...By the time Procol Harum spin-off group Freedom recorded this eponymous album, they'd long since abandoned that group's classical roots in favour of a coarser, Cream/Sabbath-style progressive blues template...The presence of three would-be lead singers helped Freedom to wring the max from the formula...They were probably cracking live... "
Classic Rock (August 2000)

"...this delightful period piece is redolent of The Who circa *Live At Leeds*...The sleeve notes also contain a brilliant anecdote about Ozzy Osbourne flinging excreta at Curved Air's Sonja Kristina."
John Hazlewood, *Q* (August 2000)

Reviews for *Is More Than A Word*: SJPCD073

"...the fact that the original LP is rated at £100, it's more than welcome for fans. Mixing blues-rock, funk, and gentle piano-based Seventies pop, the atmosphere is very upbeat...although, sadly, Freedom never made the first division of British rock, this quality package is well worth checking out."
Joe Geesin, *Record Collector* (February 2001)

"...a triumph of heavy blues rock and psychedelic pop which brought favourable comparisons with the likes of Cream and Led Zeppelin, and justifiably so...by the time of this release Freedom had abandoned their hard blues driven approach for a funkier, more soulful sound..."
Steve Ward, *Wondrous Stories* (February 2001)

See also Bobby Harrison, Snafu.

GILLAN

"The Gillan vaults have been pillaged again for some real treats...Whether it's the explosive punk-metal of Bernie Tormé or widdling by current Maiden guitarist Janick Gers, Ian Gillan's brand of metal was unsurpassed. "

Record Collector (September 2000)

If you are reading this book chronologically, I would urge you to bookmark this page first, then fast forward to Gillan's predecessor, The Ian Gillan Band.

The Ian Gillan Band had been an innovative and experimental outfit, fusing jazz and funk with traditional rock. Although the music was technically superb, it met with limited commercial success.

Ian retained the services of Colin Towns (keyboards) from the original band and recruited John McCoy (bass), Liam Glenocky (drums) and Steve Byrd (guitar) to form Gillan.

Ian took the band off in a heavier direction, playing more traditional rock, which owed much to the talent of his new musicians and the man who produced many of the new recordings, big 'bad' bald bassist John McCoy.

Gillan initially secured a deal in Japan where they released one album but the European market took notice and a deal was signed with Acrobat Records.

A new album was recorded, *Mr Universe*, which featured Bernie Tormé who had replaced Steve Byrd on guitar and Mick Underwood who took over from Liam Glenocky on drums.

The album was a major commercial success throughout Europe and reached number 11 on the U.K. album chart. It was supported by 'The Mr. Universe Tour', which unusually took in a host of Scottish venues.

A label switch saw Gillan sign to Virgin Records, where they achieved their commercial peak with the release of the album *Glory Road,* in 1980. The album reached number 3 in the U.K. and the band stormed the top twenty singles chart with the song, 'Trouble'.

This was followed by another hit album, *Future Shock (1980)* (number 2) and continued single success with 'Mutually Assured Destruction' (number 32) and 'New Orleans' (number 17). However, there was deep frustration that the band could not crack the American market. It was an enigma given their success in Europe, Japan and other territories.

In 1981, Bernie left the band and was replaced by Janick Gers. The new line-up released two albums which made the top twenty, *Double Trouble* (1981) (a live double album) and *Magic* (1982). Gillan also embarked on a massive thirty-seven date tour.

Gillan shows were always entertaining and often a tremendous spectacle, with the ample frame of John McCoy being hoisted on Kirby wires over the stage - like Peter Pan's big uncle!

Mick Underwood recalls one such occasion when John's wires became tangled with near catastrophic results:-

"Mr. McCoy was flying above me on wires, when it all started to get a little bit out of control. Here was my dear and VERY BIG friend swooping ever lower over my head with no sign of control being regained. The crew did manage to sort it out [not before John had hurdled the drum kit] and avert total mayhem thank God and the gig went well."

John's days as a human bomb are long over and his feet now remain firmly on the ground.

Gillan ground to a halt when Ian had to rest his voice. However, unknown to his band mates, he wound the band up without properly addressing outstanding financial issues which have since caused considerable hurt over the years.

Angel Air has doubled the size of Gillan's considerable back catalogue thanks to the diligence of John McCoy, who has preserved a mountain of recordings – live outings, outtakes, demos and alternative versions – all from his personal collection. These are complemented by the release of an historically important live DVD.

Despite the acrimony surrounding the split of Gillan, all artistes involved in these releases have been duly remunerated.

Review for *The Gillan Tapes Volume 1*: SJPCD004

"The album features Ian Gillan, John McCoy, Bernie Tormé, Colin Towns and Mick Underwood. McCoy has many hours of tape and a follow up to this album is on the cards for this autumn.

This compilation has been put together by bassist John McCoy... there is no doubt in my mind that this album is essential to anyone who likes Gillan...If you remember just how good Gillan were then this is an album you must get. "
Feedback

"I'll stake my split-knee loons you won't find a more enjoyable compilation this month...the set is essential for any Gillan fan and fine insight for the casual listener. "
Joe Geesin, *Record Collector* (March 2002)

Reviews for *The Gillan Tapes Volume 2*: SJPCD023

"This is an amazing collection from an amazing band that left the scene far too early...very tight, live sounding numbers that have an excitement about them that you don't find on most studio recordings. "
Music America, (July 1999)

"Like it says on the packet, this is the second volume of Gillan tapes and it's even better and more interesting than the first...This twenty track compilation is a well put together collection of alternative mixes and rarities...a must for all the group's fans and a worthwhile acquisition for those who would like to know why Gillan was so popular."
Don Craine, *Beat Goes On*, (June 1999)

Reviews for *The Gillan Tapes Volume 3*: SJPCD051

"...The seventeen tracks featured are a mix of alternative takes and live recordings, and what a selection it is. All that made Gillan, the band, what it was is on show here, from powerful rockers...to classy ballads...A classic selection from a classic band...the first 5000 pressings will be released as a numbered limited edition with a free CD entitled *For Gillan Fans Only*...A must have bonus."
Wondrous Stories (August 2000)

"...Some excellent songs, some amusing spoken interludes and a kind-of-definitive version of 'The Harry Lime Theme' await. So what are you waiting for?"
Jo-Ann Greene, Goldmine(October 2000)

Reviews for *Gillan Live At The BBC 79/80*: SJPCD055

"A great double CD for rock fans, featuring seven Gillan classics from 79's Reading Rock Festival, two sets recorded for *BBC In Concert*, 'If You Believe Me' from a 1980 *Friday Rock Show* and a couple of interviews with Ian himself... "
Andy Coleman, *Birmingham Evening Mail* 11.1.00

"Deep Purple's front man stormed the Reading Festival in 1979 with his new line-up...half-a-dozen tracks from that appearance showcase their heavy riffing, thunderous percussion and full-blown, snarling vocals...A similar set for a *BBC In Concert* broadcast is tighter, if anything...Another broadcast for the same BBC series, a year

later, saw the introduction of the fast and furious 'Unchain Your Brain'...A handful of other good rockers with trademark, spot-on vocals, a 16-page booklet, and it's time to ditch your old tapes."
Tim Jones, *Record Collector* February 2000

Reviews for *Live Tokyo 23 October 1978 Shinjuku Koseinenkin Hall*: SJPCD082

"...this release is one of the earliest recorded moments (and the first time on CD) of the newly formed Gillan line-up...A must for all Gillan fans despite the bootleg quality."
Steve Ward, *Wondrous Stories* (October 2001)

"...a real gem...a live set to die for. Great material and enjoyable sleeve notes make this a top-notch effort."
Joe Geesin, *Record Collector* (March 2002)

Reviews for *On The Rocks*: SJPCD119

"*On The Rocks* only contains strong songs, mostly genuine material and now and then a well chosen 'oldie' cover...
Time flies when you're enjoying yourself and that's exactly how to describe this CD in a few words; before you know it, it's over."
Deep Purple Fan Club (August 2002)

"The folks at Angel Air must be diehard Gillan fans because they've released more Gillan compilations, live performances, and CD's from related band members than any other label. If you're a fan of Ian Gillan or Deep Purple, you're probably well aware of the label. *On The Rocks* is a recording of a June 17, 1981 performance from Aachen, Germany. A clear and well-recorded presentation...diehards will probably want to scoop it up." Score: 3 out of 5 Battle-Axes
Chris Dugan - Metal Dreams

Reviews for *Live Wembley 17th December 1982*: SJPCD152

"At over seventy minutes you get your money's worth here with a mix of Gillan and Deep Purple material. The band was on form with classics belting out like 'Black Night', 'M.A.D.' (where Colin Towns and Janick Gers let fly) and the Beatles cover 'Helter Skelter' (who remembers Vow Wow's version of this?)
Of course 'Smoke On The Water' is here and it's time for Gillan to employ a series of bizarre vocal sounds! Interesting to speculate what the band would have done had Gillan not disbanded the group.
Worthy addition to a Gillan/Purple fans collection, with good sound quality throughout plus extensive sleeve notes." Rating ****
Jason Ritchie, *get ready to ROCK!* (January 2004)

"An excellent live recording from the last days of Gillan, 15 tracks that see the band pushing the realms of Heavy Metal so far into the future that Gillan's own imminent departure for Black Sabbath (and the reformed Deep Purple) remains a sore point for everyone who believed his band was worth much more than either. "
Jo-Ann Greene, *Goldmine* (February 2004)

Reviews for *M.A.D. Glasgow 82*: SJPCD184

"All the tracks are here you'd expect including 'Trouble', 'M.A.D.', 'Smoke On The Water' and one of my personal fave Gillan songs 'No Laughing In Heaven'. Two bonus tracks as well - 'No Easy Way' and 'If You Believe Me'. As with any Angel Air release you get very informative sleeve notes (why can't all re-issues/rarities releases be this good?) from Jerry Bloom, editor of 'More Black Than Purple'."
Jason Ritchie, www.getreadytorock.com (September 2005)

"It's a thumping line-up that can tackle techno metal as easily as straight rock 'n' roll, and Gillan himself is on enthusiastic form."
Classic Rock (November 2005)

With thanks to John McCoy and Jerry Bloom.
www.moreblackthanpurple.co.uk www.bernietorme.com
www.mickunderwood.com www.colintowns.com

See also McCoy, Mammoth, Samson/Paul Samson, Zzebra, Bernie Tormé, Sun Red Sun, Desperado.

GO WEST

Go West represent possibly the youngest of a brace of Eighties signings to Angel Air.

In 1982, musicians Peter Cox and Richard Drummie pooled their artistic talents and recorded two demos, 'Call Me' and 'We Close Our Eyes'.

On the strength of these two songs, they secured a record deal with Chrysalis which marked the beginning of a long and successful career.

The release of 'We Close Our Eyes' as a single in early 1985 saw the duo secure hits on both sides of the Atlantic. On the back of this success, their debut album *Bangs and Crashes* (1986) sold in the region of 1.5 million copies and enjoyed a chart run in the U.K lasting over a year and a half!

A string of hit singles followed, including the memorable 'King of Wishful Thinking' which was one of the most played records on American radio during that era.

Other memorable singles of the time include the hits 'Goodbye Girl' and 'Call Me' which ensured an unbroken chart run that lasted well into 1993.

Despite pursuing a number of solo projects, Cox and Drummie have in recent years performed a number of sell-out shows, proving that they still have the ability to pack out the largest of arenas.

Angel Air's 2004 release of Go West in concert – *Kings of Wishful Thinking – Live*, is a fantastic trawl through their greatest hits and features the customary interview and band history.

Such was the popularity of this release that it became a top thirty hit, thus proving that the small independent labels are more than capable of competing with the multi-nationals.

Reviews for *Kings Of Wishful Thinking – Live*: NJPDVD613

"In the 1980s they were a very popular band in the U.K. but in the rest of the world only known for their hit "When I Close My Eyes" and their appearance on one of the best soundtracks of all times (ROCKY 4).

Now a DVD is available of a recent concert they gave. Although they lost their Eighties hair look, the band still sounds like the Eighties, with a big keyboards sound and soulful lead vocals.

All their U.K. hits were performed during the concert they gave and although I had not listened to this band before it gave me a good feeling watching this professional recorded DVD...a must-have because Go West was another typical Eighties product and they still sound very strong.

Besides a full concert performance also interviews with the two main members (Peter Cox and Richard Drummie) and a history bonus feature is included on this 2 hours and 40 minutes DVD." (Points: 8.2 out of 10)

Gabor Kleinbloesem, *Strutter'Zine* (January 2006)

"There is a real rapport between the band and the crowd which makes all of the intervening time just melt away...Overall this is a DVD that will interest not only new fans who have been brought in by the appearance of Peter Cox on TV but also by those who were fans years ago but somehow lost track of them along the way. At 160 minutes long this is definitely value for money. "

Feedback, (June 2004)

With thanks to Andrew Jordan. www.gowestmusic.co.uk

MICK GRABHAM

Mick Grabham is perhaps best known for his involvement with Procol Harum. However, he has led an interesting and varied career in the music business.

Mick was born and raised in the north east of England during the gritty post-war era. As a teenager, he worked his way through a series of local bands, honing his craft as a guitarist.

He eventually chose to move south and joined Plastic Penny, who scored a hit with 'Everything I Am'.

When the project folded, he formed his own West Coast influenced rock band, Cochise, recording three albums between 1969 and 1972 (*Cochise, Swallow Tales* and *So Far*). They also cracked the Billboard Top 100 with 'Love's Made A Fool Of You'. Band mate Rick Wills later went on to join Foreigner.

In 1972, Mick joined Procol Harum, remaining with them for five years. He also found time to perform with Ray Fenwick as part of the magnificent Guitar Orchestra.

Mick's solo album has been very hard to find in record shops. Re-released by Angel Air, it was freely available for the first time and boasts the usual array of extra tracks. Mick's accompanying musicians include the late B.J. Wilson (formerly of Procol Harum), Nigel Olsson and the late Dee Murray (both formerly of Elton John's band), Pete Wingfield, Dick Parry and the belting voice of Madelaine Bell (Blue Mink).

See also Ray Fenwick, Guitar Orchestra.

133

GREENSLADE
& DAVE GREENSLADE

Dave Greenslade made his name playing keyboards with progressive rock giants Colosseum, scoring four top thirty albums and building up a following worthy of their name.

By 1972, the group had worked themselves into the ground, only to emerge as Colosseum II featuring John Hiseman, Gary Moore and Don Airey.

Dave Greenslade chose to form his own band, giving his surname and reputation to the ensemble. Consequently, public expectations were exceptionally high.

Dave was joined in Greenslade by Tony Reeves on bass (a former member of Colosseum), Dave Lawson (keyboards and vocals) and Andy McCulloch (drums).

The group was unusual because it lacked a guitarist, relying instead upon two keyboardists. The debut album, *Greenslade* (1973), boasted symphonic soundscapes and an orchestral approach that proved popular with lovers of progressive rock.

That same year, Greenslade released a second album, *Bedside Manners Are Extra*, which is regarded as their finest work of the era.

For the third album, Dave brought in his old friend Clem Clempson from Colosseum to beef up the sound, along with violinist Graham Smith and acoustic guitarist, Andy

Roberts. The end result, *Spyglass Guest* (1974) was very well received and reached number 34 in the U.K. album chart, their biggest commercial success. This album included a superb cover of 'Theme From An Imaginary Western' by Mountain.

The departure of Tony Reeves was a huge blow to the band. His replacement, Martin Briley, toured with the band and played on their final album of the era, *Time and Tide* (1975). However, the shape and sound of the band had changed and the album came in for some criticism from fans.

Interestingly, all of the Greenslade album covers came in a gatefold design, almost obligatory for any self-respecting band of this ilk. They were designed by Roger Dean and showed a man with an excessive number of arms, a symbolic gesture to the three or four keyboards played at any one time by Messrs Greenslade and Lawson.

By 1976, Dave wanted to terminate Greenslade's existing management contract. He felt a different organisation may be better suited to the band's requirements. Alas, a buy-out was the only way this could be achieved. This proved to be too costly and Dave took the sad decision to disband Greenslade.

Dave went on to record two solo albums in the Seventies before moving into the field of television drama, where he scored music for twenty-six dramas in twenty years.

The Nineties reformation of Colosseum had the knock-on effect of leading to a Greenslade reunion.

With Tony Reeves back on board, the band had its beating heart back again. The line-up was completed by Chris Cozens on drums and John Young (ex-Asia) on keyboard. John Trotter deputised for Cozens during the live shows.

An album was made in 2000 called *Large Afternoon* which was followed by a live album, *The Full Edition*, released by Angel Air in 2001.

Angel Air has also released Dave's solo album from 1999, *Going South*. Dave describes it as "an album initially inspired by the evocative sight of migrating birds. I always experience a mysterious thrill when observing these determined creatures on their way to who knows where."

Reviews for *Going South*: SJPCD168

"...a welcome reissue...a fine album which maintains the high standards set by its creator."
Steve Ward, *Classic Rock Society* (August 2004)

"This is an ambient New Age album from a keyboard player who has produced some stunning work..."
Feedback (September 2004)

See also Colosseum.

LUTHER GROSVENOR

Luther Grosvenor was born on 21st December 1946 in the town of Evesham near Worcester. The youngest of seven children, he was named after his sister's husband, an American G.I.

Luther took up the guitar from a young age and made his stage debut at the age of fifteen, playing Shadows numbers.

By the mid-Sixties, Luther had taken a giant leap and turned professional, forming the band Deep Feeling with Jim Capaldi and Poli Palmer (later of The Blossom Toes).

The project came to an end when Jim teamed up with Steve Winwood and Dave Mason to form Traffic. However, Luther wasn't forgotten and Winwood played a major role in securing him a place in a band called The V.I.Ps, who were enjoying major chart success in France at the time. The V.I.Ps featured Keith Emerson, Mike Harrison, Greg Ridley and Mike Kellie.

The V.I.Ps transformed into Art, steering away from their R 'n' B roots and taking a more progressive course. They released an album, *Supernatural Fairy Tales* (1967) on the Island label but this failed to make any commercial impact. When the future was looking decidedly dicey, Island's owner, Chris Blackwell, suggested that Art team up with American vocalist/organist, Gary Wright.

The new line-up was re-christened Spooky Tooth by Island producer Guy Stevens and so began a rich and innovative period which saw the perfect marriage between Wright and his new band mates.

Their first album, *It's All About* (1968) was well received and helped Spooky Tooth to build up a strong following. *Spooky Two* (1969) capitalised on this and is now regarded as a masterpiece. It featured the rollicking nine minute classic, 'Evil Woman'.

From then on, things seemed to go downhill. Greg Ridley left to join Humble Pie and the remainder of the group collaborated with French electronic music composer, Pierre Henry on the album *Ceremony*. This caused some confusion with the fans and the media and did little to help their cause.

Gary's departure left just Luther, Mike Harrison and Mike Kellie. With the assistance of members of The Grease Band, they pulled together a final album, *The Last Puff*, which was well received but bore witness to the band splintering as they undertook session work and pursued solo projects.

Luther took time out after the demise of Spooky Tooth, spending time at Chris Blackwell's Spanish villa, soaking up the sun and writing new material. Upon his return to England, Island Records gave him the go ahead to record his first solo album, titled *Under Open Skies* (1971). Luther tried unsuccessfully to pull a new band together but managed to lay some tracks for a second album although the project was never completed.

In 1972, Luther joined Stealer's Wheel as a replacement for Gerry Rafferty. He appeared on two singles and played a large number of gigs until 1973, when Rafferty rejoined the band. At about this time, Luther declined the opportunity to reform Spooky Tooth, viewing this as a regressive step.

By 1973, Luther had joined Mott The Hoople as replacement for Mick Ralphs who had left the band to form Bad Company with Paul Rodgers. It was an inspired move which saw Luther share in a successful chart run, which is described in more detailed later in this book.

During his time with Mott The Hoople, Luther earned the nickname of Aerial Bender, as Ian Hunter recalls:

"We were in Mannheim doing a TV show and he got drunk and put his head in a horse trough and walked down the street bending all the car aerials. And Lyndsey de Paul was with us and she goes 'Ah! Look at Arial Bender!' And I thought, 'that's a great name for a guitar player.'"

Luther (Ariel) made a massive contribution to his new band and gave 110 per cent to the group, finally departing in late 1974 to be replaced by Mick Ronson of Bowie's Spiders From Mars.

Following his adventures with Mott The Hoople, Luther reportedly tried to form a new band although this did not come to fruition. He was also invited to join the Mael Brothers in Sparks but opted instead to form his own band, a hard rock outfit called Widowmaker.

Widowmaker was funded by Luther and featured Paul Nicholls (ex-Lindisfarne), Bob

Daisley (ex-Chicken Shack) and Steve Ellis (ex-Love Affair and Ellis). Steve brought in his friend Huw Lloyd-Langton (ex-Hawkwind).

Their debut album in 1976 was well received and the band toured with ELO, The Who and Little Feat. As a live act they were powerful but off-stage, they reportedly fought like cat and dog. Consequently, Steve Ellis left to be replaced by John Butler, who featured on their second album, recorded at the end of that year.

The band toured America but with the departure of Butler coupled with managerial problems, they called it a day. In fact, Luther decided that it was time to leave the music business.

There was however, one brief exception – a low key project with Verden Allen called Verden and Luther. They released a single called 'On The Rebound'.

Luther quietly retreated to pursue life as a painter and decorator, running his own business. It was only in 1992 that he was tempted back on to the stage by friend John Ledsom, forming part time band, Blues '92.

In 1995, Luther contributed to a Peter Green tribute album which in turn, led to the release of a solo album, *Floodgates* (1996) (SJPCD088). The album featured some of Luther's old friends including Mike Kellie, Steve Dolan, Dave Moore, Jess Roden and Jim Capaldi (who sadly died recently). This album has now been released by Angel Air.

Luther's career back in the music business took an interesting twist a few years later when he partook in a Spooky Tooth reunion which generated a new album.

In 2004, Luther appeared at the memorial concert for his late friend, Greg Ridley.

He now fronts the Ariel Bender Band who are a regularly live attraction in the U.K and Europe.

See also Mott The Hoople.

GUITAR ORCHESTRA

"It's a pity that it has been delayed until now as this could have been a real classic from the Seventies featuring musicians who have worked with Pink Floyd, Procol Harum, Ian Gillan and The Spencer Davis Group. This musical extravaganza was the brainchild of Mick Grabham and Ray Fenwick. Featuring guitars and yet more guitars, it is a comfortable blend of blues/rock well expounded by the likes of Free and Eric Clapton."

Terry Craven, *Classic Rock Society*

The first ever release by Angel Air came from McCoy. The second was an all-star extravaganza from the highly unusual Guitar Orchestra.

It is fair to say that had the *Guitar Orchestra* album been released at the time it was recorded during the early Seventies, then it may well have become a classic and perhaps a familiar sight in record collections the length and breadth of the country.

The brainchild of Ray Fenwick and Mick Grabham, the album is a remarkable collection of songs performed by leading guitarists of the time. As well as Ray and Mick, the album features Dee Murray, Tony Newman, John Gilbert, Tim Renwick and Nigel Olsson.

The original release ran in to difficulties due to a ground breaking and highly original romp through Elgar's 'Pomp And Circumstance'. Disappointingly, The Elgar Society blocked the release at the time, though all copyright issues have now been resolved.

Ironically, one of the aims of the modern version of the Society is to encourage the study and performance of Elgar's work in schools and colleges. Guitar Orchestra's version of 'Pomp and Circumstance' can only seek to encourage young people to explore his music through their own clever, modern interpretation.

Reviews for *Guitar Orchestra*: SJPCD002

"...it would be easy to dismiss the CD as derivative...In its own way it could have been a groundbreaker. Even for hardcore instrumental fans, the vocal tracks are not without interest...Of the purely instrumental tracks 'Stella' has an attractive, relaxed feel, and 'Live Wire' could almost be a rather heavier out-take from the Shadows 'Rockin' With Curly Leads' Album.
Very much a case, then, of what it might have been...full marks to Mick Grabham and Ray Fenwick for allowing us to hear these tracks - albeit twenty six years too late."
George Geddes, *Pipeline*

"...at the easy listening end of rock, with both hard and jazz influences, and all very enjoyable. You need to be in the mood for it, but it's far from coffee table, so lay back, chill out and let's rock..."
Joe Geesin, *Record Collector* (November 2001)

See also Ray Fenwick, Mick Grabham, Ian Gillan Band, Minute By Minute, Fancy, Summer Wine, The Spencer Davis Group, Tee Set.

JOHN GUSTAFSON

"...his songs are inventive (incorporating jazz, funk and country influences) and make for a driving rock album."

Joel McIver, *Record Collector* (August 1999)

John Gustafson has earned himself a reputation as one of the greatest bass players of his generation.

John's career can be traced all the way back to the Cavern Club in Liverpool when he was a member of The Big Three. John rubbed shoulders with the future stars of the time, honing his skills and exploring new sounds.

He went on to join The Merseybeats, achieving considerable commercial success.

In the late Sixties, John joined the remnants of a band called Episode Six which evolved in prog rock outfit, Quatermass. They toured America and released one album but were arguably too far ahead of their time and split up.

John soon found himself much in demand as a session bassist. This included a long stint with Roxy Music, playing on three of their albums.

During the mid-Seventies, he became an integral part of The Ian Gillan Band. His unique style of playing suited Gillan's vision of fusing British rock with black American music.

Prior to this, John was presented with some studio time in which to record a solo album. He worked with some extraordinary musicians, including Mike Moran, Barry Desouza and Tony Hymas. The recordings were much in the vein of his work with Ian Gillan.

The collection of recordings were titled *Goose Grease* – reference to John's nickname of 'Gussie Goose' (after a Liverpool Echo cartoon character) and his mother's habit of keeping a jar of goose grease in the basement, which she would religiously rub into John's chest as a little lad to combat coughs and sneezes.

John's busy schedule meant that the recordings 'went off the boil' and were never released. His career progressed apace, including a seven year stint recording and touring with Mick Green's Pirates.

The album has always been worthy of release. Angel Air has seized the moment and for the first time, given the nine tracks a public airing.

Reviews for *Goose Grease*: SJPCD008

"Angel Air has really done it this time, not re-releasing a rare LP as in the past, but finding an UNRELEASED gem from 1976 from the much sought after Gustafson - everybody from Roxy Music to Ian Gillan rate him as a superb bass player and arranger/writer. It was he for example, who put the bass line to "Love Is The Drug" and completely changed the feel of the track according to Bryan Ferry, who is not one to hand out praise - full stop.

Goose Grease is a collection of mainly jazz funk tracks that unusually manage to be musically complex and clever but prove eminently listenable to. The opener 'Boogie Woogie', (although having a poor title) demonstrates this nicely, although songs like 'Precious Heart' and 'Don't Care' try hard to break this style the band are obviously comfortable with. Gustafson is backed by such luminaries as B.J.Cole, Tony Hymas and Mike Moran and they combine perfectly to produce a superb collection with many similarities with the (now) much vaunted hard funk-rock of the Ian Gillan band of the mid-late Seventies, which he joined shortly after completing this.

The only mystery is why it was never released before."
"*The Modern Dance*" Internet version #7

"It borrows the jazz-funk style fashionable at that time and combines it with hard rock, giving the resultant fusion a harder, tougher edge...Another good release from Angel Air of forgotten classic rock."
David Schofield, *Wondrous Stories* (December 2001)

See also Ian Gillan Band.

HADLEY NORMAN & KEEBLE

During the Eighties, London-based Spandau Ballet were at the cutting edge of the new romantic movement. The band comprised Tony Hadley (lead vocals), Gary Kemp (guitar), Martin Kemp (bass), Steve Norman (guitar, saxophone and percussion) and John Keeble (drums).

Their chart breakthrough came in the winter of 1980 with the pumping anthem, 'To Cut A Long Story Short' which peaked at number 5 on the U.K. singles chart. This was followed by 'The Freeze' which reached the top twenty, setting them on a meteorical course for success.

In March 1981, they released their debut album, *Journey To Glory,* which peaked at number 5 on the U.K album chart and had a chart run extending over half a year.

A string of hit singles followed leading to a domination of the charts which lasted for four years. Most notably, they hit the top spot with 'True', which has become a classic of the era. In total, they hit the top fifty on no less than twenty occasions and ten of those were top ten hits.

Their albums were equally well received, with *True* (1983) giving them their first number 1 hit album. It had a chart run which lasted for nearly two years.

In 2002, three fifths of the original band came together to perform at a club called Pennington's, in Bradford. The voice of Spandau Ballet, Tony Hadley, was joined by Steve Norman and John Keeble for a night of nostalgia and hits.

An enthusiastic and lively audience gave Messrs Hadley, Norman and Keeble a rapturous and warm welcome as they ploughed through a decade of hits including 'Gold', 'True' and a rousing version of 'Chant No.1 (I Don't Need This Pressure On)'.

The events of the evening were captured on camera for Angel Air's DVD release, which featured fourteen songs plus interviews with the band (NJPDVD610).

The following year, Tony Hadley found himself thrust back on to prime time television when he won the reality television show *Reborn in the USA*.

EDDIE HARDIN

"This splendid 1995 recording has now been granted a mid-price re-issue by the good people at Angel Air, and deserves the widest possible exposure."

Kevin Bryan, *Retford Times* (April 2002)

By the time Eddie Hardin left school, he had already shown himself to be the master of the Hammond organ as well as a talented young song writer.

His career kicked off when he joined a Mod band called The Wild Uncertainty, who released just one single. Moving on to The Spencer Davis Group, he shared the fruits of a commercially very successful era, chalking up hits around Europe with songs such as 'Mr Second Class' and 'Time Seller'.

Before the end of the Sixties, Eddie had split from the group, along with drummer Peter York. After a stint as session musicians, Hardin and York teamed together to form what they described as "the World's smallest big band". The band comprised just the two musicians, playing organ and drums. They became an instant hit in Europe and recorded three terrific albums between 1969 and 1971 (*Tomorrow Today*, *World's Smallest Big Band* and *For The World*).

In 1972, Eddie released his first solo album; *Home Is Where You Find It*.

Hardin and York were briefly thrown together again with the reformation of The Spencer Davis Group, releasing a number of albums between 1973 and 1974, prior to the line-up disbanding once again.

Eddie went on to work with Roger Glover and a host of other top musicians on the celebrated *Butterfly Ball* project, which was based upon the William Roscoe poem, *The*

Butterfly Ball And The Grasshopper Feast. The result was a beautifully animated cartoon, an album and a rock opera performed at the Royal Albert Hall. Eddie co-wrote a song for the soundtrack called 'Love Is All' which became an enormous worldwide hit. Indeed, it was for many years the biggest selling record in Holland and was recently a hit all over again in France. It was also used by a Dutch political party in their election campaign. Other musicians involved with the project included John Gustafson, Ray Fenwick, Ian Gillan and Mo Foster.

In 1976, Eddie released *Wizard's Convention*, an album he wrote and produced, recorded with the help of some famous friends in the music business, including Mike d'Abo, Roger Glover and of course, Peter York.

This was followed by a solo outing, *You Can't Teach An Old Dog New Tricks* (1977) and *Circumstantial Evidence* (1982) (re-released by Angel Air).

During the Eighties, Eddie collaborated with Zak Starkey on a musical version of *Wind In The Willows.* The end result was released as an album and staged as *Hardin And York's Wind In The Willows* for German television. The show featured Maggie Bell, Ray Fenwick, Donovan, Denny Laine, Joe Fagin and Graham Bonnet. This has also been released by Angel Air.

During the Nineties, Eddie revived *The Wizard's Convention* with two further instalments (the second has been released by Angel Air) as well as a steady flow of solo work including *When We Were Young* (1996) and *Just Passing Through* (2000).

Eddie continues to perform as a key player in The Spencer Davis Group.

Reviews for *Eddie Hardin's Wizards Convention 2* SJPCD009:

"Way back in 1974 Eddie Hardin co-wrote *The Butterfly Ball* with Roger Glover. Two years later he wrote and produced *The Wizard's Convention*. Then in 1995 he returned to the U.K from France, where he now lives, to record this album co-written with Ray Fenwick. As with the first *Wizard's Convention* Hardin assembled one hell of a group of artists, including Mike d'Abo, Paul Jones, Tony Ashton, Debbie Bonham, John Entwistle, Chris Farlowe, Denny Laine, Phil Manzanera, Zak Starkey and Snowy White. Together these great musicians produce an album that is fundamentally the blues. For your money you get Mike d'Abo and Paul Jones performing together for the first time on the lively 'Here I Go Again', the laid back 'Sultana', an instrumental featuring Snowy White and Ray Fenwick, Chris Farlowe singing 'Try A Little Tenderness' and Eddie Hardin taking on the vocals of a driving version of the Little Richard track 'Lucille'. If you like the blues then you should find something on here that you'll like, as virtually every style of blues is represented. A worthy successor to its illustrious predecessor."
Adrian Lyth, *Classic Rock Society*

"The host of guests all perform excellently...The songs are quite variable from jazzy blues to a hint of country...The skilled song writing has almost been tailor made for the particular guest performing, and it makes for a superior album."
Bernard Law, *Wondrous Stories* (Sept 2001)

See also The Spencer Davis Group, Hardin And York.

HARDIN AND YORK

"...The keyboard work throughout is of the highest order and is obviously reminiscent of The Spencer Davis Group...The album is a wonderful time capsule with real musicians playing real music on real instruments evoking memories of a time gone by when nearly all rock music was this good."

Wondrous Stories (August 2000)

Eddie Hardin (keyboards) and Peter York (drums) formed the engine room of Sixties rhythm and blues band The Spencer Davis Group.

When the band came to a halt, they decided to continue their working relationship under the banner of Hardin and York.

Described as a cross between Procol Harum and Traffic, they recorded three albums between 1969 and 1971 (*Tomorrow Today*, *World's Smallest Big Band* and *For The World*), all of which were produced by Mike Hurst.

They remained a reasonably small act in the U.K, regularly touring the college circuit. However, in Europe and particularly Germany, it was a very different story. Hardin and York built up an enormous following and could easily pull in crowds of up to 15,000 people at a time.

Angel Air has two Hardin and York releases. First is a live outing from the duo, *Live in the 70's*.

The second is a DVD release of Hardin and York's celebrated *Wind In The Willows* concert, an exceptional live extravaganza marrying music and dialogue, filmed in front of a large and enthusiastic German audience. The cast is a 'Who's Who' of British rock including Maggie Bell, Zak Starkey, Ray Fenwick, Donovan, Denny Laine, Joe Fagin, Graham Bonnet, Jon Lord and Don Airey.

Reviews for *Live In The 70s*: SJPCD016

"...This live album suggests we missed out - the way Eddie attacks his organ on 'Freedom Suite' is positively Emerson-esque in its aggression. L*ive In The 70s* is lovingly documented, as are all Angel Air releases..."
Mike Heatley, *Classic Rock* (September 2000)

"...an excellent set recorded at the London Marquee on June 15 1971...it's a high-octane performance that occasionally leaves you wondering how just two men could create such a vast amount of energy and noise..."
Jo-Ann Greene, *Goldmine* (October 2000)

See also The Spencer Davis Group, Eddie Hardin and Peter York's New York, Mike Hurst.

BOBBY HARRISON

"For me, Harrison stands for part of my musical past and this album has enough to intrigue me."

Adrian Lyth, *Classic Rock Society*

We have already met Bobby Harrison through his band Freedom. Between 1968 and 1972, they produced a handful of superb albums, all of which have been re-released by Angel Air.

When Freedom disbanded, Bobby chose to pursue a solo career. Pulling together some of the biggest names in the business, he recorded a funk-driven album, appropriately named *Funkist*. The recordings featured Herbie Flowers, Clem Cattini (ex-Johnny Kidd) Tony Iommi, Ray Owen and Micky Moody, to name but a few.

The album was released by Capitol Records in America and peaked at number 76 on the Billboard chart. Despite selling tens of thousands of units, Bobby failed to see a dollar in royalties. The album was never released in the U.K.

Funkist served as a bridge between Bobby's old band, Freedom and his new project, Snafu.

Bobby founded Snafu with old friend Micky Moody. They recruited Terry Popple on drums (ex-Tramline), and Colin Gibson (ex-Ginger Baker's Air Force) on bass. The line-up was completed by keyboard wizard and fiddle player, Pete Solley. So began one of the finest and most soulful British acts of the mid-Seventies.

The chemistry between the five musicians was very special and they ploughed a creative but uncommercial furrow, much in the vein of Little Feat and The Allman Brothers.

They recorded three albums before disbanding. All three have been re-released by Angel Air and are featured later in this book.

Following the break up of Snafu, Bobby relocated to Chicago where he spent a couple of years gigging.

Whilst in America, he met an Icelandic lady and settled with her in Reykjavik, opting for a quieter life away from the rush and chaos of the Windy City.

He recorded an album in the mid-Eighties with Icelandic jazzers, Mezzoforte with a view to promoting himself in his new homeland:-

"It was all done very basically, very 'first take etc'. I think we recorded the whole of that album in three days flat. It was done at a really good studio in Reykjavik though, called Steema."

The end result was called *Solid Silver* which has now been re-released by Angel Air, complementing and concluding the Bobby Harrison career retrospective. This is the first time the album has been made available outside of Iceland.

Bobby had a hankering for his roots and returned to his native Southend. He now leads a quiet life as a committed Born Again Christian.

Reviews for *Funkist*: SJPCD056

"...a first-time-on-CD reissue for what many fans consider the missing link between his careers with Freedom and Snafu...Funkist featured contributions from fellow future Snafu man Micky Moody, Humble Pie's Clem Cattini, Deep Purple's Ian Paice, Black Sabbath's Tony Iommi, Procol Harum's Matthew Fisher, Wings' Henry McCulloch and Juicy Lucy's Ray Owen..."
Jo-Ann Greene, *Goldmine* (April 2000)

"...there is plenty of funk and soul mixed with the blues-based rock that Bobby is best known for...The whole album is an easy mix, and Purple or Sabbath fans shouldn't expect too much heaviness. But it's a real gem, nonetheless."
Record Collector (June 2000)

Reviews for *Solid Silver*: SJPCD011

"It's always pleasing to get something from a musician that you remember from the 70's but you wondered what he was doing now. The original drummer with Procol Harum, founding member of Freedom and lead singer with Seventies rockers Snafu, Bobby Harrison has a pedigree. This album is a step in another direction, a lot more blues and AOR but the aforementioned pedigree shines through.

It's one of those albums where Harrison's voice is supported by neat jazz saxophone and piano solos and is always upbeat except where Harrison sings a purposeful ballad like the opener 'It's Over' or if he gets ultra bluesy as on 'Hot Stuff'. Second track, 'The Hunter', has opening bars that reminded me so much of 'Spirit In The Sky' while the sax is covered superbly on 'Overload' by Stefan Stefanson.

For me Harrison stands for part of my musical past and this album has enough to intrigue me."

Adrian Lyth, *Classic Rock Society*

"The album features many differing musical styles, from big, clenched fist, AOR ballads to blues rock...Mezzaforte's influence on the sound is immense and the jazzy saxophone and luscious electric piano chords are an unusual but effective accompaniment to Harrison's blues soaked delivery...by and large this is an enjoyable album of jazz tinged blues rock.

Steve Ward, *Wondrous Stories* (Feb 2002)

See also Snafu, Freedom.

STEVE HOLLEY

"Mix one part Wings and one part Badfinger, and you have a rocking album filled with thirteen, intelligent, catchy pop tracks. Assisted by Keith Lentin...and a number of other top players including Denny Laine, Holley shines on *The Reluctant Dog*."

Robert Silverstein, *20th Century Guitar* magazine (May 2003)

Stephen Jeffrey Holley was born into a musical family in London. His father, Jeffrey, led a swing band and his mother, Irene, was the band's singer.

By the age of five, Steve had become fascinated by the drums and, by the time he was eleven, he had formed his first group, The Formula.

The Formula was successful at a local level and won a talent competition at the local Methodist church. From thenceforth, music became Steve's first priority.

Upon leaving school, he spent a couple of years in Holland with G.T. Moore and the Reggae Guitars (Gerald T. Moore was co-founder of the hippie folk group Heron who were signed to the Dawn label), where they recorded an album for Polygram in 1975.

Looking for a new direction, Steve turned his attention to session work:-

"It became apparent to me that there had to be a market for a group that could handle any given situation and could guarantee the effectiveness of each facet of the music and the individual performances. I liked the idea of putting together a band who could work as session guys behind anybody."

This new group of session players, dubbed Vapour Trails, attracted the attention of Warner Brothers who they signed with. They soon found work backing Kiki Dee who had just hit the big time. Steve also found himself working on Elton John's album, *A Single Man*.

Indeed, such was his reputation as a drummer that he found himself in an impossible situation:-

"Elton had asked me to join his band permanently and at the same time I was asked to join [Paul] McCartney. It was a difficult decision."

Ultimately, Steve went with Paul McCartney and Wings. In just eighteen months, he had progressed from a fledgling studio artist to a major rock drummer, backing some of the biggest stars in modern music history.

With the dissolution of Wings in the early Eighties, Steve relocated with his girlfriend (now wife) to America with a suitcase of clothing and a drum set. Steadily making a name for himself, he worked on many prestigious recordings including Julian Lennon's debut album. His new career culminated with a three year stint in The Joe Cocker Band with whom he performed 'A Little Help From My Friends' in Berlin on the day the Wall came down.

Steve is now a record producer, based at Pilot Studios in New York and has recently recorded with various country and blues artists, including Katy Moffat and Grammy-nominated Junior Brown. He has also been recording and performing with Sean Fleming, The Handsome Dogs, Catherine Russell, Kevin Bacon, G.E. Smith, Ian Hunter and Dar Williams.

In the late Nineties, Steve played a benefit concert for orphan children in Bosnia-Herzegovina titled *Lilies In The Field*, backing such artists as Justin Hayward, Steve Howe, Phoebe Snow, Gary Brooker, Annie Haslam and Ian McDonald.

Despite being in demand as a producer and session musician, Steve still found time to record his own album, between June 2001 and December 2002. The result is his first solo outing, released by Angel Air in 2003.

Reviews for *The Reluctant Dog*: SJPCD133

"...a thirteen track collection of melodies and feelings that is well worth the wait...It's more than an impressive first album and one that should have seen the light of day long before 2003."
Joe Viglione, *All Music Guide* (March 2003)

"An album of laid back tunes, ideal for late night listening. You get the added bonus of some fine guitar playing and a wide variety of instruments from accordion to flute. Not an instant album by any means but a definite grower."
Jason Ritchie, *getreadytorock!* (March 2003)

With thanks to all at www.steveholley.com.

LINDA HOYLE

"...They don't make 'em like this anymore...it's just so exquisite..."

Modern Dance, (Issue 41 November 2002)

The early part of Linda Hoyle's career with Sixties jazz-rock outfit Affinity has been briefly chronicled earlier in this book.

Following her departure from the band, Linda teamed up with musician and song writer Karl Jenkins with a view to making a solo album. It was Ronnie Scott's suggestion that they worked together. Linda takes up the story:-

"In some ways making this record was a 'get it off your chest' exercise. There were so many people and styles I admired and listened to – some since I was very young – but my one regret was that I didn't include a Billie Holiday song because she is, of all people, my greatest influence. There is no question that my first major musical influences were the shouting blues singers of the early Twenties, particularly Bessie Smith. I grew up listening to jazz – Fats Waller, Bix Biederbecke and Louis Armstrong –

played by my father every weekend on breakable, meltable 78s. I probably have the largest repertoire of Fats Waller songs of any living middle-aged white woman!"

With this incredible grounding in jazz, Linda and Karl set about writing an album of original material. The songs they recorded were vibrant, at times semi-autobiographical and always told a story. These were complemented by superb renditions of Mildred Bailey's 'Barrelhouse' and Nina Simone's 'Backlash Blues'.

The album was named *Pieces Of Me*, after one of the songs, which Linda considered very appropriate:

"*Pieces Of Me* was meant to be as anarchic as it sounds. It was the title piece of the album because all the tracks were reflective of some aspects of me – sentimental, nostalgic, nasty, hopeful."

Ronnie Scott made a concerted effort to 'improve' Linda's image but she was having none of it:

"There was an attempt (largely unsuccessful) to tidy up my scruffy image. I was much happier in my green pearlised leather jacket and cut off shorts – quite pioneering! I had my own idea of how I wanted to look and would buy vintage clothes – some of them from the turn of the century - which I would wear on stage as well as off."

Reviews for *Pieces Of Me*: SJPCD117

"Hoyle and writing partner Jenkins (keys) crafted impressive, progressive rock/jazz numbers of considerable power and nuance. No wonder the vinyl of this is/was so collectable, it's bloody good."
Colin Bryce, *Mohair Sweets* (November 2002)

"…she pays a vocal tribute to many of the great blues singers who inspired her, including Bessie Smith, Mildred Bailey and Laura Nyro…And damn fine it is too!"
Tony Shevlin, *East Anglian Magazine* (November 2002)

With thanks to Linda Hoyle.

See also Affinity.

MIKE HURST

"Hurst goes through his attic, dusts off the tapes and shares the treasures and trinkets he unearths…There are some absolute gems here…"

Tony Shevlin, *East Anglian Magazine*, (November 2002)

It is rumoured that Mike Hurst has no need to redecorate his living room. All he has to do is re-arrange his gold discs once in a while.

We have already met Mike in this book and there is more from him later in this weighty tome.

For now, we have a total of four Angel Air releases which explore Mike's successful career both as a record producer and as a musician and singer.

Mike's career took off in the early Sixties when he joined the Springfields as a replacement for Tim Field. Within months, the trio were enjoying massive chart success on both sides of the Atlantic.

As Mike observes, "the writing was on the wall when the Beatles graduated from the bottom of the bill to the top," and in October 1963, the Springfields split up.

Mike's career subsequently followed a fascinating path. He recorded songs as a solo artist, formed a band called The Methods (with Jimmy Page, Albert Lee and Tony Ashton) and presented a BBC radio show called *Teen Scene*.

At the suggestion of his wife, Marjorie, Mike became a record producer and undertook work for Mickie Most and Andrew Loog Oldham.

Mike also produced a string of hits for Cat Stevens as well as 'She's Not There' for Colin Blunstone and 'Mighty Quinn' for Manfred Mann.

Between 1970 and 1971, Mike recorded two albums for Capitol Records (*Home* and *In My Time*) which collectively make up Mike's first Angel Air release.

He also managed to rack up hits with vocal harmony group Summer Wine and rock band Fancy.

Mike continued to produce records for a score of different artistes throughout the Seventies including Hello, The Four Tops, Shakin' Stevens (whom he managed) and Cilla Black. Most notably perhaps, Mike produced seventeen top forty hits for Showaddywaddy.

In the Eighties, he formed a trio called Sundance (featured later) and scored a hit in France with his son, Jonas.

Upon the passing of his mother, Mike took over the running of her children's theatre group. He set up a new theatre group when he relocated to the West Country.

Mike regularly embarks upon lecture tours for which he has built up a considerable reputation.

As well as releasing Mike's two albums from his Capitol days (packaged together on one disc), we also have an offering from The Mike Hurst Orchestra from 1969 called *Drivetime*, which was originally made for Decca to demonstrate Len Levy's revolutionary Phase 4 Stereo, a concept which (through echo) was designed to create a wall of sound.

The third and fourth releases are two compilations of songs produced by Mike over three decades and include tracks from Episode Six, the original version of 'Video Killed The Radio Star' and songs from Hardin and York and Colin Blunstone to name but a few.

The Mike Hurst cake is metaphorically iced with an absolutely superb live concert DVD which acts as an ideal career retrospective and gives the listener a chance to see the man himself, who has spent so many years locked away at the mixing desk. The all-star line-up for the show features Ray Fenwick and Clem Cattini.

Reviews for *Home/In My Time*: SJPCD098

"Long out of print, the two albums are entertaining in an adult-rock kind of way. Lushly produced, exquisitely played and boasting any number of pleasantly memorable songs...."
Goldmine, (March 2002)

"…this entertaining listen (boasting the talents of Jon Lord, Ian Paice, Tony Ashton, Rod Argent and more) showcases the singer's rich voice.

The music may sound dated but the delivery is polished and well worth a replay."

Peter French, Hartlepool Mail (6 July 2002

Reviews for *Producers Archives Volume 1*: SJPCD123

"Legendary producer Mike Hurst produced some of pop music's biggest names during his time with labels such as the cutting-edge Deram.

Names that pop up on this new compilation include Paul and Barry Ryan…New World, Eddy Grant and Colin Blunstone…The whole album is full of quirky little stories and quirky little songs…"

The Mercury (January 2003)

"…The Episode Six track here, 'My Little One', is nothing less than a Sixties rock classic…Although other tracks blend into a mish-mash of Sixties and Seventies pop, there are some real gems and rarities too. The Four Tops' 'For Your Love' is a previously unreleased treasure while Eddie Hardin's 'Resurrection Shuffle' is a classy new wave rocker…"

Record Collector (January 2003)

Reviews for *Drivetime*: SJPCD125

"…a nifty collection of anthemic classics…plus there's a chance to hear the unique stereo effects of the day. "

East Anglian Preview (May 2003)

"…Tony Hatch meets Parnell! Very different but strangely warm and cosy!"

Modern Dance (March 2004)

Review for *Producers Archives Volume 2*: SJPCD172

"Every song has a great story behind it, as well as Hurst's distinctive imprimatur. Fashions changed, stars came and went, but the producer was always up for something fresh and new, shifting with the times, and lavishing attention on even the least deserving."

Jo-Ann Greene, *Goldmine* (February 2005)

See also Hardin and York, Sundance, Minute By Minute, Summer Wine, The Favourite Sons, Fancy.

www.mikehurst.co.uk

GARY HUSBAND

"...what we have is a pianist interpreting music originally produced by an avant-garde guitarist and the result is something that works magnificently...It is music that takes the listener on a voyage, one that can have unexpected twists yet at the same time is always safe and interesting."

Feedback (November 2004)

Gary Husband is one of those rare breeds of musician who has managed to succeed on a professional level both as a drummer and a pianist.

Born into a family steeped in music, Gary studied classical piano and theory from a very young age.

He went on to broaden his horizons by taking up the drums, securing a place in The Syd Lawrence Orchestra by the age of sixteen.

Gary also started composing jingles and incidental music for BBC and YTV, as well as freelancing alongside the various jazz stars that regularly passed through Leeds in his native Yorkshire.

Gary's relocation to London saw his career thrive, in both the jazz and jazz-rock scenes. He drummed for Paraphernalia, The Jim Mullen/Dick Morrissey Band, The Gary Boyle Band and Turning Point. He also cropped up from time to time with the BBC Radio Big Band, Ronnie Scott's Quintet, Gil Evans and RMS (Ray Russell, Mo Foster and Simon Phillips). The late Seventies also bore witness to the start of Gary's fabulous musical association with the legendary guitarist, Allan Holdsworth.

The Eighties and Nineties were equally busy for Gary who served for long periods with Billy Cobham, Andy Summers, Jack Bruce, Zakir Hussain, Gary Moore and American fusion/jam band, Gongzilla. The list is seemingly endless. Gary's forays into the more commercial arena have included a five year stint with Level 42 which has been reprised again in recent years.

As well as lending his services to other musicians, he has pursued his own projects including The Gary Husband New Trio, which has been described as "...a totally contemporary, original and quite 'cinematic' take on the more traditional piano-led concept that explored Gary's far-reaching original compositional style with imaginative re-workings of jazz standards."

One of Gary's greatest successes has been the release of his first piano solo album, *The Things I See - Interpretations Of The Music Of Allan Holdsworth*, which has been released by Angel Air. The album was a huge hit with fans and critics and was selected as one of the best albums of 2001 by *Jazz On 3* (BBC Radio 3). The Guardian newspaper made it their album of the week.

In 2003, Gary was awarded a place on the Arts Council Of England's Contemporary Music Network touring scheme with a view to leading a hand-picked ensemble of world-class jazz musicians on a tour across the U.K. He is generally regarded as one of the greatest drummers of his generation.

Gary continues to record and has released an album interpreting the music of John McLaughlin.

Review for *The Things I See*: SJPCD182

"The recording is a testament to Holdsworth's writing and to Husband's not inconsiderable skills as a pianist as he refashions ten of Holdsworth's compositions...Maybe it's because Holdsworth is so careful at crafting his tunes that people can't see past the detailed arrangements to the broader potential of the material but Husband clearly does, and hopefully *The Things I See* will encourage others to do the same."

John Kelman, *All About Jazz* (November 2004)

www.garyhusband.com
See also Igginbottom's Wrench.

STEVE HYAMS

"Bracing…the interplay between the musicians is top-drawer."

Rich Wilson *Record Collector* (April 2002)

Steve was born in Fifties London to a shop keeper who hit the big time importing cameras from the Soviet Union.

As a young lad, Steve was sent to a strict boarding school, which proved to be an horrendous experience. Salvation came in the form of the few albums he took with him by The Who, Yardbirds and The Pretty Things.

By the mid-Sixties, Steve had started playing the guitar. He also went on his travels, playing bass with a blues band in France, cover versions in Ireland and hitting the hippie trail via Afghanistan and India.

By 1972, Steve was based in Brighton playing in The Sam Prody Blues Band. When the band fell apart, he formed The Steve Hyams Band with Bruce Irvine.

Steve and his new band of musicians caught the attention of manager Tony Hall, who saw in Hyams a tremendous amount of potential. He sent Steve off to America to work with Elliot Mazer (Neil Young's producer). Upon his arrival in San Francisco, Steve found that Mazer was unavailable due to touring commitments.

The situation was exacerbated by Steve's heroin habit. He went through cold turkey during his first few days the States and the recordings that eventually emerged (with Denny Siewell producing) were disappointing.

Returning to the U.K. empty handed, Steve teamed up with Paul Kossoff with a view to launching a new project. Paul had been with the band Free and was later to form Back Street Crawler. But at this stage, he was fighting his own demons. His addiction to 'downers' rendered him sadly incapable of playing his guitar and this led to their planned project floundering.

Out of the ashes of the Kossoff project came a new version of The Steve Hyams Band, again featuring Bruce Irvine on guitar, with Bryson Graham on drums and Nick Potter on bass. They were talented but criminally undersold. They released a single but only a few promotional copies of the album were ever pressed.

During the Eighties, Steve found work outside the music business before returning to the fray with The Dig Band.

Two Steve Hyams albums have been released by Angel Alr. The first, *Mistaken Identities*, pulls together Steve's work from the Seventies. The second, *Feather And A Tomahawk*, brings us nicely up to date.

Review for *Mistaken Identities*: SJPCD015

"...first time...available on CD...it is one of those elusive gems full of juicy lead guitar, rhythm guitar and subtle vocals that the Seventies gave as such a sound base to follow. The album has excellent sleeve notes to bring the uneducated up to the moment and boasting that Hyams was the one who introduced Mott The Hoople to David Bowie, something that proved essential to their success. I feel lovers of bands like 10CC, America, Crosby Stills & Nash and even Quo would enjoy the sound of Steve Hyams. Hey, he's even got Madeleine Bell on backing vocals."
Martin Hudson, *Classic Rock Society*

Reviews for *Feather And A Tomahawk*: SJPCD039

"...probably one of the best albums released this year...The album is a real mixture of sounds, ranging from country to straight rock and boogie via Dire Straits and Pink Floyd..."
Kingston Comet, (August 1999)

With thanks to Claes Johansen.

See also Crawler.

THE IAN GILLAN BAND

"...Ian Gillan's powerful vocals and Ray Fenwick's excellent guitar work give the music an extra dimension. My highlights: a very surprising and subdued version of "Child In Time" (with fine twanging guitar and good electric guitar solo) and an enthusiastic rock 'n' roll medley..."

Background (October 2001)

If you have been reading this book chronologically, you would have encountered Gillan, successor to The Ian Gillan Band.

Ian Gillan's career started in the mid Sixties with a group called Episode Six. By 1970, he found himself in the spotlight as lead singer with Deep Purple, his incredible vocal style lending itself perfectly to the sound of his new band. A string of colossal selling albums followed and the blue print for rock was set in stone with anthems such as 'Smoke On The Water'.

After four years, Ian left Deep Purple and pursued a number of commercial ventures.

It was at about this time that Roger Glover (ex-Deep Purple) staged his performance of the soundtrack to *The Butterfly Ball* (based around the poem *The Butterfly And The Grasshopper's Feast* by William Roscoe). The show featured a whole host of talented musicians including John Gustafson (bass), Ray Fenwick (guitar) and Ian.

Ian teamed up with John and Ray, drummer Mark Nauseef and keyboardist Mike Moran and The Ian Gillan Band was born.

Each and every musician involved in the new band had had some involvement with the jazz scene and it was therefore agreed that they would pursue a jazz-rock/jazz-funk sound. An album was recorded called *Child In Time,* which reached the lower end of the U.K. album charts. However, the timing could not have been worse. Despite being recorded in 1974, it was only released in 1976 when the British music scene was going through some enormous changes. The record label, Oyster Records, lost a fortune on the album, having ploughed about £100,000 into the band.

A line-up change followed with the departure of Mike Moran, who was eventually replaced by Colin Towns.

The Ian Gillan Band signed a new record deal, this time with leading independent, Island. They recorded a new album, *Clear Air Turbulence,* which took the band further towards jazz, funk and rock experimentation. The fusion was seamless and owed much to the talents of Mark Nauseef who had mastered new and distinctive rhythms with an Indonesian orchestra. John Gustafson developed his own style of funk bass and Ray Fenwick (who had played every conceivable type of music to date) honed his own approach to The Ian Gillan Band sound. Towns was a marvel at the keyboard and Ian Gillan remained in full voice, his screaming vocals continuing to be his distinctive calling card.

Prior to the release of *Clear Air Turbulence,* Ian was unhappy with the mixes and arranged for the whole album to be remixed. The impending tour was duly re-scheduled. It finally kicked off four months late (April 1977) and took in a total of nineteen dates, including The Rainbow in London.

Clear Air Turbulence picked up cult status in Europe and was well received in Japan. It turned out to be the band's creative pinnacle.

The Ian Gillan Band had up until now toured heavily and there was disappointment within the ranks that they had not made more of an impact.

Ian had the answer which was to return to the old rock formula with shorter songs. Perhaps the world wasn't ready for their groundbreaking brand of music.

The third album, *Scarabus* (1977), was supported by an enormously successful tour of Japan. The enthusiastic Japanese record company released one of the shows as a live album (*Live At The Budokan* (1978)), which became The Ian Gillan Band's final release...until now.

Ian Gillan took the decision to disband the band, retaining the services of Colin Towns and generally surrounding himself with musicians with a traditionally more rock-orientated background. The band was to be called Gillan.

Thanks to the diligence of guitarist Ray Fenwick, a heap of unreleased recordings have been dusted off to complement the original Seventies albums. These have been released by Angel Air and include the original mix of *Clear Air Turbulence* (*The Rockfield Mixes Plus*), a stack of rarities (*Rarities 1975-1977*) and *Live Yubin Chokin Hall, Hiroshima 1977* lifted from the same tour as the original Japanese release, *Live At The Budokan.*

Finally, there is an important rediscovery - *Live At The Rainbow.* This has been issued both as a CD and DVD. The DVD includes an interview with Ray, an interview from the Japanese tour and various rarities.

Reviews for *Live At The Rainbow*: SJPCD017

"Contained within the six tracks on the album are two Deep Purple classics, namely 'Child In Time' and 'Smoke On The Water' with the added joy of some shattering guitar from the vastly overlooked Ray Fenwick. Serious rock fans overlook it if you dare. "
Colin Bell, *On The Record* (regional newspapers)

"*Live At The Rainbow* was recorded on 14th May 1977 in front of a packed house at the famous Rainbow Theatre in London...we are treated to storming renditions of 'Smoke On The Water' and 'Woman From Tokyo'. 'Twin Exhausted' rounds off one hell of an album, a timely reminder that there was something between Deep Purple and Gillan that was definitely worth listening to."
Adrian Lyth, *Classic Rock Society*

Reviews for *Live Yubin Chokin Hall, Hiroshima 1977*: SJPCD076

"...this monster live show captures the band in full throttle in Japan. There's a superb classic rock 'n' roll medley, plus the first ever release of 'Trying To Get To You'."
Norfolk & Suffolk Preview, (July 2001)

"...guitarist Ray Fenwick has raided his vaults for this excellent set and come up with some real gems. Not only are there plenty of alternate versions...and backing tracks but several numbers unreleased in any form...Essential."
East Anglian Daily Times (March 2003)

Reviews for *The Rockfield Mixes...Plus*: SJPCD166

"A great CD package with very informative sleeve notes by Jerry Bloom. A must for Gillan fans and anyone who likes the varied sounds that were Seventies rock.
Jason Ritchie, *getreadytorock!* (March 2003)

"...a jazzy, inventive record driven by the 'wristy' rhythms of Nauseef, Towns' eclectic piano and Fenwick's funky guitar, was arresting...Gillan has never explained why he remixed the album, but it's tempting to conclude that he found the original sessions a little too outré."
Classic Rock (June 2004)

With thanks to Ray Fenwick, Andrew Bedford, Jerry Bloom and Claes Johansen.
www.colintowns.com

See also Minute By Minute, Ray Fenwick, Fancy, Summer Wine, Gillan, John Gustafson, The Spencer Davis Group, Tee Set, Guitar Orchestra.

ICE

"...an absolute must for Sixties completists."

University of Sussex Alumni News, 2005

An earlier chapter in this book touched upon the history and recordings of a band called Affinity.

The predecessor to Affinity was a band by the name of Ice.

Ice was fronted by the owner of one of the 'fruitiest' voices in the music business, Glyn James.

Glyn; along with Grant Serpell (drums), John Carter (bass and backing vocals), Lynton Naiff (Hammond organ and piano) and Steve Turner (electric guitar and acoustic guitar) set out to conquer the music business at the first attempt. They failed.

However, in the process, they left behind a rich and varied selection of material worthy of a second hearing.

In 1967, Ice found themselves signed to the mighty Decca label. Billed as 'one of the brightest signings of 1967', they released their debut single 'Anniversary (Of Love)' backed with 'So Many Times'.

'Walk On The Water' was earmarked as the follow up but despite a certain amount of radio play on Radio One, the song was shelved in favour of 'Ice Man'.

Both singles are now highly collectable and change hands for in the region of £50 a copy.

Angel Air has pulled together both singles, together with 'Walk On The Water' and a rake of other exceptional recordings to make a very desirable nineteen track album. Highlights are 'Ice Man', 'Whisper Her Name (Maria Lane)', 'Open The Door To Your Heart' and the stunning 'Skyline'.

Sadly, Ice did not survive beyond 1968 as Glyn explains:-

"Despite our differences, we were all deadly serious about Ice. The group broke up because we could not get from the publisher or the record company the terms and conditions we had to have in order for us to sustain and develop as a band."

Reviews for *Ice Man*: SJPCD176

"...whilst there are hints of the later jazz-rock of Affinity, the core tracks are more pure Sixties psychedelic pop. It's fairly evocative, if hardly mind-blowing fare but it does complete the jigsaw. One suspects that there were a few Association and Fifth Dimension albums lying round the Dansette at Uni.

So comprehensive is this musical nugget-mining, one wonders where to next, early-fifties recordings of Naiff in pram with a plastic xylophone? Bring it on!"

David Randall, (March 2005)

"Here's a treat. The last few years have seen Angel Air delve deeper into the Affinity catalogue that many fans were aware was even possible. Well, the digging continues, with the release of *Ice Man*, a 19 track compilation that gathers up the entire recorded works of Ice, a band fronted by Glyn James and John Carter but of interest here for keyboard player Lynton Naiff, and the presence as 'additional musicians' of Mo Foster and Linda Hoyle...

Ice Man certainly ranks among the most thrilling exhumations so far."

Jo-Ann Greene, *Goldmine* (March 2005)

With thanks to Glyn James and Grant Serpell.

See also Affinity, Sailor.

'IGGINBOTTOM

...a dazzling album with a depth and musicality that is quite awesome...

Colin Bell, *On The Record* (May 2000)

'Igginbottom (Higginbottom pronounced with a broad Yorkshire accent!) emerged from the Bradford area in the late Sixties.

The group was 'discovered' and managed by three members of teen sensations, Love Affair – Michael Jackson, Maurice ('Mo') Bacon and Morgan Fisher.

'Igginbottom featured guitarist, Steve Robinson (a one-time band mate of Jackson), Allan Holdsworth (guitar), Dave Freeman (drums) and Mike Skelly (bass).

The band was special not only for the talented line-up, but for the glorious brand of jazz-pop they religiously peddled.

They received their big break when Ronnie Scott was talked into setting up a special guitar evening for them at his club, an event that featured John Williams and Barney Kessel.

Williams and Kessel received a rapturous welcome but 'Igginbottom found themselves up against an indifferent and unreceptive audience of seasoned jazzers. However, as their set progressed, the room began to heave with bodies and by the end of their performance they had successfully won over the entire audience with their unique and glorious brand of music.

The band went on to record the album *Igginbottom's Wrench* (1969) which was supported by a number of live shows. Sadly, they were short-lived and drifted apart. It seems that their young managers were finding the entrepreneurial world tough going and a tall order to juggle with their own careers.

Allan Holdsworth went on to achieve worldwide success as an accomplished and innovative guitarist.

Reviews for *'Igginbottom's Wrench*: (SJPCD064)

"...Tough guitar-led jazz-rock, very classy, very smart."
Jo-Ann Greene, *Goldmine* (July 2000)

"Holdsworth was a technically awesome guitarist even at this early stage of his career...This is where he began and as such it's of interest to jazz buffs."
Zabadak, No.18

www.therealallanholdsworth.com

See also Mott, Mott The Hoople, Morgan, Morgan Fisher, British Lions.

JAGUAR

"No other label is currently doing a better job at keeping alive the best of classic hard rock/heavy metal…*Run Ragged* is the ultimate comeback from one of the finest NWoBHM bands of all time…pure sonic aggression from start to finish…"

www.metal-gods.net (July 2003)

The New Wave of British Heavy Metal has spawned a generation of fabulous bands.

Jaguar, formed in the late Seventies, represented everything that was good about the movement.

The band was formed in the West Country by Garry Pepperd (guitar), who joined forces with Jeff Cox (bass) Rob Reiss (vocals) and Chris Lovell (drums).

They debuted with the song 'Stormchild' on the *Heavy Metal Heroes* compilation and won many friends in the process.

Changing record label and vocalist (Rob Reiss was replaced with Stormtrooper's Paul Merrill); they released the single 'Axe Crazy' and developed a form of speed Metal that was to have an enormous influence on the music scene. They released the album

Power Games which is acknowledged as a classic of its genre.

A change in label witnessed the band shifting direction, taking a more melodic approach which was not universally popular with fans.

Jaguar underwent a number of personnel changes and regularly toured until they split in 1985.

In 1998, on the strength of the successful CD release of the album *Power Games*, Garry and Jeff reformed the band. Nathan Cox (formerly of Andy Scott's Sweet) joined on drums with Jamie Manton on lead vocals. They recorded a new album, *Wake Me*, which was inspired by the band's heavier roots.

Jeff Cox subsequently left for personal reasons but was replaced by Darren Furze, described at the time as a calming influence on his band mates. This line-up recorded *Run Ragged*, which has the fitting honour of being Angel Air's 150th release.

Darren has since left the band and been replaced by Simon Patel.

Reviews for *Run Ragged*: SJPCD150

"Recorded in 2002, *Run Ragged* is a fine album bursting with classic heavy Metal style choruses and riffs that makes me think of bands like Iron Maiden and Saxon etc. The production is superb and the album just clicks from start to finish.
Nicky Baldrian, www.aordreamzones.com

"Breakneck speed riffing collides with thunderous drumming and creates a maelstrom of sound over which the vocals are delivered in typical Heavy Metal fashion and the end result is a powerful album which should please Jaguar fans as well as devotees of the more extreme factions of Metal."
Classic Rock Society (August 2003)

With thanks to Joe Geesin.
www.jaguar-online.com

CHAS JANKEL

"...what a treat...this album has a charm and groove which many modern artists should aspire to. Well worth checking out."

Record Collector, November 2005

Responsibility for the re-release of Chas Jankel's self-titled solo album can be laid squarely at the feet of senior broadcast journalist, Stephen Foster.

As a young man, Stephen first encountered Chas when he was playing a live gig at the Gaumont in Ipswich with Ian Dury And The Blockheads. Some twenty five years later, they found themselves in a pub together...and the rest they say is history.

The success of Dury owed a lot to his chief 'Blockhead' and Jankel played a major part in developing the sounds that accompanied Dury's weird and wonderful and often 'colourful' lyrics.

The classic albums *New Boots And Panties* and its successor, *Do It Yourself* spawned a multitude of incredibly clever, funky and jazz-tinged numbers which set the charts alight in the late Seventies.

By the end of that decade, Dury and Jankel went in separate directions, Ian producing the album *Laughter* and Chas releasing the self-titled *Chas Jankel* on A And M Records.

Without doubt, the highlight of Chas's album is the opening track, 'Ai No Corrida', a gorgeous slice of music he wrote in Amsterdam, with lyrics by Kenny Young (famous for writing 'Under the Boardwalk'). Quincy Jones was so taken by the song that he re-recorded it for Atlantic Records and scored a massive worldwide hit, reaching number 14 on the U.K singles chart in 1981.

The album maintains a similar high standard throughout, concluding with the bonus song 'Little Eva', co-written by Chas and Ian in 1983/84.

A grateful Chas was delighted to see this album out on the shelves again:-

"Many thanks to Stephen Foster for suggesting I get in touch with Peter Purnell at Angel Air Records. This is the first time this album has been available on CD. The record was released 25 years ago and I have to say that the mastering process by Sound Recording Technology has brought out the subtlest details that were hard to distinguish on the original album release…25 years ago!!!!!!!! So thanks Peter, Stephen and the good folk at S.R.T."

Reviews for *Chas Jankel*: SJPCD202

"…slick solo set for A&M in 1979…well nigh indispensable."
Kevin Bryan, *Belfast Telegraph*

"The upbeat numbers are the highlights of the album, containing catchy grooves infected with meticulous arrangements of keyboards, guitars, drums and horns; and while Jankel handles nearly every instrument as well as the vocals, he is joined by fellow musicians (including Mark Isham and Peter Van-Hooke) who make the recording all the more vivid. The longest of these jazzy, crazed cuts runs for nearly fifteen minutes without losing its grip.

For some reason though, Jankel contrasts these songs with basic, mellow pieces that are far less exclusive, giving away the momentum for a relaxing, classically oriented break.

Still, this is a work filled with vision and subtleties that are rare amongst its natural territory and way ahead of contemporary club/acid jazz outfits such as Jamiroquai.

The Angel Air release delivers the album with fine, remastered sound for the first time on CD, as well as a bonus track co-written by Jankel and Ian Dury."
Avi Shaked (October 2005) (8/10)

With thanks to Stephen Foster.
chazjankel@gmail.com www.chazjankel.com or www.theblockheads.com.

THE KORGIS

"...there are some lovely melodies floating around in there..."

Record Collector (July 2005)

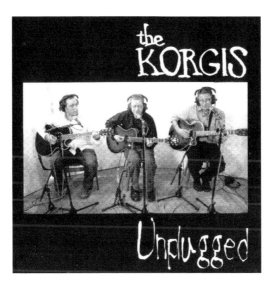

The Korgis originally comprised two musicians from the West Country, Andy Davis and James Warren.

Andy and James were members of a prolific and popular Seventies band by the name of Stackridge (formerly called Stackridge Lemon), who released some consistently strong and quirky albums (one produced by George Martin) and a whole host of singles besides (see later in this book).

The Korgis recorded their first album in 1979 and had near instantaneous chart success with 'If I Had You', which peaked at number 13 in the U.K. singles chart.

However, their greatest commercial success was with a song called 'Everybody's Got To Learn Sometimes', which was a worldwide smash hit, reaching number 11 on the American singles chart and number 5 at home. David Lord's sumptuous production leant itself to the song perfectly.

The Korgis released a handful of consistently strong singles which have stood the test of time, but these didn't emulate the commercial success of their predecessors.

'Everybody's Got To Learn Sometimes' was re-released in 1989 in order to raise awareness and funds for the hostage situation in The Lebanon and underwent a remix by D.N.A. in 1993. It proved to be a dance floor hit, some fourteen years after it first saw the light of day.

Such is the beauty and timelessness of this song, that it has been repeatedly covered by one generation of musicians after another, last charting for Baby D in 1997 (reaching number 3).

The Korgis have released a number of albums featuring different personnel (*The Korgis* (1979) *Dumb Waiters* (1980) and *Sticky George* (1981)) but Davis, Warren and 'new' boy John Baker now form what many people view as the definitive line-up.

Through Angel Air, The Korgis have received a new lease of life, with the release of *The Korgis Kollection*.

The feast for Korgis fans continued with the release of an *Unplugged* DVD and album, recorded in a studio with keyboards and acoustic guitars. The musicianship and vocals are excellent with some inspiring new re-interpretations of old classics.

To bring the Korgis story up to date, Angel Air has released a Korgis three track single, 'Something About The Beatles' which is supported by a new video.

Review for *The Korgis Kollection*: SJPCD204

"The Korgis had brief chart success between 1979 and 1980 with two U.K hit singles, 'If I Had You' and 'Everybody's Got To Learn Sometime' – both included on here. Both of these are certifiable pop classics with their lush arrangements and melodious vocals. This collection has the added bonus for fans of some newly recorded tracks, which carry on the band's core sound of gentle melodies plus extensive sleeve notes. There are some demos dating back from 1978 that have aged remarkably well.

An enjoyable collection from a band who certainly deserve more credit and exposure than they got. One for fans of well crafted and timeless pop melodies. ***1/2."

Jason Ritchie, *www.getreadytorock.com* (April 2005)

Reviews for *Unplugged*: SJPCD213

"Recreating hits like 'Everybody's Got To Learn Sometime' on three acoustic guitars (with a hint of piano) takes them to a simple, beautiful level often not immediately apparent in their earlier incarnation...A stylish songbook from two of Britain's vastly underrated artists."

Maverick (April 2006)

"...by simply unplugging their guitars and creating sumptuous new arrangements, The Korgis breathe such new life into these golden numbers that it's amazing how fresh they all now sound...Although it may look like just another best-of package, Unplugged actually walks The Korgis to brand new heights. A must for all fans."

Jo-Ann Greene, *Goldmine* (May 26, 2006)

With thanks to the Korgis website (www.thekorgis.co.uk), Gavin Mulroney, James Warren and Andy Davis.

See also Stackridge, Andy Davis, James Warren.

KROKUS

Angel Air has never been shy to stray into Europe to secure new signings. Here we have Switzerland's very own answer to AC/DC – Krokus.

Heralding from the land of high mountains, clean air, delicious chocolate and an abundance of cuckoo clocks, Krokus played their first ever gig in 1975 and disbanded shortly thereafter.

They reformed with a new line-up consisting of Fernando Von Arb (guitar), Chris Von Rohr (vocals), Jug Naively (bass and keyboards) and Freddy Steady (drums).

The band immediately looked beyond the borders of their own country and proved a popular draw in Spain's Costa Brava. They released three albums between 1976 and 1979.

A line-up change saw the departure of Naively who was replaced by Marc Storace. This new version of Krokus embarked upon a European tour and recorded the breakthrough album *Metal Rendez-Vous*, which achieved gold status (and now stands at double Platinum).

Krokus toured England, sold out everywhere and topped the British Metal charts with the single, 'Heatstrokes'.

A gruelling amount of touring followed, together with the release of two albums, *Hardware* and *One Vice At The Time,* both of which were highly successful. In 1982, Freddy Steady left the band.

In 1983, Krokus broke America with the album, *Headhunter,* selling a million copies in the process. They followed this up with *The Blitz* and played to 80,000 people at a Chilean festival.

Despite their success, all was not well in the Krokus camp. Their success had been hard earned and much deserved but the effects of the punishing lifestyle were beginning to bite. In 1988, lynch-pin Fernando Van Arb left the band thus ending the first phase in their history.

In 1990, Van Arb pulled together a new version of Krokus which featured Peter Tanner (vocals), Many Maurer (guitar), Peter 'Rabbit' Haas (drums) and Tony Castell (guitar, vocals). They recorded *Stampede,* which has been re-released by Angel Air as part of a double CD set.

Shockingly, in 1992, Fernando Van Arb was diagnosed with lymphoma and spent the next couple of years battling the illness. Happily, he made a full recovery and returned with a new version of the band in 1994.

Krokus went on tour, selling out venues where ever they went. They also recorded the classic album, *To Rock or Not To Be,* which featured Freddy Steady and Marc Storace. This album makes up the other half of the aforementioned Angel Air double CD set.

Krokus continue to go from strength to strength, with Fernando still at the helm, although personnel have changed around him over the years.

Angel Air has released a third Krokus album, *Round 13,* recorded in the spring of 1999. The album features such crunching numbers as 'Blood Comes Easy' and the Spinal Tap-esque 'Suck My Guitar'.

In 2006, they remain active and continue to record regularly. Their new album peaked at number 2 on the Swiss album chart.

Review for *Round 13*: SJPCD031

"I have always been a big fan of Krokus but when original lead singer Marc Storace left the band and in came new singer Carl Sentance I had my doubts if this would bring back the classic Krokus sound. The band released with Carl a few albums, of which *Round 13* was released by Angel Air Records. The album had a high class production by Tony Platt and musically it was typical Krokus/AC/DC riff orientated hard rock but definitely not as good as classy Krokus. Especially the opener 'Heya' was a bit too simple to make it an interesting tune, but happily the rest of the CD is sometimes good old Krokus hard rock with mostly sing-a-long songs such as 'Money Back', 'Break Free', 'Witch Hunt' and 'Wild Times'. On the other hand, there are also plenty of weaker tunes on the album, such as 'Guitar Rules', 'Suck My Guitar', 'Blood Comes Easy' and the aforementioned 'Heya'.

Anyway, the band brought back Marc Storace on their new CD which was released earlier this year, but the CD still hasn't had an official release over here, although it went to number one in Switzerland! Check out this Krokus CD from 1999 if you want to hear someone else singing, but I rather prefer the Marc Storace era Krokus." (Points: 7.5 out of 10)
Strutter Magazine (September 2003)

Review for *Stampede/To Rock Or Not To Be*: SJPCD042

"The legendary Swiss hard rock band Krokus made a return to the scene in 1990 with the album *Stampede*, an album that saw the replacement of original singer Marc Storace. A new singer was found in the shape of Peter Tanner, who was a good replacement. The album's opener and title track 'Stampede' saw the band moving into faster paced pure melodic metal, like Judas Priest, yet a bit more melodic. The rest of the album was just pure Krokus, so rough and ready hard rock with singable choruses, with as highlights 'Electric Man', 'Nova-Zand' (pure Led Zeppelin mid-tempo 'Kashmir' style), 'Good Times' and 'In The Heat Of The Night' (a seven-minute classy melodic rocker).

Four years later the band released *To Rock Or Not To Be*, which saw the return of Marc Storace, although musically a bit simpler hard rock and not as good as classic Krokus, but still with songs like 'Flying Through The Night', 'In The Dead Of The Night', 'Talking Like A Shotgun' and 'Stormy Nights' - an interesting record for the fans of the band. Both albums have been released onto a double CD in the U.K by Angel Air Records, with the addition of a few bonus tracks, such as the BTO cover 'You Ain't Seen Nothin' Yet' and the unreleased Krokus originals 'Wasteland' and 'Stormy Night'. In other words, highly recommended to the Krokus fan!" (8/10)

Strutter magazine (October 2003)

With thanks to Philip S. Walker.

http://krokusonline.seven49.net

DEKE LEONARD

"...an album of great songs, all carved firmly in the classic Leonard mould – and, though Leonard's own liner notes suggest he is confining his solo albums to once-every-quarter-century, *Freedom And Chains* is so good that we hope he may well relent."

Jo-Ann Greene, *Goldmine* (March 2005)

Deke Leonard is an extremely popular and well known figure on the rock music scene, particularly in his native Wales.

Deke's career can be traced back to the Sixties when he was a recognisable figure on the Welsh gigging circuit. He served with a number of different bands including The Corncrackers, The Jets, The Blackjacks and The Dream. He also played in Hamburg during this era, performing for seven or eight hours a day to punters.

Deke's big break came when he was in a band called The Bystander, a singles-orientated act who renamed themselves Man, switching to an album-based deal with their label, Pye Records. This was nirvana for Deke, who describes himself as "a compulsive song writer".

Man recorded two albums for Pye, *Revelation* (1969) and the amusingly titled *2oz's Of Plastic With A Hole In The Middle* (also 1969).

The band toured Europe and based themselves in Germany for a year.

A new decade brought a new record deal. Man signed to United Artists and embarked upon their most successful era, which saw the release of a total of seven studio albums and two live outings. The band worked hard and it seemed that they were doing something everyday of the year.

Deke left Man in the early Seventies and was offered a solo deal, recording the albums *Iceberg* (1973) and *Kamikaze* (1974). He and went on to form a band called Iceberg prior to joining a reconstituted Man line-up some years later.

In 1981, Deke recorded a third solo album, *Before Your Very Eyes* before teaming up with Sean Tyler of Ducks Deluxe and forming The Force. Sadly, Sean suffered a breakdown and as a consequence, the group transformed into a new version of Iceberg.

In 1983, Deke received an offer to reform Man. The band embarked upon a successful revival, regularly recording and touring until some twenty one years later, he left again ("given half a chance, I'd get rid of me!")

Deke carved out a new niche for himself as a writer, penning two critically acclaimed books, *Rhinos Winos and Lunatics* and *Maybe I Should've Stayed in Bed?*

Recently, he was reminded by his wife, Mary, that it had been a good many years since he recorded his last solo album. Deke took steps to rectify this oversight and trawled through hundred of his songs, settling upon a worthy selection. The end result, *Freedom and Chains*, was released by Angel Air in 2005.

Reviews for *Freedom And Chains*: SJPCD197

"This rollicking collection of hummable, self-penned numbers is linked to Man's driving rock only by dint of Deke's gravelly vocals and sometimes squealing slide guitar.

It's almost like a melting pot of 20th century music...As one might expect from wit, raconteur and author Deke there's a great deal of wry humour - girly backing vocals and lyrical twists - which along with inspired playing and Nick Lowe-like recycling of influences creates a hugely enjoyable record..."

Nick Dalton, *Record Collector* (April 2005)

"Deke's solo albums have been...a rarity...and this fine offering is actually the great man's first since 1976. Man devotees and supporters of rock in general should seek out the delights of tracks such as 'Queen Of My Heart', 'The Thrill Of Revolution' and the Buddy Holly influenced 'Something In My Heart Says No.'"

Kevin Bryan, *www.maelstrom.nu* (April 2005)

With thanks to Deke Leonard www.dekeleonard.com www.manband.co.uk

HUW LLOYD-LANGTON

"..An album of very warm and very convincingly genuine 70s-inspired hard rock. Huw Lloyd's inspiring, melodic vocals and his guitar playing are absolutely superb!"

Psychedelic, No.9 (December 2001)

The career of Huw Lloyd-Langton can be traced back to 1968 when he played his first professional gigs in Germany with Winston G. and Manfred Mann's drummer, John Lingwood.

Huw received his big break when he joined a band called Group X, who became Hawkwind Zoo, which was eventually shortened to Hawkwind.

Huw stayed with the band until 1970, appearing on their debut album, but left due to health problems. He is quick to stress that there was not a problem with any of the personalities within the band – he simply needed "a bit of a rest."

Huw's career took a number of interesting twists and turns, including a stint with Salt and Ariel Bender's Widowmaker.

In 1979, Huw was invited to rejoin his old band, Hawkwind. This time, he stayed with the band for ten years, appearing on no less than ten albums.

However, he grew weary of the constant line-up changes and called it a day, choosing to focus own his own band, Lloyd-Langton Group, which he had been running in parallel with Hawkwind since 1983.

On the Move…Plus is a re-release of Huw's 1997 album, originally released in Sweden. Featuring three bonus tracks and original artwork by Huw, it is a very personal album drawing on a lifetime of musical influences.

Reviews for *On the Move…Plus*: SJPCD093

"...this CD is a triumph of guitar driven bluesy hard rock....The twelve original tracks...highlight what a great (and underrated) guitarist he is and his ear for a great melody means that the majority of the songs are punctuated by some superb, irresistibly catchy riffs...In my ignorance I expected this album to be Hawkwind style space rock but the reality was a pleasant surprise. Guitar rock of the highest order."
Steve Ward, *Wondrous Stories* (Sep 2001)

"...very much a guitar based songs album that is full of class...It will probably appeal to ageing old gits...and will never feature in Kerrang! But this is very solid indeed
Feedback, (November 2001)

With thanks to Keith Smith. http://www.huwlloyd-langton.co.uk/

THE LOOK

"If this were twenty years ago then undoubtedly there are a few songs on here that could do serious damage to the singles charts..."

Feedback, May 2005

In the winter of 1980, there was a song which dominated the airwaves. It was one of the catchiest songs of the year and soared into the U.K. top ten. 'I Am The Beat' was unashamedly new wave and seemed destined to launch The Look on a long and illustrious career.

During this exciting era, the band built up a steady following and regularly filled thousand seat auditoriums up and down the country.

The Look recorded an album on the MCA label but this took a whole year to complete. According to band members, MCA were reluctant to pay them for their services, which led to the inevitable delays.

Failing to capitalise commercially on their big hit, band and label eventually parted company.

This left the four band members (Jonny Whetstone, Mick Bass, Gus Goad and Trevor Walter) in a nightmare scenario, having built up a following but without a record label.

Salvation appeared to come in the form of an independent label called Towerbell, who subsequently folded, as Mick recalls:-

"We had a single out, 'Drumming Up Love' and got on Crackerjack with it; but Snowy White was doing slightly better than us at the time with 'Bird of Paradise' and the label could only concentrate on one thing at a time. Two weeks later, we went to the offices and they were boarded up!"

The Look soldiered on, but never signed to another label…until 2004, when they signed to Angel Air. Pulling together songs recorded over the previous five years (as well as 'I Am The Beat' as a bonus track), they were at long last presented with the opportunity to follow up their debut album. The only change to the line up was the replacement of Trevor (drums) with Chris Wyles, the former having gone into teaching and losing touch with his band mates.

For Jonny, Mick and Gus it has been an immensely satisfying experience, as Mick explains:

"This has inspired us to record another one. We won't leave it 25 years this time!"

Reviews for *Pop Yowlin'*: SJPCD192

"This stuff is poppy and vaguely familiar, done with a great deal of class and delivery. It's light, fun stuff that leaves a smile on the face and a tap from the foot."
Marty Dodge, *www.getreadytorock.com* (February 2005)

"Tight, melodic and powerfully pop-ish, it is indeed the successor that the band's debut demanded, suitably updated of course, but still bristling with all the hooks and hummable parts that its reputation demands.

'I Am The Beat' nearly pales compared to these new hit-worthy contenders, with the rest of the set almost as strong. A welcome return for this classic group of pop-rockers."
Jo-Ann Greene, *Goldmine* (2005)

RAY MAJORS

Ray Majors career can be traced back to an exciting hard rock band called Hackensack who emerged during the late Sixties and early Seventies. The band was fronted by Nicky Moore (later of Mammoth, Tiger, Samson and Electric Sun), and featured Ray on guitar. They played over 200 shows, toured with Mott The Hoople and released an album, called *Up The Hard Way* (1974). They were considered to be one of the heaviest and hardest sounding bands of their day.

Hackensack disbanded in 1974 and Ray moved swiftly on to join Mott, a band that emerged from the ashes of Mott The Hoople. Together, they achieved moderate commercial success before re-inventing themselves as British Lions, a hard rocking outfit fronted by John Fiddler. The British Lions released two albums and threatened to take America by storm, hitting the Billboard chart with 'Wild In The Streets'. Alas, management and financial issues brought a promising band to a premature end.

In 2000, Ray was presented with the opportunity to 'spread his wings' and record a solo album. The result, *First Poison*, has been released by Angel Air and features fifteen cracking tracks and a fantastic cover, prepared especially for Ray by Peter Praconovik.

MAMA'S BOYS

"...A thunderous treat for fans of the Irish end of the New Wave of British Heavy Metal..."

Jo Ann-Greene, Goldmine, (June 2001)

The Mama's Boys emerged from Derrylin, County Fermanagh, Ireland in the early Eighties.

Brothers Pat and John McManus had earned a reputation as the All-Ireland fiddle and tin-whistle champions. The formation of a hard rock band was not therefore a natural progression from their folk roots.

Pat and John were joined by Brother Tommy, a percussionist. Together, they set out on tour in support of their heroes, Irish folk-rockers, Horslip. In so doing, they developed a sound inspired by Horslip and their other heroes, Thin Lizzy.

Mama's Boys initially signed for the delightfully named Pussy Records before steaming through a considerable number of labels, including Ultra-Noise, Lyntone, Spartan and Jive.

Throughout the Eighties they released a steady run of singles, including their own interpretation of Stevie Wonder's 'Higher Ground', previously covered by new romantics Tik and Tok and successfully re-appraised by The Red Hot Chilli Peppers.

They also released a number of albums and hit the billboard top two hundred twice; with *Mama's Boys* (1984) and *Power and Passion* (1985) - (the latter reaching number 55 in the U.K. album chart).

The final album, *Relativity* (1992), has been picked up by Angel Air and is available in America for the first time. It is the only album the band released which featured Mike Wilson on lead vocals.

Sadly, the band came to an end when Tommy died of leukaemia after a brave battle. No one felt like carrying on without him.

Pat and John re-emerged as Celtus, exploring their Irish roots, mixing folk themes with drum loops.

Reviews for *Relativity*: SJPCD081

"...the band's last album, released in 1992...is quite a mixed batch of songs. Listening to the opening two songs...and you would label the band as Seventies rockers with a bluesy vocalist, not too far from the sound Whitesnake had...but don't think this is purely a bluesy influenced hard rock album. As early as the third track...the guys show their Celtic roots...Mama's Boys were always more of a force live than in the studio...The bonus tracks...were recorded during the band's European tour in the winter of 1990. Excellent stuff!"
Rockhaven (February 2001)

"Mama's Boys were an out and out rock outfit in the mould of Foreigner...Anyone expecting to hear the folk/Celtic roots of Celtus will be disappointed although the sounds which later influenced the Celtus recordings are not always that deeply hidden...The combination of these more ethnic instruments with the more traditional power rock chords work superbly well...enjoy this CD for what it is, a superb slice of brilliantly performed, superbly produced classic rock."
Steve Ward, *Wondrous Stories* (April 2001)

MAMMOTH

"If these guys were as pretty as Bon Jovi then they could have been huge...This is a good album, certainly one that hard rock lovers of the old school should seek out..."
Feedback (Nov 2003)

When Mammoth arrived on the Eighties music scene, they were billed as the biggest and heaviest band around. It wasn't just the music that was heavy; the band members were too!

Mammoth were formed by two giants of the rock world - John McCoy, the bassist from Gillan and Zzebra and Nicky Moore, who had made his name with Hackensack and Samson.

John and Nicky crossed paths whilst working on Paul Samson's 1986 solo album. They worked well together and came up with the idea of writing songs for other artists to perform.

John hit upon the suggestion for a band. He was aware that Nicky possessed an extraordinary singing voice and wanted to build a band around 'the big man'. Given that John himself was...ample, it seemed a reasonable proposition to use this as a clever marketing tool. Mammoth were born!

Kenny Cox of More was recruited on guitar and the appropriately sized and named 'Tubby' Vinnie Reed joined on drums. The line-up and image were complete.

John raised some investment and a series of demos were made. They also recorded a Radio One session and signed a record deal with Jive Records, part of the Zomba Group.

An album was recorded but Kenny left mid-session. His parts were completed by John and an old friend, Bernie Tormé. Indeed, Bernie would have been an ideal addition to the group given his talents…but the stick-thin guitarist would have looked decidedly out of place!

The end result was melodic hard rock. The debut single, appropriately titled 'Fatman', was one of the first ever CD singles and is now sought after by collectors.

Mammoth made their debut at a Radio One 20th Anniversary show at Prestatyn and were well received. A second guitarist was soon recruited, Big Mac Baker, and a second single was released by Jive, 'All The Days'.

Both singles had been well received and there was great anticipation in the music press regarding the forthcoming album but there were problems; Jive and Mammoth saw the band very differently.

Mammoth could see themselves breaking America, promoting the fun image whilst maintaining their dignity. Jive wanted them to appear on children's television.

The music press seized upon these problems and slowly but surely, Mammoth were beginning to be viewed as a joke, despite the strong reviews.

A year later than planned, the debut album was eventually released along with a third single, the aptly titled 'Can't Take The Hurt'. A tour followed (along with another Radio One session) but the momentum had been lost and Nicky left the band.

Mammoth were a terrific opportunity wasted.

Thankfully, enough material has been left in the vaults to complete the Mammoth legacy with two Angel Air albums, *XXXL* and *Larger And Live*.

The former features early demos and material from a second album that was never released. *Larger And Live*, includes six tracks that were recorded at the aforesaid Radio One 20th Anniversary show at Prestatyn.

Reviews for *XXXL*: SJPCD006

"First up we have *XXXL*…the long awaited second album by Mammoth, probably the heaviest band ever, at least physically. Formed by John McCoy (ex-Gillan), with Nicky Moore (ex-Samson) on vocals, Mammoth burst onto the scene with the singles 'Fatman' and 'All The Days'. From the opening weirdness of 'White Mammoth On The M1' we are thrown into a previously unreleased version of 'Fatman', featuring original guitarist Kenny Cox, which sets out what this band are about, hard rocking music with a sense of humour. As well as unreleased versions of 'All The Days' and 'Can't Take The Hurt' we are also treated to new tracks such as the ZZ Top like 'Dressed To Kill' and the manic 'Monster Mania'. This album shows Mammoth at their best, showing why they could be said to be the heaviest, biggest band ever."
Adrian Lyth, *Classic Rock Society*

"It is a great mix of music and Nicky Moore's bluesy vocals, here being utilised in a much more commercial-sounding environment than it was with Samson...if you sit down and play this album without any preconceived ideas of what they were going to sound like then I assure you that you will be pleasantly surprised. The more I have played this the more I got into it. The Mammoth is extinct. Now could not be a better time to let one mess all over your stereo system."
Feedback

Reviews for *Larger And Live*: SJPCD144

"Built around the novel idea of having heavy musicians playing heavy music, they released one full studio album and had single success with 'Fatman'. This release contains six live tracks from a Radio One road show in Prestatyn in 1987 (with the legendary DJ Tommy Vance compering) plus songs that would have made a second album had there ever been one released.

The live tracks show Moore in great form. He has a bluesy voice (his Samson era work is a must in any rock fans collection) and can really belt it out when needed...Worth a listen just to here what could have been with their second album had it ever seen the light of day. Despite the fat gimmick there were good tunes and music in the band and it's a shame they never carried on. In Moore and McCoy they had a strong writing partnership and produced some classic AOR/melodic rock tunes, not unlike latter day Slade at times. Nicely packaged with informative sleeve notes from Record Collector's Joe Geesin."
Jason Ritchie, *getreadytorock!* (September 2003)

"...Altogether this album shows that Mammoth was a really great hard rock band, absolutely magnificent."
Adrian Lyth, *Classic Rock Society*, (January 2004)

With thanks to Joe Geesin.
See also McCoy, Gillan, Bernie Tormé, Samson/Paul Samson, Zzebra, Sun Red Sun.

MCCOY

"The gems are so plentiful that it is difficult to single out a few for discussion...Fans of British hard rock are highly encouraged to pick up these discs, all others should trade in their N'SYNC and Spice Girls for a real bit of rock before you rot your brains with that stuff!"

"On The Record", Music America Magazine.

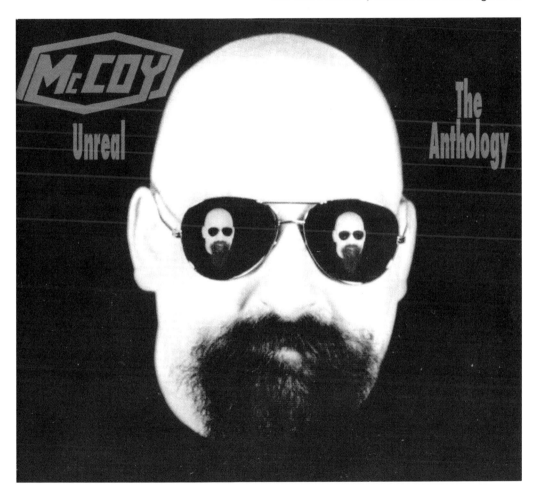

Welcome to the very early days of Angel Air. As you may have gleaned from the Foreword to this book, John McCoy came up with the suggestion for the label and it therefore seemed wholly fitting, he should enjoy the very first release. McCoy's *Think Hard. Again* became SJPCD001.

The son of a miner, John grew up in a working class household in Huddersfield, enjoying the influence of his father's traditional taste in Irish music and his sister's Classical piano playing. By the age of seven, John had taken up his first instrument - the cello.

John went on to learn the trumpet and played in local youth orchestras and brass bands until he heard his cousin play in a local rock 'n' roll combo. At that point, he decided to trade in his trumpet for an electric guitar.

In 1967, John applied for the job of lead guitarist with a Leeds band called Mama's Little Children. The vacancy had been filled but they required a bass player. John there and then decided to trade in his guitar for a bass, thus shaping his destiny.

Turning professional, John (who was still a minor at this stage) found that he had to grow up very quickly, touring the American Army bases in Europe and the Beat Clubs of Germany.

In 1968, John relocated to London and experienced poverty first hand, living hand to mouth until he secured a job with Clyde McPhatter of the Drifters. He moved on to a seven piece progressive rock group called Welcome, who toured the college and club circuit. They secured a deal with Pye, recording songs written by John and singer Tony (T-Bone) Rees.

By 1970, John had moved on to a band called Curtiss Maldoon, who recorded and toured extensively, supporting Bad Finger and Deep Purple. Indeed, both John and the band's drummer, Liam Genockey, had become a much sought after rhythm section, working for anyone from Gerry Anderson (Space 1999) to Julie Felix.

In between engagements, John and Liam formed Zzebra with Loughty Lassisi Amao – an extraordinary group that released three albums between 1974 and 1975 (a fourth has recently seen the light of day on Angel Air).

John continued to build on his reputation as a first-class bass player and found work with the likes of Bernie Tormé, Scrapyard, Francis Rossi, Atomic Rooster and Samson. He also formed the first incarnation of his band, McCoy. At the time, he was a very hairy and almost unrecognisable character, but he was slowly transforming into the bald, bearded bassist that many people recognise today. He was also developing an entertaining stage presence, balancing menace with humour, much to the delight of his fans.

By the mid-Seventies, John was approached by Colin Towns to join the Ian Gillan Band, which was flagging badly at the time. Liam also came on board along with ex-Zzebra band mate, Steve Byrd and the group became known as Gillan.

John helped to steer Gillan on a heavy rock path which has been documented earlier in this book. Perhaps the classic album of the era was *Glory Road* (1980) which featured Bernie Tormé. Gillan eventually came to an end in 1982.

During his spare time, John turned record producer and worked with a whole host of musicians, including punk band, UK Subs!

John went on to relaunch his pet project from the Seventies, McCoy. With a dynamite collection of musicians (Tony (T-Bone) Rees, Paul Samson, Liam Genockey,

Steve Lynton, Ron Rebel and Colin Towns) coupled with a legion of new fans, success was an inevitability.

The debut mini LP spent an eternity on the Music Week Metal chart. It was followed by the album, *Think Again*, which was badly hampered by distribution problems.

Both albums have been married together by Angel Air and released on CD as *Think Hard. Again*. John has also released two other McCoy albums through Angel Air, *Brainstorm* (featuring the talents of Al Romano, Michael Sciotti, Bobby Rondinelli and Arthur Guitar) and *Live 1977* from the first incarnation of the band (featuring Roger Hunt and Paul Samson).

Mammoth was John's next big project, which gave new meaning to the term 'heavy rock'. Teaming up with Nicky Moore, they made a huge visual and audible impact and deserved far more success than ultimately came their way.

John McCoy remains in demand as a bass player. He has worked in America, regularly tours and his songs have repeatedly turned up on television and film. He is now performing as one third of Guy McCoy Tormé.

In celebration of Angel Air's tenth anniversary, a McCoy 30 track double CD anthology has been released (*Unreal The Anthology*), pulling together tracks spanning John's career, including songs from Welcome, Zzebra, McCoy, Samson, Gillan and GMT to name but a few.

Reviews for *Think Hard. Again*: SJPCD001

"McCoy is John McCoy, best known as the Big Bad Bearded Bass player with Gillan, plus fellow ex-Gillan member Colin Towns, Paul Samson (of Samson fame), Ron Rebel (Iron Maiden's original drummer) and vocalist T-Bone Rees. The newly released CD, *Think Hard...Again*, was originally two albums, *The Mini Album* from 1982 and *Think Hard* from 1985. Musically we're talking the sort of heavy rock you would expect from the musicians featured. A mixture of hard rocking tracks and ballads. Of particular note are 'Because You Lied' (a song for Ian Gillan), which came out of the way McCoy and the rest of Gillan were treated when the band split, and a high energy version of the Fleetwood Mac classic 'Oh Well!'"
Classic Rock Society

"The big bald bassist who made his name with Zzebra in the Seventies and with Gillan at the turn of the Eighties went solo in 1983 and produced two superb metal albums, featured on this package…With help from Gillan pianist Colin Towns…you get a pretty essential collection. "
Record Collector (March 2002)

Reviews for *Brainstorm*: SJPCD026

"Solid and slick hard rock throughout, it's guaranteed to get your head nodding…Slip on them split-knee 'loons for a smile or two in between the more serious offerings."

Joe Geesin, *Record Collector* (October 2002)

"Bassist John McCoy is best known as Gillan member but he also released a bunch of records under the moniker McCoy. *Brainstorm* is one of these albums, a very diverse record that contains hard rock, AOR, and instrumental soundtrack pieces...I can really recommend this CD to AOR fans, although McCoy/Gillan fans should also grab this album a.s.a.p!" (8/10)
Strutter magazine (August 2003)

Reviews for *Live 1977*: SJPCD068

"This 'new' McCoy album actually pre-dates the previous three offerings...by at least six years and is the only surviving recording of the original three piece of John McCoy, Paul Samson and Roger Hunt. For that reason alone it is a truly indispensable piece of rock history...

It features all the familiar McCoy trademarks - thunderous bass (which threatens to shake your cabinets apart), incendiary riffing and sledgehammer drumming, but all played with John McCoy's distinctive ear for a great melody..."
Steve Ward, *Wondrous Stories* (November 2000)

"...Angel Air is to be commended at putting together this package with colour cover notes and up to date thoughts from the band members. As is standard with Angel Air releases it has a colour picture disc and shrunk wrapped to protect it from grubby fingers before you get it. There is a generous 16 songs which are typical for the time; it's quite an exciting live vintage sound and well worth being in your collection. "
Modern Dance (April 2001)

With thanks to Steve Pearson.
www.gmtrocks.com
See also Gillan, Bernie Tormé, Samson/Paul Samson, Mammoth, Sun Red Sun, John Du Cann, Zzebra.

MEDICINE HEAD

"Two Man Band is a defiantly contrary collection of rootsy, bluesy gems…One reaches the end astonished that a band that still sounded this vital, vibrant and vivacious should have felt the need to break up."

Jo-Ann Green, *Goldmine*, January 2002

John Fiddler has already been featured in this book under his own section as well as British Lions, a superb late Seventies rock band that took America by storm…for a short while anyway.

Prior to his 'poodle cut' days, he was better known as one half of the delightful hippie duo, Medicine Head.

John was born in 1947 in Darlston, Staffordshire. He never got to know his father, who died the following year. John's mother was left to bring up three children on her own. There was very little money for luxuries.

The main source of entertainment in the house was the radio. John spent many an hour tuning in to Radio Luxembourg and experienced something of an epiphany when he heard the sounds of Muddy Waters filling the living room.

An American by the name of Charles Kirinich introduced John to his massive blues collection and taught him how to play a few chords on his bass guitar. Lack of money prevented John from buying a guitar and he was in his early twenties before he owned his own instrument.

The other half of the duo was Peter Hope-Evans, born in Brecon, Powys, just three days after John. When Peter's father was transferred with his job to the Midlands, Peter found himself at the same school as John, Wednesfield Grammar.

John and Peter forged a strong friendship based upon the mutual appreciation of the great blues men. From time to time, musicians such as Howlin' Wolf and Big Joe Turner would visit the Midlands. John and Peter never let their empty pockets get in the way of their love of music. A seventeen mile walk to a venue was not unthinkable in those days!

John and Peter went on to art school together, though Peter left before John and the two friends drifted apart. It was two years before a chance meeting brought them back together again. It was agreed that they would form a band and various names were bandied around, including Dr. Feelgood, The Mission and Blue Telephone, before settling on Medicine Head. John explains the thinking behind the name:-

"I called the band Medicine Head 'cos it was literally medicine for my head. I was going through some major angst and the band and the name came along in the nick of time!"

The beginnings of the band were humble. John was living in digs in Burton-On-Trent. At the end of his bed happened to be a piano, so Peter would visit, harmonica in hand and John would crawl out of the bed and sit up at the piano. There were no guitars or drums…just the two of them and their basic instruments.

They tried a couple of gigs but found that the pianos in the local pubs were invariably broken or out of tune.

At about this time, Peter came into some money, so they travelled to Denmark Street in London (Tin Pan Alley) and bought a guitar and two amplifiers. To complete the sound at this stage, John found a bass drum in a junk shop, which suited some of the blues numbers they were learning to play at this time.

Initially, Medicine Head would play parties, and then they started gate crashing gigs asking if they could play. With such a simple amount of equipment, they could easily fit everything into the back of their Vauxhall Victor (bought from a scrap yard for £10.00). As word spread, they found they were getting invited back to play venues…and were getting paid!

A chance for a big break came when John and Peter found out that John Peel would be showing his face at The Lafayette Club in Wolverhampton. Seizing the moment, they turned up with their gear and, mistaken for the main act, were allowed to set everything up. All hell broke loose when the real act arrived (possibly Jethro Tull?) but Medicine

Head were allowed to play some numbers. Peel caught part of the act and was intrigued.

John and Peter capitalised on this by sending the famous D.J. a recording they had made in John's kitchen, which featured a song called 'His Guiding Hand'. Peel liked it, played it to John Lennon and Yoko Ono who felt the demo should be released just as it stood.

Consequently, Medicine Head became one of the first bands ever to sign to Peel's Dandelion Records (a lovely label with a similar philosophy to Angel Air).

In 1970, Medicine Head recorded their first album, *New Bottles Old Medicine*. It was a special moment for all involved, recorded at the CBS studios in Regent Street, surrounded by candles. The album was taped as a straight gig and is a very spiritual affair with a great deal of atmosphere. They also recorded the first of over twenty sessions for John Peel, becoming regulars at the BBC for the next seven years.

Medicine Head hit the road, supporting major acts of the time and playing the club and college circuit, winning friends and admirers on the way.

Their second album, *Heavy On The Drum*, was recorded the following year and produced their first hit single, '(And The) Pictures In The Sky' which had an eight week chart run and peaked at number 22. Astonishingly, just as they hit the big time, Peter decided to leave the band. The reasons are unclear but John kept his place open for him and soldiered on with bassist, Keith Relf and drummer, John Davies. This line-up recorded an album, *Dark Side Of The Moon* (1971) which remains a disappointment to John, who was unhappy with his playing.

By the following year, Peter had returned to the fold and a new record deal was signed with the more commercially-minded Polydor label. The ensuing album, *One And One Is One* proved to be their biggest seller and produced the massive single of the same name (number 3 in the U.K. singles chart on the back of an amazing thirteen week chart run) and 'Rising Sun' which peaked at number 11.

For their fifth album (and second for Polydor), Medicine Head became a five-piece band featuring Roger Saunders (guitar), Rob Townsend (drums) and George Ford (bass). The album, *Thru' A Five* produced the top thirty hit single, 'Slip And Slide' which was to be their last flirtation with the charts.

It was a strange time for John and Peter. The dynamics of a five-piece were alien to them and the cost of keeping so many musicians on the road was crippling. They were also ploughing through managers at a rate of knots.

In 1974, Medicine Head signed to the WWA organisation and released a superb single, 'Mama Come Out'. By this stage, the line-up had changed, with George being replaced by Charlie McCracken. Disastrously, WWA financially crashed, taking Medicine Head with them. The band were unable to release their album and the group, as a five-piece, died on its feet.

1976 saw John and Peter go 'back to basics', returning to the pub, club and college circuit as a two-piece, doing what they did best. Signing to Chas Chandler's Barn label, they released their final album of the era, *Two Man Band*. Two singles were released, 'It's Natural' and 'Me And Suzy Hit The Floor'.

Peter then left the band for a second time, with both musicians acknowledging that the project and run its course for the time being. John concluded the remaining Medicine Head dates with Roger Saunders and keyboardist Morgan Fisher.

Review for *Live At The Marquee 1975*: SJPCD091

"Excellent quality recording...the gig itself is top quality and a reminder how underrated this rather obscure duo were...an essential purchase for any Medicine Head/John Fiddler fans." 8/10
Jilly's Rock World (June 2001)

"They rock in a way that predates punk yet manage to sound as if they're in a sleazy Louisiana roadhouse rather than London's Soho...Thrown in for good measure is an 'echoey' demo version of 'Pictures' that could have come from Sun Studios, circa 1959. Awesome."
Nick Dalton, *Country Music International* (July 2001)

Reviews for *Two Man Band*: SJPCD095

"This is a surprisingly laid back, almost dreamy album which has a lovely innocent quality which permeates through the majority of the tracks...Great stuff from one of the better and most original bands from the Seventies."
Steve Ward, *Wondrous Stories* (October 2001)

"This is a great introduction to the band, as it encompasses many of their styles from blues to singer song writer, lots of acoustic as well as some electric...This was the last release as Peter and John parted ways permanently soon afterwards but they left on a strong note. A goody."
Feedback, (November 2001)

Reviews for *Fiddlers Anthology - Greatest Hits Live*: SJPCD147

"This CD, with tracks taken from that show, highlights some great music taken from across Fiddler's career. Recorded with ex-Ian Hunter Band guitarist Darrell Bath, the duo produces a great sound. Mixing both electric and acoustic guitars, Fiddler also adds vocals and harmonica.

Many of John's bands released singles that get replayed here, including the Medicine Head cuts `Pictures In The Sky' and `One And One Is One' (the latter a top three hit).

The music's great but largely acoustic throughout. It is still very enjoyable and atmospheric and enjoyed by the audience."
Joe Geesin, www.getreadytorock.com (April 2004)

"Twelve brilliant songs...These two musicians make a tremendous sound and is a great release from the boys and should captivate a lot of music fans over here as it does in the rest of Europe and the USA."
Rimmer, *Modern Dance* (August 2004)

Review for *Only The Roses* (Single): RAJP902

"...pleasant pop/rock...and retains the links with the band's illustrious past whilst at the same time proving that they still have much to offer in the 21st century."
Classic Rock Society (November 2004)

Review for *Don't Stop The Dance*: SJPCD185

"...this just unearthed, unreleased and unfinished...album from 1974 shows that, had they persevered, they could have cracked it. Fiddler's songs rock more, his growling guitar is to the fore and Hope-Evans' harmonica leads the show."
Record Collector (June 2005)

"...Full of harmonica, Jew's harp and blues rock, these recordings sound like a crossover between the free-spirit white-blues of Peter Green's Fleetwood Mac, the R&B psychedelia of The Rolling Stones and the fierce folk romanticism of Thin Lizzy."
www.maelstrom.nu (June 2005)

With thanks to Keith Smith and John Fiddler. www.johnfiddler.com.

See also John Fiddler, Morgan, Mott The Hoople, Mott, British Lions, CryBabys.

MELANIE

"…a superb double album…for all who do know Melanie's music with that oh so powerful voice also know how beautiful it is."

Modern Dance #39 (August 2002)

From Melanie's official website:-

"With guitar in hand and a talent that combined amazing vocal equipment, disarming humour and a vibrant engagement with life, she was booked as the first solo pop/rock artist ever to appear at Carnegie Hall, the Metropolitan Opera House, the Sydney Opera House and in the General Assembly of the United Nations, where delegates greeted her performances with standing ovations. The top television hosts of the time - Ed Sullivan, Johnny Carson and Dick Cavett all battled to book her. (After her stunning performance on his show, Sullivan goggled that he had not seen such a "dedicated and responsive audience since Elvis Presley.")

Accolades rolled in, from critics ('Melanie's cult has long been famous but it's a cult that's responding to something genuine and powerful - which is maybe another way of saying that this writer counts himself as part of the cult too,' wrote John Rockwell in *The New York Times*) as well as peers ('Melanie,' insisted jazz piano virtuoso Roger Kellaway, 'is extraordinary to the point that she could be sitting in front of us in this room and sing something like 'Momma Momma' right to us and it would just go right through your entire being.')

In the years that followed Melanie continued to record, continued to tour. UNICEF made her its spokesperson; Jimi Hendrix's father introduced her to the multitude assembled for the twentieth anniversary of Woodstock. Her records continued to sell -- more than eighty million to date. She's had her songs covered by singers as diverse as Cher, Dolly Parton and Macy Gray. She's raised a family, won an Emmy, opened a restaurant, and written a musical about Wild Bill Hickok and Calamity Jane…

She has, in short, lived a rare life, but all of it was just a prelude to what's about to come.

Many of the tracks featured on Angel Air's *Melanie – unplugged and solo powered* double CD were originally included on her *Silver Anniversary* album from 1993. The songs are crisp, beautifully recorded and include superb re-recordings of Melanie's four top forty U.K. hits."

Review for *Melanie – Unplugged And Solo Powered*: SJPCD103

"Ms. Safka's voice is as distinctive and strong as ever…She treats her material, old and new, with refreshing care, and the project proves not to be the expected barrel-scraping but a triumphant…celebration of a Woodstock-era icon."
Peter Doggett, *Record Collector* (July 2002)

MICK ABRAHAMS' BLODWYN PIG

"Mick's soulful guitar and vocals really showcase this fine album and are as superb as ever…Blues don't come much better than this!!!!"

Paul Bufton, *Blues Matters* (Sept 2002)

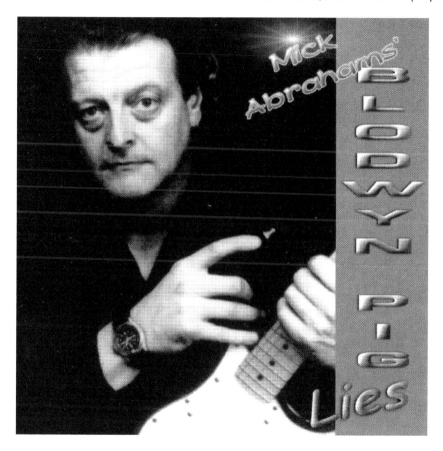

It is very difficult to imagine Blodwyn Pig without thinking of Jethro Tull. Both bands are inextricably linked by history.

Mick cut his teeth in the Sixties music scene, playing in a succession of bands which included a stint in the seedy dives of Hamburg as Jimmy Page's replacement in The Crusaders.

Upon his return from Germany, Mick joined The Toggery Five prior to forming his own blues band, McGregor's Engine, which featured Clive Bunker on drums.

By late 1967, Mick and Clive had joined forces with Ian Anderson and Glenn Cornick to form Jethro Tull. Tull were predominantly a blues band at this stage, incorporating elements of jazz and rock into their sound.

Their debut album, *This Was*, laid the foundations for a long and successful career. However Ian and Mick wanted to take the band in different directions. At the end of 1968, Mick left, forming his own band - Blodwyn Pig (a name suggested by a stoned hippie friend).

Blodwyn Pig released two albums of progressive blues (*Ahead Rings Out* (1969) and *Getting To This* (1970)), both reaching the top ten in the U.K. album charts. Alas, political differences loomed within the band and Mick left, leaving the remaining band members to soldier on before the group dissolved.

Mick formed The Mick Abrahams Band which gave way to a short-lived Blodwyn Pig reunion in 1974, prior to him leaving the music business and pursuing a career in the world of finance.

In 1988, Mick was lured into a jamming session with former musical colleagues. Such was the reception they received, that Blodwyn Pig was resurrected...and hasn't looked back since! Mick Abraham has regularly recorded and toured both with and without 'The Pig'. Angel Air has relaunched the 1993 album *Lies*, catching Mick and Blodwyn Pig at their best.

Reviews for *Lies*: SJPCD058

"Jethro Tull completists, pay attention! It is more than a decade since original guitarist Mick Abrahams re-formed Blodwyn Pig, his first post-Tull band but few of the new band's recordings ever matched *Lies*. Originally released in 1993, *Lies* received little attention (and even less exposure) when it first appeared. But the years since have seen its legend grow, both at home (where it was deleted soon after release) and abroad - where it never even appeared. Now Angel Air...have restored it to the racks, a twelve-track set upgraded with an eight-page booklet featuring liner notes by one of Abrahams' own best-known fans, Mott The Hoople drummer Buffin."
Jo-Ann Greene, *Goldmine* (April 2000)

"The music is tasty, guitar-dominated commercial FM rock that never panders to the baser elements of that style...Mick Abrahams never sounded better."
Bob Cianci, *River Reporter* (April-May 2000)

MICKEY FINN'S T-REX

"...it has to be said that Mickey Finn and co have done an admirable job..."

Hartlepool Mail, May 2002

In the autumn of 1997, Mickey Finn and Paul Fenton (both former members of T-Rex) were invited to Cambridge Corn Exchange for the unveiling of a memorial commemorating the 20th anniversary of the untimely death of their lead singer, Marc Bolan. It was a defining moment which led to the reformation of a band that seemed destined never to see the light of day again.

Finn's involvement with Bolan can be traced back to the departure of Steve Peregrine Took, Marc's original sideman, whose story is briefly chronicled elsewhere in this book.

Bolan was on the lookout for a new collaborator and his prayers were answered in the form of Mickey Finn, an ex-Croydon College of Art student who shared Bolan's taste in fashion and art.

So began the start of a new chapter and era which saw Finn and Bolan chalk up massive commercial success with hits such as 'Get it On', 'Jeepster' and 'Telegram Sam'.

Mickey left T-Rex in 1975, pursuing an active career which involved working with bands such as The Blow Monkeys and The Soupdragons, before coming full circle.

For the new T-Rex (re-branded Mickey Finn's T-Rex), Paul Fenton reclaimed his place on the drum stool which he had occupied for Bolan from 1973 onwards. Mickey resumed his place on bongos, Tony Allday joined on bass and Alan Silson on lead guitar. Silson was also no stranger to the charts, having featured on no less than fifteen top twenty hits with Smokie.

And last but by no means least; Rob Benson became the new lead vocalist. Despite Bolan being an impossibly hard act to follow, Benson proved to be so near the mark that it was difficult to tell the difference between the vocal styles of the two singers.

This highly experienced new line-up recorded a brand new album, *Renaissance*, re-working and re-recording classics from the old T-Rex back catalogue. They also put together a superb live DVD. Both have been released through Angel Air.

Sadly, Mickey Finn died in 2003 aged 55. His legacy as co-founder of glam rock is assured.

Reviews for *Renaissance*: SJPCD101

"The band's set is a tribute to Marc and I guess they are probably the only 'real' tribute band out there. They have original band members, the backing of Marc's family and the official Bolan fan club. Listen to the band - and you will hear friends and fans paying a real tribute to the man they knew and loved. This isn't just a bunch of musicians cashing in on someone else's music!

…listening to Mickey Finn's T-Rex is as good as the real thing to me. And like my friends in The Rolling Stones tribute band got me into the Stones, I think Mickey Finn's T-Rex might get me into T-Rex…"
Alternate View, (March 2002)

"Vocalist Rob Benson does indeed sound a lot like Marc Bolan which does occasionally feel a little eerie it must be said. But the overall results are OK and this pop release is bound to be of interest to T-Rex fans at least..."
Bernard Law, *Classic Rock Society* (Nov/Dec 2003)

See also Carmen.

MIDNIGHT FLYER

"...keep turning up the volume and when the roof starts shaking you can finally hear the power intrinsic to the original vinyl."

Jo-Ann Greene, *Goldmine* (July 2005)

Maggie Bell was Britain's most famous female vocalist during the Seventies. Her powerful vocal range and soulful voice made her an instant live draw and her albums sold well. A more detailed and comprehensive résumé of her career can be found earlier in this book.

At the start of the Eighties, Maggie formed Midnight Flyer with Tony Stevens (ex-Foghat). David Dowle was recruited on drums, Anthony Glynne on guitar and John Cook on keyboards.

Midnight Flyer went through a long and intense period of rehearsals and song writing before signing to Led Zeppelin's Swan Song label, who booked them into Ringo Starr's Tittenhurst Park Studio.

The recording of the album was a happy experience for the band. Mick Ralphs (Bad Company and Mott The Hoople) produced the album, lending it a power and clarity that complemented Maggie's belting vocals.

Following the completion of the album, John Cook returned to session work and was replaced by Chris Parren.

In November 1980, Midnight Flyer went on tour with Bob Seger And The Silver Bullet Band, which in turn was followed by some dates with AC/DC on their *Back In Black* tour.

Swan Song released the debut album in February 1981. Titled *Midnight Flyer*, it was followed in March by the single, 'Rough Trade'.

In July, Midnight Flyer played Montreux Jazz Festival and the following winter, went on tour once again with AC/DC. This time, the destination was North America.

An EP and single were also released, the lead track being 'Waiting For You'. A brief sabbatical was then planned before the band returned to the studio to record a second album.

However, things had gone drastically wrong at Swan Song.

John Bonham, Led Zeppelin's drummer, had died in September 1980 and the effect this had on their manager, Peter Grant, was devastating.

Peter had run Swan Song and guided the bands on the label, including Bad Company. Sadly he slumped into a dreadful depression leaving the artists at sea - directionless. Consequently, Midnight Flyer came to a halt and disintegrated by the middle of 1982. Swan Song closed its offices the following year.

It was a disappointing conclusion to a fantastic band (and label).

Reviews for *Midnight Flyer*: SJPCD198

"It's an album of well-played and crafted blues rock with a touch of soul, mainly due to the wonderfully earthy tones of Maggie Bell (nearest comparison would be Tina Turner in her classic Seventies guise)...

There are plenty of rockers like 'Hey Boy' and 'French Kisses' but Bell comes alive on the slower, soul tinged tracks like 'In My Eyes'. There are two bonus tracks on this remastered re-release including the good time feel of 'Rock 'N' Roll Party' plus very informative and interesting sleeve notes..."

Certainly one for Maggie Bell fans and those who enjoy classic blues rock.
Jason Ritchie, *www.getreadytorock.com*

"This is one of those that really seem to have slipped through the net for some reason as this is a great album that powers along with the band playing strong songs and Mick Ralphs doing a fine job on the production...loads of great melodies...a strong polished rock album with great vocals which definitely deserves to be heard by a wider audience and this reissue does it plenty of justice with copious sleeve notes and photos in the 24 page booklet, and two extra songs not originally featured on the album."
Feedback, May 2005

See also Maggie Bell, Tony Stevens, Stone The Crows.

BUDDY MILES

"These guys are fine musicians…and if you want to hear some fine covers…then this is the album for you."

Feedback (March 2002)

Buddy Miles is best known as the drummer of Jimi Hendrix's Band Of Gypsies. However, Buddy has enjoyed a lengthy solo career that has embraced rock, blues, soul and funk.

Buddy Miles was born in Omaha on 5th September 1947. He started playing the drums at the age of nine and joined his father's jazz band, The Bebops, at the age of twelve.

As a teenager, he went on to play with several jazz and rhythm & blues outfits, most prominently backing The Ink Spots and The Delfonics.

In 1966, Buddy joined Wilson Pickett's touring revue, where he was spotted by blues-rock guitarist Mike Bloomfield. Mike had left the Paul Butterfield Blues Band earlier in 1967 and was putting together a new group, The Electric Flag, which ambitiously fused rock, soul, blues, psychedelia and jazz. He invited Buddy to join and the band made a monumental and historic debut at the Monterey Pop Festival.

They recorded an album together but by 1968, Bloomfield had left the band. A second album was recorded with Miles at the helm but it was not a commercial success.

With the Electric Flag's horn section in tow, Miles formed his own group, Buddy Miles Express. They signed to Mercury Records and recorded their debut album, *Expressway To Your Skull* (1968). Jimi Hendrix produced the album.

Miles reciprocated this good turn by playing on Hendrix's *Electric Ladyland* album. He also partook in an all-star jam session which resulted in Muddy Waters' *Fathers and Sons* album. Hendrix also produced the second Buddy Miles Express album, *Electric Church* (1969).

Later that same year, Buddy, Jimi and bassist Billy Cox formed Band Of Gypsies. The line-up did not last long, with Buddy leaving the following year to be replaced by Experience drummer Mitch Mitchell. They recorded one live album together.

Buddy went on to back guitarist John McLaughlin on his album *Devotion* before returning to the role of bandleader on his most popular album, *Them Changes,* which stayed on the American chart for over a year.

 Between December 1971 to April 1972, Buddy toured with Carlos Santana. In so doing, they recorded a live album inside an inactive volcano in Hawaii (a first, surely?) which became an American top ten hit.

Buddy also participated in a short-lived Electric Flag reunion in 1974 prior to relocating to Casablanca in 1975, where he recorded two albums.

In 1981, Buddy recorded the album *Sneak Attack* for Atlantic Records. Throughout the Eighties he generally maintained a low profile, partly as a consequence of personal problems.

However, in 1986, he became the lead voice in a television advertising campaign that featured clay-animated raisins singing 'I Heard It Through The Grapevine'. It proved to be one of the greatest marketing campaigns in television history and led to him recording two albums as front man of The California Raisins, as well as a Christmas special.

Buddy also teamed up briefly once again with old friend Carlos Santana as the official lead vocalist of Santana appearing on the album *Freedom* (1987).

In the early Nineties, Buddy Miles played with Bootsy Collins before reforming Buddy Miles Express, recording the albums *Hell and Back* and *Miles Away From Home*. It was this line-up that recorded the live set which is featured on the Angel Air release, *Hey Jimi - Tribute To Hendrix*.

Miles continued to tour throughout the Nineties and formed The Blues Berries with Rocky Athas (guitar), releasing an album in 2002.

Reviews for *Hey Jimi - Tribute To Hendrix*: SJPCD107

"Recorded live in 1995, it is the spirit of the album that re-animates Hendrix, not the material. Only one of the tracks, 'Red House' is at all associated with the man but the flair and fire are unmistakable…the sound quality and booklet are as fine as one could hope. Recommended."
Jo-Ann Greene, *Goldmine* (May 2002)

"…it features the strongest trio Miles put together in over a decade…Miles' voice is strong and the band is powerful…"
Voodoo Child (Summer 2002)

With thanks to www.buddymiles.com.

MINUTE BY MINUTE

"…Played live in the studio the result is pretty hot, with well-crafted tunes to the fore...Interesting stuff."

Bernard Law, *Classic Rock Society* (Nov/Dec 2003)

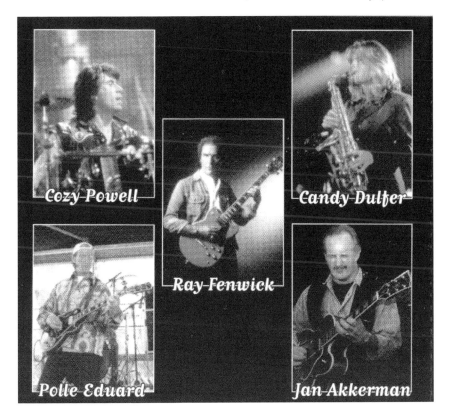

Minute By Minute emerged during the latter half of the Eighties and comprised a group of seasoned musicians who had been at the forefront of their profession since the mid-Sixties.

The group was the brainchild of two individuals, Ray Fenwick and Polle Eduard.

Ray Fenwick earned a formidable reputation in the Sixties and Seventies as guitarist with The Spencer Davis Group, Fancy, Ian Gillan Band and in recent times, as part of Mike Hurst's 'All Star' Band.

Prior to life with Spencer Davis, Ray was a member of Tee Set, one of the most successful Dutch chart acts of all.

Tee Set featured an articulate gentleman by the name of Polle Eduard on bass.

207

Polle and Ray were dissatisfied with their standing within the group and in 1967 formed a break-away band called After Tea. Again, they built on their previous Dutch successes scoring a string of top forty hits in Holland.

Polle and Ray stayed in touch through the years and came together almost two decades later to record the album *Long Hot Night* under the banner Minute By Minute.

They recruited a formidable band around them, featuring Dutch maestro Jan Akkerman, legendary drummer Cozy Powell, Graham Bonnet (ex-Rainbow and Michael Schenker), and Tony Martin. Bobby Van Den Berg joined on keyboards and he in turn recommended Candy Dulfer. Lisa Boray completed the line-up of this gifted and eclectic group.

Ray has fond memories of making *Long Hot Night*:-

"All the musicians on this album give '100% performances' and not least my musical partner Polle Eduard. His vocals are always fresh and exciting and his song writing skills shine through. I love his use of the English language; he always manages to convey so much with so few words. Not bad for a Dutchman!

Since these recordings were made, Cozy Powell is sadly no longer with us, having been killed tragically in a car accident. He once told me that he loved this album and often played it. With this in mind, Polle and I would like to dedicate this release to the memory of Cozy."

Reviews for *Long Hot Night*: SJPCD108

"…a quality album of R & B. With Polle Eduard's smooth vocals bouncing along with the beat and Ray Fenwick's excellent blues guitar this shows the quality of the music. 'Katie's Love' is a soulful track with saxophone by Candy Dulfer and with four (demo) bonus tracks added on its well worth a look."
Alistair Flynn, *Wondrous Stories* (May 2002)

"No outlandish solos or heavy situations but pop music with much variation…more or less like *Butterfly Ball* with R&B roots.

The songs are very catchy as well. Candy Dulfer delivers some amazing sax…look out for 'Katie's Love' with Jan Akkerman setting the mood…"
Het Paarste News, June 15 2002

With thanks to Ray Fenwick.
www.rayfenwick.com

See also Ray Fenwick, The Ian Gillan Band, Fancy, The Spencer Davis Group, Mike Hurst, Tee Set, Fancy, Guitar Orchestra, Jan Akkerman.

MORGAN &
MORGAN FISHER

"...Morgan is very much influenced by King Crimson...Overall the whole sound reminds me of a melting pot of several bands but mainly the aforementioned KC with early ELP thrown in...A treat for Seventies aficionados."

Background (May 2000)

Morgan Fisher was born on 1st January 1950. By the time he had reached his eighteenth birthday, he had already shared in the roller coaster experience of having a number 1 hit single.

In the late Sixties, Morgan played the Hammond organ with teen idols Love Affair, appearing on a string of hits including 'Everlasting Love' (number 1), 'Rainbow Valley' (number 5), 'A Day Without Love' (number 6), 'One Road' (number 16) and 'Bringing Back The Good Times' (number 9).

Morgan also created electronic music for London's Institute Of Contemporary Art.

In 1971, he formed his own band to which he leant his name. Morgan was a progressive rock band with a long pedigree.

Tim Staffell joined as lead vocalist, having previously fronted a band called Smile (the predecessor of Queen). Maurice Bacon joined on drums and Bob Sapsed on bass. Maurice and Bob had previously played alongside Morgan in Love Affair.

Progressive rock was booming in parts of Europe and before long, the band had been offered a deal by RCA Italy. They headed out to Rome and recorded their debut album, *Nova Solis,* in a studio that was apparently 'floated' on a layer of oil in order to negate the effects of traffic vibration.

Morgan returned to Rome to make a second album, *The Sleeper Wakes*. On this occasion, Morgan (the artiste, not the band) found time to squeeze out an album's worth of solo material. Dubiously titled *Morgan Fisher's Hand Job,* RCA declined to release the end product. However, the additional studio time presented Morgan with the opportunity to explore beyond the boundaries of his band and dip a toe into areas he had been passionate about for years, including modern classical music, film scores from France and Italy and electronic music. It was eventually released on Maurice Bacon's private label in the early Eighties, featuring two extra tracks. It has also received a release on compact disc through Angel Air under the more dignified title of *Ivories (along with Nova Solis and The Sleeper Wakes)*.

Around this time, Morgan became professionally involved with world-famous fusion guitarist Alan Holdsworth, co-producing an album for him.

Morgan moved on briefly to The Third Ear Band before joining Mott The Hoople.

The Mott The Hoople story is told in some detail in this book. During his time with the band, Morgan had the delight of working with Bowie, toured America and was part of the first ever rock band to perform for a week on Broadway (Uris Theatre). They scored a string of hits including 'All The Young Dudes'. When Mott The Hoople dissolved, some of the remaining members (including Morgan) formed Mott and then British Lions, though Morgan also continued to plough his own furrow, which included working with artists as diverse as American punks Wayne County And The Electric Chairs and The Dead Kennedy's.

In 1978, Morgan set up his own London-based independent studio and record label called Pipe Music.

A prolific period followed, when Morgan recorded an album of ambient music called *Slow Music*, an art-punk album called *Hybrid Kids* and a sensational and now quite famous compilation called *Miniatures*, which featured no less than fifty one tracks, each a minute in length, by some of the most extraordinary and diverse musicians of the time, including Robert Fripp, Robert Wyatt, Michael Nyman, XTC, The Penguin Cafe Orchestra and The Damned.

In 1982, Morgan played keyboards for Queen on their 1982 European tour.

By the middle of the decade, he had relocated to Japan and set about building The Handmade Studio.

Morgan also recorded a series of ambient albums – *Look At Life, Inside Satie, Water Music, Flow Overflow, Life Under The Floor, Peace In The Heart Of The City* as well as music for art videos, films and television.

In 1989, he had the rare honour of performing at the Heian Shrine for the 1200th anniversary of Kyoto City with the Japanese dancer, Kisanuki Kuniko.

The following year, Morgan played at a diverse number of events and venues, including Expo 90 in Osaka, Tenkawa Jinja (Shinto shrine), Tsubosakadera (Buddhist temple) and Kobe City Museum.

He also recorded a new album, *Echoes of Lennon* with guest, Yoko Ono.

1991 saw Morgan head off in an entirely different direction when he dipped a toe into the world of Techno, playing with Japanese band Dip In The Pool.

In 1992, he recorded a triple set of ambient/polyrhythmic music which he christened *The Re-Series* (*Relax, Refresh* and *Recharge*). Staggeringly, he also found the time to create the soundtrack to the animated film, *The Apfel Land Story* and perform the music from *Twin Peaks* with Haruomi Hosono of Yellow Magic Orchestra (the performance included Julee Cruise who sang on the original *Twin Peaks* soundtrack).

In 1993 Morgan performed with a major Japanese band called The Boom. He also toured China with Yasuaki Shimizu, Aska Kaneko, Ryu Hon Jin and Wasis Diop. In contrast, the following year he played in London at the Mick Ronson memorial concert.

Morgan added to *The Re-Series* with the fourth instalment in the collection, *Rebalance* and went on a tour of Japan with The Boom, having co-produced and played on their *Far East Samba* album.

In 1995, Morgan re-visited his first two *Re-Series* albums with Japanese musicians (singer Sizzle Ohtaka and violinist Aska Kaneko). He also continued to perform with The Boom and wrote a book about their tour called 'Far East Tour Diary'. Indeed, his adventure with them continued with the *Tropicalism-0* album and tours of Japan and Brazil. He also appeared at Montreux with them.

Morgan went on to produce *Moth Poet Hotel*, a Mott The Hoople tribute album with major Japanese bands.

In 1997, he re-visited the Miniatures project with *Miniatures 2* (a sixty track sequel which was eventually released in 2000). The following year, Morgan pulled together a compilation album of his own music called *Echoes Of A City Life* and released a new ambient album, *Flower Music*. He also recorded *Home*, an album with Sizzle Ohtaka and Hamza-El-in (a well-known musician from Sudan).

In 1999, Morgan expanded The *Re-Series* with *Remix* and performed on an album by The Minus 5 (featuring Peter Buck of REM).

Morgan's first soundtrack of the new millennium was for the DVD animation film *Traja*. He went on to join a new art/music performance unit featuring Sizzle Ohtaka (voice performer), Etsuko Takezawa (koto, shamisen, sho), Bruce Osborn (photos, video), Kozo Chiba (computer graphics).

Morgan played on the new album of his old friend Tim Staffell and collaborated on an album with Hans Joachim Roedelius (formerly of Seventies Austrian ambient band Cluster).

In 2003, Morgan performed a number of shows including a performance at London's Institute of Contemporary Art with Futon Logic. The following year, he embarked upon a Monthly series of 'Morgan's Organ' solo concerts at Super Deluxe, Tokyo, featuring his own photos and videos.

Few artists have achieved quite so much in a lifetime of music.

Reviews for *Nova Solis*: SJPCD067

"...Forget the label 'prog rock', with its connotations of over-long compositions and extravagant solos, what we have here is an album full of good tunes and, dare I say it, songs...The CD comes with an excellent twelve-page booklet, complete with lyrics, track-by-track notes and the inside story of the making of the album, written by Morgan Fisher...this is a darn good album..."
Adrian Perkins, (August 2000)

"Another album from the vaults of the now legendary Angel Air archives...The packaging and quality is up to Angel Air's usual (high) standards and the music ain't bad either! ...If you like your prog with a combination of a keyboard virtuoso and out of this world vocals, then you'll love this. Another piece of heaven on earth from Angel Air."
Wondrous Stories, (September 2000)

Reviews for *The Sleeper Wakes*: SJPCD049

"...This is in fact a very good progressive album, one that would sit proudly in any proghead's collection...They come across at times as a cross between ELP and King Crimson...Overall an album that will be enjoyed by many..."
Feedback, October 1999

"Morgan was influenced by the likes of King Crimson and Frank Zappa, with a classical approach that (Morgan) Fisher used to great effect in constructing his arrangements. Of the four tracks, the highlight is the twenty-minute 'What is - is What' which may be naive and pretentious in places but is a real highlight of the prog genre, invoking memories of Yes during their *Close To The Edge* period or early Queen. Unexpectedly good."
Rich Wilson, *Record Collector*, January 2000

Reviews for *Ivories*: SJPCD072

"...an album of fifteen musical snippets recorded in 1972 and issued in 1984 to little acclaim...Morgan's a fascinating chap, and his solo work is gradually coming out through Angel Air who keep the Mott flag flying. "
Michael Heatley, *Record Buyer* (April 2001)

"Marvellously cinematic in scope and sound...There are also short recorded conversations that took place at various times during his Mott career that Fisher has added to the original LP that further enhance the quirky charm."
Colin Bryce, *Mohair Sweets* (March 2001)

See also Greg Ridley (for Alan Holdsworth connection), Mott The Hoople, 'Igginbottom's Wrench, Mott, British Lions.

MOTT

"...a more than competent rock band with a good ear for melodies. The accompanying sleeve notes have some interesting information and photos..."

Wondrous Stories (August 2000)

I would suggest that you skip on to Mott The Hoople (next chapter), then return to this page.

On 14th December 1974, Mott The Hoople were in disarray. The only remaining members were Overend Watts, Dale Griffin and Morgan Fisher.

With a succession of hits behind them and a heap of best selling albums, it came as a terrible shock to find that the group were hopelessly in debt. In the spirit of Dale Griffin's wonderful sleeve notes, the band members for this segment shall herein be known as 'Overdraft Watts', 'Mortgaged Fisher' and 'Dole Griffin'.

Urgent meetings with management were convened with a view to salvaging something out of the situation.

'Overdraft' and 'Mortgaged' wanted to take a new band off into a different direction from its predecessor but the powers-that-be decreed that any new band should carry the

Mott The Hoople brand. So Mott was born.

Auditions were held and Ray Majors (ex-Hackensack) was recruited on guitar and Terry Wilson-Slessor on lead vocals. However, Terry also accepted an invitation to join Paul Kossoff's Backstreet Crawler and ruled himself out of the frame. Nigel Benjamin stepped in to the breach and the five-piece was once again complete.

Mott recorded two albums for CBS (both of which hit the top 40), released three singles and toured the U.K and America (twice).

Angel Air has released two Mott albums to complement the original CBS releases. The first is a live offering salvaged from the band's vaults, pulling together recordings from the U.K. and America. The second is a treasure trove of demos in part culled from sessions at the Gooseberry Studios.

Reviews for *Live Over Here & Over There '75/'76*: SJPCD025

"The presentation and the liner notes...are superb...as it seems with all Angel Air releases. In summary then as live albums go this is pretty good and coupled with the interest factor (like this being the first live album from what many rated as the best live band of the early Seventies) then comes recommended."
Zabadak, August 1999

"Ladies and gentlemen this is one fun album. Forget about comparisons and just revel in the angry maelstrom of Seventies Brit' rock...bloody good. "
M Dyas, *Wondrous Stories* (August 1999)

Review for *The Gooseberry Sessions And Rarities*: SJPCD054

"...All but the maddest Mott fans should turn off their players after track twelve and immerse themselves instead in the voluminous sleeve notes by drummer Griffin that accurately reflect the problems Mott faced in the immediate post-Hunter era."
Mike Heatley, *Classic Rock* (September 2000)

"...the material is powerful in the main and maintain some of The Hoople's allure...Undoubtedly of interest to completists will be the original audition tapes of potential vocalist Brian Parrish and eventual guitarist Ray Majors...A worthwhile release."
Rich Wilson, *Record Collector* (August 2002)

With thanks to Dale 'Buffin' Griffin.

See also Mott The Hoople, Morgan/Morgan Fisher, Overend Watts, Ray Majors, British Lions.

MOTT THE HOOPLE

"...Excellent packaging, lengthy liner notes, great photos and an unimpeachable track listing are the good news...Mott remind us once again why, on their night, there wasn't a band in town to touch them."

Jo-Ann Greene, Goldmine (September 2000)

The roots of Mott The Hoople can be traced back to a mid-Sixties band called The Silence and its successor, The Doc Thomas Group (also called Silence).

Emerging from Hereford, at one time or another, the band featured Stan Tippins (vocals), Mick Ralphs (guitar), Peter Overend Watts (bass), Dale 'Buffin' Griffin (drums) and Terry Allen (Organ).

215

Like many acts of the time, they grew up the hard way, earning their stripes on the pub and club circuit as well as playing in Hamburg.

Their career showed signs of flourishing when Mick Ralphs persuaded Guy Stevens (manager of Free and an executive at Island Records) to listen to their demo tape. Guy liked what he heard, auditioned the band and signed them up.

Guy Stevens had a vision for his new signing, which he christened Mott The Hoople (after a book by Willard Manus). However, he felt that Stan didn't quite fit the image he had in mind. In good grace, their lead singer bowed out and pursued a solo career in Italy (returning as Road Manager in 1970).

Auditions for a new singer were held in a small studio but without success. Eventually, the engineer Bill Farley suggested a musician he knew called Ian Hunter.

Hunter was an experienced bassist who had grown up playing gigs in small venues. He had also spent time playing in Hamburg. He secured the Mott The Hoople job with a rendition of Dylan's 'Like a Rolling Stone'.

The new band started rehearsals prior to recording their debut album, simply titled *Mott The Hoople* (1969). It was a powerful album mixing cover versions with original material and was influenced heavily by Bob Dylan.

They soon honed their stage act and before long had picked up a following, based upon the explosive chemistry between the musicians who were a superb live unit. On the strength of this, the debut album nudged the lower reaches of the album charts.

In 1970, Mott The Hoople recorded their second album live in the studio. The end result, *Mad Shadows*, was a dark album which broke into the U.K. top fifty album charts but failed to make a major impact, despite being backed by a punishing U.K. tour. The band also toured America at this time.

A third album was recorded showcasing the more melodic side of Mott The Hoople. *Wildlife* was released in 1971 and stalled just outside the top forty. Again, another tour followed but there was still frustration at the band's inability to translate the power, enthusiasm and euphoria of live shows into hard record sales.

Mott The Hoople returned to the studio for a fourth album, trying the live approach once again. The end result, *Brain Capers* took just four days to record. It was a mad affair with Guy Stevens and engineer Andy Johns dressing as highwaymen in the hope of creating the right atmosphere.

A trip to America bore witness to the band's first attempt at recording a commercial single. The result, 'Midnight Lady', earned the band a place on Top Of The Pops, resulting in a dip in sales!

Both *Brain Capers* and a second single, 'Downtown', failed to make an impression, despite extensive touring. Consequently, the band's financial position was starting to look decidedly dicey, their management seemed to be losing interest and Island Records were losing enthusiasm for Mott The Hoople. It seemed that they had finally hit the buffers.

Overend Watts contacted David Bowie to see if he had a vacancy for a bassist but Bowie was aghast that one of his favourite bands had thrown in the towel. He offered them one of his songs, 'All The Young Dudes' and arranged for his management company, Mainman, to take over Mott The Hoople's affairs. Mainman secured them a deal with CBS. 'All The Young Dudes' was a dream come true and encapsulated the spirit of the band.

Rejuvenated, the band returned to the studio for their first CBS album. With Bowie in the producer's chair, they cut an album that was destined to be a hit. *All The Young Dudes* (1972) (both album and single went by the same name) climbed to number 21 in the U.K. album chart and the single peaked at number 3. Mott The Hoople had arrived!

An autumn tour of the U.K. followed along with a tour of America, their first as a headline act.

Changes were afoot on the home front when Mott The Hoople were dropped by Mainman, who were concentrating on Bowie. In fact, contracts had never been completed so it was in many ways academic. Verden Allen also left the band at this time, apparently unhappy that his song writing was being overlooked. He was also worried about the direction the band was going in.

The next album, *Mott* (1973) was recorded for the first time as a four piece band and was a huge hit, peaking at number 7. They also recorded a new single, 'Roll Away the Stone' which was a top ten hit (their fourth hit single in total, following 'Honaloochie Boogie' and 'All The Way From Memphis' into the charts).

Yet another American tour followed, with Morgan Fisher eventually replacing Verden on keyboards. However, further problems loomed when Mick Ralphs left the fold, feeling sidelined. He went on to form Bad Company with Paul Rodgers.

Luther Grosvenor ('Ariel Bender') was brought in as replacement. The year finished with a highly successful U.K. tour, culminating in two shows at Hammersmith Odeon (Queen supported them).

In January 1974, the new line-up recorded the seventh Mott The Hoople album, simply titled *The Hoople*. The high point of the recording was Morgan's keyboards…the low point was the poor quality of the sound as a consequence of faulty studio equipment.

The first single from the album, 'The Golden Age Of Rock 'n' Roll', was a U.K. top twenty hit and the album peaked at number 11 in the album charts. It was a hit in America too.

A ten week tour of America followed, again with Queen in support. The shows were exciting and explosive, with Luther and Ian acting as sparring partners, much to the delight of the audience.

A live album (*Live*), which was recorded on the preceding tour, made the U.K. top forty in November 1974.

This proved to be Luther's last recording for Mott The Hoople. Mick Ronson was brought in as his replacement, fresh from playing in David Bowie's Spiders From Mars.

A European tour followed with Ronson on board but this proved to be the end of the road. Whilst Ian took some time out in America buying a new house, he collapsed, suffering from mental exhaustion. Some planned U.K. dates were re-arranged but then cancelled.

It was all over when it became apparent that Ian no longer wanted to continue. Mick Ronson headed off to pursue his solo career, leaving Overend Watts, Dale Griffin and Morgan Fisher as the only members prepared to soldier on.

Angel Air has managed to bottle the very 'essence' of Mott The Hoople with a stack of releases and re-releases spanning their entire career.

Reviews for *Mott The Hoople*: SJPCD157

"...Truth is, Mott The Hoople were one of the finest, loudest rock bands England ever produced, a rampaging thrash that was never heavy rock, with the angst and anger of the Stooges, yet often 'rootsy', even country...Their 1969 debut...A curious collection of covers...along with self-penned screams of anguish...set the tone for the next several years..."
Nick Dalton, *Record Collector*, (January 2004)

"Excellent and exhaustive liner notes provide fascinating historical data, while each beautifully remastered disc avoids overkill by only adding a couple of well-chosen bonus tracks...Ultimately, none are expendable."
Bernard Perusse, *The Gazette* (France), (December 2003)

Reviews for *Mad Shadows*: SJPCD158

"...This is a tremendously strong album, with some great performances...and the band really moving away from their debut..."
Feedback (Nov 2003)

...altogether darker and louder, personified by the glorious opener 'Thunderbuck Ram' and mixing up feelgood rockers ('Walkin' With A Mountain') with Hunter's more tortured outpourings ('When My Mind's Gone').
Nick Dalton, *Record Collector*, (January 2004)

Reviews for *Wildlife*: SJPCD159

"Excellent and exhaustive liner notes provide fascinating historical data, while each beautifully remastered disc avoids overkill by only adding a couple of well-chosen bonus tracks...Ultimately, none are expendable."
Bernard Perusse, *The Gazette* (France), (December 2003)

"...a much more sedate and song based affair...this album does have some beautiful song writing...This issue of *Wildlife*; has a great version of Mountain's 'Long Red' in the bonus section..."
Free Appreciation Society (January 2004)

Reviews for *Brain Capers*: SJPCD160

"Mott's last album for Island is a belter...a raw, heavy metal punk album six years ahead of its time. Of the pre-Bowie albums, this is easily the fans' favourite...

Sleeve notes as always are excellent, as is the sound quality."

Adrian Perkins (Nov 2003)

"...The twenty page booklet is full of interesting things about the songs and the recordings. A nice raw sound is captured on the album and helps adds life to some of the songs."

Alistair Flynn, *Classic Rock Society*, (January 2004)

Reviews for *Two Miles From Heaven*: SJPCD161

"What an absolute peach this collection is. Unreleased tracks, rare B-sides and early versions of songs that would be recorded later on...this album has long been sought after by fans, and is now at long last available on CD.

...As always with Angel Air, packaging is excellent with excellent and informative sleeve notes by Dale Griffin...

Sound quality throughout is excellent (a lot better than the original LP)."

Adrian Perkins (Nov 2003)

"...a masterpiece. It has definitely been worth the wait. Sound quality is much better than I had hoped. For all fans of Mott The Hoople, this album is a must....Of course what sets this album apart is not only the good quality live recordings but the four demo tracks that are included on the first disc...Disc 2 has the more familiar live set from 1974...again the sound quality is right up there with the best live recordings...If you need any persuasion to buy this double CD set, then what can I say - you must be a very casual fan! The booklet has some excellent and rare photos of Mott The Hoople supplied from the personal collections of Mick Ralphs and Dale Griffin. Liner notes are by Keith Smith. All in all, a really good release. Definitely worth the 5 stars I have rated it." *****

Phil Holbrook, *'Pleasure Doing Business With You'*

(October 2001)

Reviews for *All The Way From Stockholm*: SJPCD029

"...Both shows have been available as bootlegs before, but the superior sound quality and official status are a welcome improvement...

The packaging is up to the usual Angel Air standards, with a clear jewel case and a sixteen-page booklet penned by Campbell Devine and stuffed with twenty rare photographs of the band..."

Just A Buzz

"...important for MTH fans and rock historians alike...this two-CD set captures these guys at their rowdy, snotty best, showing exactly how influential they really were.

Both discs are full of great classic rock tones courtesy of guitarist Mick Ralphs and vocalist/guitarist Ian Hunter...their chord progressions obviously made a lasting impression on would-be rock stars of the time. 'Jerkin' Crocus' sounds like every Kiss track ever written and selections such as 'Thunderbuck', reveal the impact 'The Motts' had on bands such as Oasis, Queen, Def Leppard and Sweet...

Anyone who has ever loved or hated glam rock should give this a spin."
"*Guitar Player*", (USA), May 1999

Reviews for *Rock 'n' Roll Circus Live*: SJPCD061

"...It captures a moment in time as off kilter as rock should be. In many ways, it's comparable to the equally seminal *Velvet Underground Live At Max's Kansas City* album..."
Zorilla.Com (July 2000)

"Recorded live in Wolverhampton on 6th April 1972, this special collector's edition CD features what many consider the classic line-up of the band...The release includes a twenty page booklet with lots of information and rare photos supplied by Mick Ralphs...one for the fans."
Wondrous Stories (August 2000)

Reviews for *Hoopling - Best Of Live*: SJPCD121

"...One of the greatest rock and roll bands in the world at their best - playing live. Splendid stuff."
Modern Dance, (Issue 41 November 2002)

"...it really does cherry-pick some fantastic performances including a dynamic 'Roll Away The Stone/Sweet Jane' medley from Santa Monica in 1974 and a savage 'Golden Age Of Rock 'N' Roll' from the same show. An excellent booklet features band members' own recollections of the songs..."
Jo-Anne Greene, *Goldmine* (November 2002)

Reviews for *Family Anthology*: SJPCD196

"Angel Air have done a fine job in packaging the whole complicated Mott family tree over the last couple of years, and this compilation highlights that pretty well...Not only a good compilation, there's a fine mix of essential classics and rarities, a couple of previously unreleased numbers and even a new number by Overend Watts."
Record Collector (September 2005)

"…this compilation is going to tickle most Mott fans' palate."
Classic Rock (August 2005)

Reviews for *Live Fillmore West, San Francisco*: SJPCD226

"It's thunderous stuff throughout. Mick Ralphs' guitar and Verden Allen's' keyboards dominate the mix, establishing a wall of dense energy through which Ian Hunter's vocals crack and crackle like alien radio waves, to ferment a seething brew that leaves the unsuspecting listener breathless with excitement."

Neither is that the end of it. Opening the disc are four tracks from the band's 1971 return to the Fillmore, this time riding their third album, *Wildlife*; while the package closes with 'The Wreck of the Liberty Belle', a previously unreleased demo from around the same time as the main *Fillmore* show. It's raw and unfinished, but you can taste the song's potential regardless."

Jo-Anne Greene, *Goldmine* (October 2006)

"Truly excellent live material from the personal vaults of Overend Watts....This is what Mott The Hoople were really about."
Maverick (August 2006)

With thanks to Keith Smith and Adrian Perkins.
www.justabuzz.com; www.hunter-mott.com. Fanzine Mott@start.no; www.ianhunter.com.

See also Mott, British Lions, Ray Majors, Verden Allen, Overend Watts, Mick Ralphs, Silence/Doc Thomas Group, Morgan & Morgan Fisher, Bad Company, The Rats.

For The Mott The Hoople Appreciation Society write to:
Two Miles From heaven, PO Box 14, Stowmarket, Suffolk, IP14 1EN. England.

MOUSE

"...The material is song-orientated with a groove that is both precise and mighty, rooted in hard rock trends but taken further by the creative band... "

www.maelstrom.nu (July 2005)

Angel Air Records have taken a huge amount of pride in re-releasing little gems that would otherwise have been by-passed by the music industry. *Lady Killer* by Mouse is one such example.

Mouse comprised Alan Clare (vocals and keyboards), Ray Russell (guitar), Jeff Watts (bass guitar) and Al Rushton (drums).

In the summer of 1973, these four highly talented and exceptionally hairy musicians entered the De Lane Lea's Studios in Wembley and cut their first and only album. The end result was a polished and well executed album of progressive rock music, played to a high standard and boasting some lovely vocals.

Mouse were launched onto an unsuspecting public with the single 'We Can Make It', but it failed to make any commercial impression.

This was followed by the album, *Lady Killer* (1974) and a second single, 'All The Fallen Teen Angels'. Both faired poorly and Mouse disbanded without achieving their full potential.

Original copies of the singles sell for in the region of £15 a piece. The album, a true rarity, will cost in excess of £100 for a good copy.

Alternatively, a delve into the Angel Air back catalogue will secure you a copy of *Lady Killer* on compact disc, inclusive of the two singles and a brace of bonus tracks.

Reviews for *Mouse*: SJPCD189

"...a classic progressive/psych rock album. It should certainly have received more attention at the time..."
Music Week, 23.05.05

"With more credits to his C.V than most can dream of, Russell can play most styles. This set is more toned down yet more solid than Running Man. It's a fine slice of mid-Seventies rock/pop, with some decent tunes along the way. There's even a hint of reggae in the moving 'All The Fallen Teen-Angels'.

Although much of the booklet replicates that of Running Man (well, Russell's biog' was pretty similar at the time), with four bonus tracks it's a good package and for fans very welcome on CD." ***
Joe Geesin. (April 2005)

With thanks to Ray Russell.
See also Ray Russell, RMS, Rock Workshop, Running Man.
www.rayrussell.co.uk

MR BIG

"...Mr Big were very much a hard rock band but with a very melodic edge and a penchant for luscious vocal harmonies accentuated by the wonderful voice of main vocalist/guitarist/chief songwriter Dicken...Each track is melodic rock at it's very best...One of the great lost albums and lost bands of the Seventies..."

Steve Ward, *Wondrous Stories* (March 2001)

The roots of Mr Big can be traced back to a band called Chaulkies Painful Legg which was formed in 1967 by Jeffrey Pain (also known as Dicken), his brother Dave and Vince Chaulk, an old friend from the same street.

The trio played local village halls, incorporating a mix of original material and cover versions into their set.

Growing in confidence, they recorded a demo tape and boldly set off for Abbey Road Studios. Dave managed to catch the attention of Mary Hopkin who was arriving for a recording session. He offered her their demo tape and she graciously agreed to pass it on to George Martin.

Mary was true to her word because the band were invited back to Abbey Road for an audition. Devastatingly, they blew their big chance and turned in a below par performance.

Around 1969/1970, Chaulkies Painful Legg underwent a radical change. Pete Crowther joined on bass and the band were renamed Burnt Oak. In 1972, Vince got married and left the band. He was replaced by drummer John Burnip, who had been Bryan Ferry's first drummer in Roxy Music.

The band started gigging and built up a reputation on the live circuit, changing their name to Mr Big. They were rejoined by Vince, becoming a two-drummer outfit with a punchy sound.

In 1974, Mr Big signed to Epic Records and released the single, 'Eee I'm All Right'. They were photographed dressed as pearly kings, an image that Dicken is philosophical about:-

"It was definitely not the right scene for us but we got a lot of publicity out of it, which later proved to be more of a help than the hindrance we thought it would be. I still have my pearly suit at home in an old chest."

This was a busy era for the band, who found themselves constantly in demand. They made a host of television appearances (including the popular police drama *Softly Softly*) and played a stack of regular gigs, including over twenty appearances at the Marquee.

It was during a performance at The Speakeasy that Mr Big were spotted by Morgan Fisher and Stan Tippins. Tippins introduced Mr Big to Mott's manager, Bob Hirschman, who took them on, ditched the pearly suits and knocked their image into shape.

In 1975, they released their first album, *Sweet Silence*, which Record Mirror proclaimed to be one of the best albums of the year from a new band.

Mr Big supported Queen on a six week tour, which they followed with a headline tour of their own.

The sound of the band was bolstered by the inclusion of Eddie Carter (vocals and guitar). Eddie joined them for a European tour supporting Sweet, possibly the biggest act in Germany at this time.

Bob Hirschman negotiated a new record deal with a view to breaking Mr Big in America.

They became the first British act to sign to the Arista label, releasing their second album, *Mr Big* (renamed *Photographic Smile* in America).

Mr Big included the song 'Romeo' which was released as a single. It was an enormous hit, reaching number 4 in the U.K. singles chart. The follow up, 'Feel Like Calling Home' also made the top forty.

Around this time, John Burnip became the band's personal assistant. His place in the band was taken by John Marter. Mickey Llewellyn also came on board, filling in as second guitarist.

The making of the third album took the band to both sides of the Atlantic but was fraught with record company politics. The end result, *Seppuku*, failed to meet with record label approval, despite being an excellent selection of tracks.

A brief tour followed but lack of money and enthusiasm resulted in the inevitable collapse of the band.

Angel Air has now given the Ian Hunter-produced *Seppuku* a long overdue release, thus completing Mr Big's back catalogue for the first time.

In 1989, Dicken reformed Mr Big as Mr Big (UK) (an American band had 'hijacked' the original name which was registered to Dicken and Pete).

Mr Big (UK) featured Mike Higgins (bass and vocals), Ian Campbell (drums) and Chris Hutchinson (keyboards and vocals). Ian was later replaced by Simon Saunders.

The band recorded a number of tracks over the years which have made their way on to Broken Home's album *Life*, also released on Angel Air.

Reviews for *Seppuku*: SJPCD076

"I find it unbelievable that EMI chose not to release this album first time round (in 1978). It is to Angel Air's credit they have tracked down the master tapes and finally released this album. It is not just a good album; it is a great album that will appeal to anyone who likes guitar-based rock. Essential."
Adrian Perkins (February 2001)

"...it's a very, very good album indeed and EMI should be bloody well ashamed that they didn't put it out first time around...thanks to Angel Air, justice is finally done."
Two Miles From Heaven, (November 2001)

With thanks to Dicken, John Burnip, Shaun Godfrey and Sven Gusevik.

See also Broken Home.

MARIA MULDAUR

"Muldaur approaches her material with a jeweller's precision, cutting each tune scrupulously into a fine gem. She can sing circles around the young thrushes who dominate today's pop charts."

San Francisco Chronicle

Maria Muldaur's career has embraced a wide range of musical styles which have earned her a reputation for her adaptability and versatility as a singer. She has often avoided the more lucrative and commercial paths to pursue the songs and music that have truly inspired her.

Maria Grazia Rosa Domenica d'Amato was born and raised in Greenwich Village, a district of New York. In the Fifties, Greenwich Village was a glorious mix of Italian and

Irish communities, chequered with immigrants from a diversity of backgrounds. She was surrounded by a melting pot of different cultural sounds and knew from an early age that music was to be an integral part of her own life.

By 1963, she had developed her own singing style, combining blues, R and B and Louisiana music which she christened 'bluesiana'.

Maria's first album was made as a member of the Even Dozen Jug Band who were signed to Elektra. They built up a regional following, playing two nights at the Carnegie Hall.

Maria moved on to The Jim Kweskin Jug Band where she met her husband, Geoff Muldaur. The band built up a reputation on the college and festival circuits and released a number of well received recordings before splitting.

Maria and Geoff relocated to Woodstock. However, following their divorce, Maria relocated to the West Coast where she kicked off her solo career.

Aided and abetted by the likes of Ry Cooder and Dr John, Maria recorded her debut album. Released in 1974, it became a benchmark in her career, hit the best seller lists and included 'Midnight At The Oasis'. She describes this superb offering as "God's way of blessing me."

Maria pursued a prolific recording career which embraced gospel, swing and jazz.

In the autumn of 1984, Maria undertook a residency at Ronnie Scotts' in London. The results can be heard on *Live In London*, which was originally released in the mid-Eighties but soon disappeared from the music racks when the record label folded. The recording benefits from some additional work from Mo Foster, Peter Van Hooke, Chas Jankel and Ray Russell.

Maria still continues to record and tour and has recently been nominated for a Grammy.

Reviews for *Live In London*: SJPCD109

"...you've got to hand it to her; she's one hell of a singer. This is the first time this album has appeared on CD. Just love it."
Modern Dance, (Issue 41 November 2002)

"...this gospel tinged live set is a much more gutsy and powerful piece of work...It's been unavailable for many years, but this more than merits this rather belated re-issue now. Vastly impressive fare."
Kevin Bryan, (August 2002)

www.mariamuldaur.com

MUSICIANS UNION BAND

"This is a little bit of an oddity from 1971. Twenty-one musicians from Britain and Holland collaborating on a collection of tunes...The recording was actually the brainchild of Ray Fenwick and Hans Vermeulen and is typically untypical of the period....Interesting."

Bernard Law, *Wondrous Stories* (Sept 2001)

Musicians Union Band was the brainchild of Ray Fenwick and Dutch friend, musician Hans Vermeulen.

In 1971, Ray and Hans brought a group of musicians together to record a glorious double album of cover versions and original material. The musicians were drawn from Britain and Holland and were a veritable 'Who's Who' of the music business during this era.

The album was only ever released in Holland and as a consequence, had limited availability.

For those of you content to hear good music without scouring ebay for the original, Angel Air has released the album in all its glory, preserving it for another generation.

Musicians were drawn from a host of bands including The Spencer Davis Group, The Elton John Band, Tee Set, After Tea and Golden Earring.

Tracks include 'Jailhouse Rock', 'Love Me Tender' and Brian Wilson's 'In My Room'.

Review for *Musicians Union Band*: SJPCD010

Musicians Union Band was a unique idea, even for 1971 when it happened, in bringing together a bunch of British and Dutch rock musicians from the likes of Golden Earring, Shocking Blue, The Tee Set, Motions, Elton John Band and the Spencer Davis Group. Originally a double album, the eighteen cuts are largely the work of one of the men behind the idea, Ray Fenwick, plus covers of material by the Beach Boys, Clapton, Presley, Willie Dixon and others. Hardly the most essential album of all times and definitely an oddity but the fact there's a distinct 'rootsy'/American influence to proceedings and it has that shaggy dog persona of all that early seventies stuff gains it a thumbs up.

Steve Caseman, *Rock 'N' Reel*

See also The Spencer Davis Group, Ray Fenwick, Tee Set, Fancy, Minute By Minute.

CHRIS NORMAN

"...shows him to be quite a formidable performer...in fine voice throughout and...further enhanced by great sound quality. Not only a must for Smokie/ Chris Norman fans but worth investigation by all lovers of quality pop music."

Classic Rock Society (March 2006)

Chris Norman and Smokie fans were in for an enormous treat when in 2005, Angel Air released a double CD of Chris and his band playing live in concert.

An Acoustic Evening With Chris Norman spanned two incredible shows in which the singer showcased both his solo work and hits with Smokie. For good measure, he threw in some of his favourite rock 'n' roll numbers. The first of the two performances was 'unplugged' and the second was performed live in front of 50,000 Austrian fans.

231

To complement the new album, Angel Air also released a Chris Norman DVD, featuring both the aforementioned concerts as well as a sack full of extras, including a fifty minute interview with Chris.

Both releases were hits in Germany. The DVD peaked at number 5 in the charts.

Chris co-founded Smokie in 1974. Although their roots were grounded firmly in folk-rock, they found themselves drifting towards the glam market and scored a string of colossal worldwide hits including 'If You Think You Know How To Love Me', 'Living Next Door To Alice', 'I'll Meet You At Midnight' and 'Lay Back In The Arms Of Someone' (all featured on the above Angel Air releases). Such was their success that they could comfortably pack out arenas around the globe.

In 1982, Chris took the decision to spend more time writing and working in the studio, co-writing songs with Peter Spence for artists such as Donovan and Agnetha from Abba.

In 1985, Smokie reformed to play a charity show in aid of the Bradford F.C. fire disaster and decided to go back on the road. Tours of Germany and Australia followed but in the latter part of 1985, Chris recorded a project for a German TV movie *Tatort* and decided to once again concentrate on his solo career.

Chris's solo work took off in 1986 with the song, 'Midnight Lady', which was a massive hit throughout Europe, holding the number 1 spot in Germany for six weeks.

In 1994, Chris was awarded 'International Video Star Of The Year' by CMT Europe for the videos 'Jealous Heart', 'The Growing Years' and 'Red Hot Screaming Love'. That same year Chris formed a new band and went on tour for the first time in six years. Since that time he has continued to tour extensively all over the world.

In 2004, Chris won a German television show called *Comeback – die Grosse Chance* and in the wake of this success, scored a German top ten hit single with 'Amazing' and top 30 album 'Breakaway'.

Following the success of *An Acoustic Evening With Chris Norman*, Chris is very much in demand as a performer, with new works in the pipeline.

Review for *An Acoustic Evening With Chris Norman*: SJPCD215

"Not only is the music good, so too are the songs, and there's also a twelve-track bonus CD on offer here, making this an excellent release. Value, versatility and very good music."
Hartlepool Mail (March 2006)

With thanks to Chris Norman's and www.chris-norman.co.uk.

GRAHAM OLIVER

"…this is a superb piece of work with some exceptional 'guitaring' and some inspirational lyrics…It's a moving album in places and a rocker in others."

Modern Dance #39 (August 2002)

Graham Oliver has been at the forefront of the New Wave of British Heavy Metal since its inception.

His musical career began with SOB (Son Of A Bitch), who changed their name to Saxon and achieved phenomenal success. Graham was the band's guitarist and played on all eight top forty albums and five top forty singles.

He left the group in 1995, teaming up with former Saxon bassist Steve Dawson, initially to reform Son Of A Bitch before kick-starting their own version of Saxon - the much celebrated Oliver Dawson Saxon.

233

At the invitation of Angel Air, Graham recorded his first ever solo album, *End Of An Era*. He was ably assisted by Steve Dawson, Pete Gill, Kev' Moore, Richard Spencer, Steve Tudberry, Chris Archer and his son Paul.

Graham explains the creative process and his thinking behind the album:

"While preparing songs for the version of Saxon which features myself and Steve Dawson, it was clear a number of great ideas and compositions just weren't suitable for the up-coming Oliver Dawson Saxon album. Like all guitarists, I have compositions and personal favourites which never see the light because of the style of band you're associated with. So it was suggested to me by Angel Air that I put out a solo album. Among the songs you'll find here are some from Jimi Hendrix. I've had a life-long love of Jimi's music and saw him in concert in Sheffield as a schoolboy. Years later, I visited Jimi's dad, Al, and his one hundred year old grandmother Nora, in Seattle. I had always wanted to record a Hendrix song or two and having started recording with my son Paul on drums, the results are here. 'Sippin' Wine' came from an idea I had nurtured since reading some of Jimi's unfinished lyrics in 'Cherokee Mist'. Inspirational guitarists like Jimi are getting fewer and fewer. *End of an Era* is not about finality but recognising the changing face of music and the decline of guitar heroes."

Graham is still recording and playing live. He recently teamed up with John McCoy, playing dates as Twin Dragons. He has also been playing Hendrix songs to European audiences with Scorpions legend Uli Jon Roth.

Reviews for *End of an Era*: SJPCD085

"This is a collection of classic old songs and new material that shows the full range of what he is capable...This is a must-have collection of classic rock songs..."
Adrian Lyth, *Highway To Hell* (Sept 2001)

"Old and new is amalgamated and it works well...Graham shows that he's not a one-dimensional Eighties guitarist and that he still has a few surprises up his sleeve."
Miggo, June 2002

With thanks to Graham Oliver.

See also Saxon, Oliver Dawson Saxon, Steve Dawson, Son Of A Bitch.

www.oliver-dawson-saxon.com

OLIVER DAWSON SAXON

"... a storming live album...A tremulous barrage of hard riffs and banshee vocals, it's a thunderous collection that highlights both older Saxon classics and new material..."

Jo-Anne Greene, *Goldmine* (April 2003)

We have encountered Steve Dawson and Graham Oliver through their solo entries in this book. Together, they perform as Oliver Dawson Saxon. This is their story.

Steve and Graham, along with Biff Byford, Paul Quinn and Pete Gill were collectively the definitive line-up of the original band known as Saxon. They spearheaded the New Wave of British Heavy Metal, paving the way for others to follow. Remarkably for a heavy Metal band, they scored an extraordinary run of hit singles, including '747 (Stranger in the Night)', 'Wheels of Steel' and 'Never Surrender'. Their albums became classics, including *Wheels Of Steel*, *Strong Arm Of The Law*, *Denim And Leather* and *The Eagle Has Landed*.

By 1986, Steve Dawson (the bassist) had left the group. A series of further personnel changes ensued and in 1995, Graham (guitarist) left as well.

Graham and Steve teamed up together to form their own version of Saxon.

In 1996, they released the album *Victim You* under the banner of Son Of A Bitch (the original name of Saxon prior to a re-branding). The album was under promoted by the record label, Hengest, and with the band name meaning little to a new generation of fans, faired poorly. It has since been re-released by Angel Air.

Graham and Steve decided to re-name the group Oliver Dawson Saxon in order to reach their intended fan base, thereby offering Saxon fans two versions of the band. However, they are also adamant that there is only one true version of Saxon – the original line-up of Dawson, Oliver, Byford, Quinn and Gill.

Oliver Dawson Saxon began a heavy touring schedule, joined by Nigel Durham on drums (a former member of Saxon), Haydn Conway (ex-Saracen) and John Ward on lead vocals (ex-Shy). They recorded the album, *re://Landed.*

In 2003, Angel Air released *It's Alive,* a superb DVD which caught Oliver Dawson Saxon in storming form at a night club in Bradford, playing to a large and appreciative audience. The band played a mix of old and new material, including a feast of Saxon classics. The result was electric and can be found on both the aforesaid DVD and on CD.

A new album is currently in production.

Reviews for *It's Alive*: SJPCD130

"...a legitimate slab of thundering old-school metal...Definitely rawer and in-your-face than Biff/Quinn Saxon, The OD's speed through generation anthems like 'Strong Arm Of The Law', 'Motorcycle Man', '747' and 'Power And The Glory' with all the enthusiasm of the good old times..."
Goblin, _Metal Gods_ (March 2003)

"Instrumentally, the band is tight, powerful, and delivers the Saxon classics as you would hope to hear them. Even the Son Of A Bitch tracks ('Past The Point' and 'Bitch Of A Place To Be') are good metal songs."
Chris Dugan - METAL DREAMS

With thanks to Graham Oliver, Steve Dawson and Joe Geesin.
www.oliver-dawson-saxon.com

See also Saxon, Graham Oliver, Steve Dawson, Son Of A Bitch.

GARY PICKFORD-HOPKINS

"This is a 'grown-up' album where the main concentration is on his melodious vocals, the songs being a vehicle for his talents. There are no panderings to fashion, just a man content in his art, accompanied by guys who can rock a little or slow it down as the need arises. There are so many good songs on this album but the favourite is probably 'Loving You Means Leaving You' which is a duet with Bonnie Tyler. If his name was Rod Stewart this would be a monster smash."

Kevin Rowland, *ghostland.com* (June 2003)

We have already touched upon the history of one band that evolved from the roots of Jethro Tull – Blodwyn Pig, formed by bluesman, Mick Abrahams.

Another band to emerge from Jethro Tull was Wild Turkey, formed by Glenn Cornick and Gary Pickford-Hopkins in 1971. Glenn played bass on the first three Tull albums, seeing them develop from a blues band into full blown folk-rockers. Gary had served with V.I.Ps, Smokestack and Eyes Of Blue.

Gary and Glenn toured Wild Turkey relentlessly around the globe, touring the U.K., America, Canada and Europe. In so doing, they found themselves working alongside Black Sabbath, Ten Years After, Yes, ZZ Top, Bo Diddley, Procol Harum, Frank Zappa, Tower of Power, Tim Buckley, Roxy Music and The Eagles.

When they weren't on the road, they somehow managed to record two albums for Chrysalis Records (*Battle Hymn* (1972) and *Turkey* (1973)).

Gary also found time to record an album with Chick Churchill of Ten Years After called *You And Me,* which was released by Chrysalis in 1973.

Following the demise of Wild Turkey, Gary became involved in the glorious madness weaved by Yes keyboardist, Rick Wakeman. Two famously ambitious albums were recorded, *Journey To The Centre Of The Earth* (1974) and *The Myths And Legends of King Arthur And The Knights Of The Round Table* (1975).

Following the end of the Rick Wakeman adventure, Gary travelled to Japan and toured with Tetsu Yamauchi (Free and The Faces), recording a live album, *The Good Times Roll Band.*

In 1976, Gary sang with a band called Network, who were signed to Phonogram. Network featured Andy Pyle (bass), John Gosling (keyboards), Graham Foster (guitar) and Ron Berg (drums). They recorded an album which the label chose not to release, channelling their resources instead into a new act called Dire Straits, who were making a name for themselves on the pub rock circuit.

Following a stint working with Quincy Jones, Gary teamed up with long term friend Ray 'Taff' Williams, forming a band called The Broadcasters.

Gary also secured a publishing deal with Chrysalis and wrote a catalogue of songs, including 'Shooting Star' which featured on Elkie Brooks third album. He also recorded a number of demos with Morgan Fisher (an Angel Air stable mate).

G.P.H. is Gary's first ever solo offering, pulling songs from different periods of his life. The album features Brian Thomas (drums), Andy Collins (bass), Alan Thomas (keyboards), 'Taff' (lead guitar) and a guest appearance from Bonnie Tyler.

Gary continues to tour with his current band, Steel Water Band, which features his old mate 'Taff'.

Reviews for *G.P.H.*: SJPCD138

"A very rounded collection of songs, all of which are well produced and played. You get blues rock, AOR and more, good chilling out music."
Jason Ritchie, *getreadytorock!* (March 2003)

"'The songs came together over a long period of time,' Gary explains. 'Some come from the Wild Turkey period, some were written in a basement flat in Paddington and one in Lanzarote. It's quite R&B-ish in places, I've tried to keep it bluesy, but there are one or two sweet songs on it. All in all I'd like to think it shows a good range of what I can do.'

This is definitely a feel-good album, the self penned lyrics, the guitar, the beats and Gary's original voice create a naturally addictive sound...If you like a bit of what I call smooth rock then long awaited masterpiece is a definite must."
The Welsh Connection, April-May 2003

See also Racing Cars.

THE PIRATES

"...Green's guitar playing is legendary so what more can be said except CRANK IT UP LOUD and enjoy!"

Nuclear Submarine (February 2000)

On 25th June 1977, the New Musical Express Magazine ran an article on The Pirates with the headline 'Old Farts Mount Massive Counter-Offensive'. The article, by Roy Carr, was celebrating the return of the classic Pirates line up, who had become the darlings of the punk movement. Indeed, compared with bands such as Sex Pistols and The Damned, they were indeed 'mature'.

Fast forward some twenty plus years and Mick Green could still be found fronting The Pirates, entertaining fans with his highly complex technique of playing both lead and rhythm guitar simultaneously (perhaps he should be paid twice for each gig!)

Angel Air has served The Pirates well. Various incarnations and line-ups of the band have churned out a succession of great albums since the days of Johnny Kidd and no less than three of these can be found in the Angel Air catalogue.

The first Pirates release on the label is *Home And Away – Live In The 90s*. This

239

album showcases a version of The Pirates fronted by Peter Taylor, who by all accounts, had a fabulous time touring with Green and co.

The second release, *Land Of The Blind*, features 'senior partner' Mick Green, this time with Romek Parol on drums and B.J. Anders on bass and vocals. The album contains a series of new and energetic songs and recordings, breathing fresh life into the Pirates' long and illustrious legacy.

The third and final release on Angel Air is *Rock Bottom*, a thumping studio album from the same line-up. The album features some cracking re-recordings of old Pirates classics (including 'Please Don't Touch') as well as a brace of new songs. The album closes with a hard-bitten version of Carl Perkins' 'Blue Suede Shoes', fronted by the gravel-voiced Lemmy from Motörhead.

Reviews for *Land Of The Blind*: SJPCD047

"...Excellent return from one of the originators of British roots-rocking guitar...From the slide rocking of 'Danger Zone' to the cheery 'My Old Radio', it's tuneful, enjoyable stuff with a stiff enough kick to make it more than just something for old fans...Who knows, with Macca's patronage, Green could be on the road for a stylish comeback..."
Nick Dalton, *Country Music International* (March 2000)

"...Pirates' guitar legend Mick Green has fronted more than a couple of 'Pirates' outfits over the past few years but this is probably one of the best I've heard since Frank Farley and Johnny Spence jumped ship...We get a whole heap of classic Pirate style rock 'n' roll...For sure, this release is definitely one Pirates fans are gonna wanna hear."
Mohair Sweets

Reviews for *Rock Bottom*: SJPCD083

"The Pirates can lay claim to have being at the birth of British rock but on the evidence here they still deserve to draw crowds on merit, not just for old time's sake. Superb booklet as per normal with Angel Air."
Feedback (May 2001)

"This is stripped-down timeless rock music - the sort that might be called 'garage' today if The Pirates were new on the block...the venerable Green knocks out some smart tunes, including a superb re-working of that first 1959 single, 'Please Don't Touch'. There's also an impressively atmospheric version of Buddy Holly's 'Not Fade Away'. And the originals here are also gloriously knockabout. This is an album of timeless, dirty rock 'n' roll from The Pirates - a band who can still joust riffs with the best."
Malcolm Dome, *Classic Rock* magazine (October 2003)

With thanks to Roy Carr, Dale Griffin and Mick Green.
www.thepirates.co.uk.

HONEST JOHN PLAIN

"...if straight-to-hell rock 'n' roll is to your taste (and it jolly well ought to be), *Honest John Plain & Amigos* will certainly be to your taste."

Jo-Anne Greene, *Goldmine* (July 2003)

Honest John Plain has already been featured briefly in this book, as a member of The Crybabys. Now it is his big moment.

First – the tag. Why 'Honest' John?

Well, he earned himself a hefty reputation for a number of alleged dodgy deals. By far the most spectacular was reputedly selling his band's equipment for £500 and placing the proceeds on a horse…which came second!

John was born in Yorkshire in 1952. He was attuned to popular music from a young age, buying his first guitar from his local Woolworths. College friend Matt Dangerfield showed him his first chords and John never looked back.

In 1971, John and Matt relocated to Maida Vale in London. Matt joined the now famous London SS (featuring Casino Steel, Mick Jones, Brian James and Tony James) for whom John also drummed during a session.

The London SS disbanded in 1975, with Casino (keyboards/vocals) and Matt (guitar) teaming up with John (acoustic guitar) to form The London Boys. They were joined by Andrew Matheson (vocals), Geir Waade (drums) and Wayne Manor (bass) – the latter three left after a handful of rehearsals.

Casino, Matt and John kept the band going, shortening the name of the group to The Boys. They were joined by Duncan 'Kid' Reid (bass/vocals) and Jack Black (drums).

During this time, John also drummed for an early version of Generation X.

The Boys managed to secure a record deal and were tipped for major chart success but due to bad planning, bad luck and poor marketing, this did not happen. However, they made four solid albums and built up a following before splitting in 1981 (their fan club had been run by Alan Anger, Siobhan Fahey and Hazel O'Connor).

Rather than put the band to bed, it was agreed that they would resurrect it every Christmas for a gig as The Yobs – they even released an album, *The Yobs Christmas Album.*

John drifted through a number of different projects and co-wrote the Lurkers minor hit 'New Guitar in Town'. He also played in The Dirty Strangers which featured Keith Richard and Ronnie Wood, though his contributions were charitably erased prior to the release of the album!

In the late Eighties, John formed Brat Boy with Brady from Hollywood Brats. They recorded some demos and toured France until Brady quit the line-up.

John then moved on to Tower Block Rockers, which featured Darrell Bath (vocals/guitar) and supported celebrated German punks Die Toten Hosen on tour.

John and Darrell made a formidable partnership and decided to form a new band, the Crybabys, whose story has already been told elsewhere in this book.

The Nineties proved to be a fruitful decade for John.

In 1991, the Yobs released a second Christmas album which was complemented by the release of a collection of outtakes from the Boys called *Odds and Sods.*

Die Toten Hosen also continued to feature in John's life. He regularly appeared on their albums and joined them on stage.

In 1993, John recorded the album *Honest John Plain And Friends*. He also made an album with Ian Hunter, Glen Matlock, Casino Steel, Darrell Bath and Vom (Dr and the Medics) on the Grammy nominated album, *Dirty Laundry* (1994).

John put out a third album with the Crybabys and also a third Yobs album, *Leads 3 Amps Utd 0.*

In 1996, The Boys recorded their first album in over fifteen years, *Power Cut.*

At about this time, a band called Michelle Gun Elephant had a massive hit in Japan with two Boys cover versions. Encouraged by this development, Captain Oi! Records re-released The Boys back catalogue which sold 30,000 copies in Japan alone!

The 21st Century has seen John more in demand now than he has ever been, regularly travelling the globe to fulfil engagements. He has also become accustomed to selling sell out gigs in Germany where he has developed a formidable reputation.

In 2002, John travelled to Argentina to record *Honest John Plain And The Amigos*, his second solo album. The result has been picked up by Angel Air and is released in all its glory.

The Boys made a massive comeback in 2006, playing sold-out gigs and receiving superb reviews.

Reviews for *Honest John Plain And The Amigos*: SJPCD1443

"Hunter-style mock Cockney vocals…and memorable power pop with punk overtones and the end result is a fine album which deserves a large audience."
Steve Ward, *Classic Rock Society* (July 2003)

"…many of the songs on here would not sound out of place on a (Ian) Hunter or even on a Mott album…This is an interesting album that shows that even 26 years after his first single, Honest John still has a lot to offer a new audience, particularly if that audience is partial to Ian Hunter-style material."
Kevin Rowland, *ghostland.com* (June 2003)

With thanks to Steve Metcalfe. www.theboys.co.uk
See also The Crybabys.

QUATERMASS II

"This is an absolute cracker of an album and should ensure that Quatermass II makes more of an impact than the original band..."

Terry Craven, *Wondrous Stories* (May 1999)

In 1969, the band Quatermass were at the forefront of the progressive rock movement. Formed from the remnants of a band called Episode Six, the group featured John Gustafson on bass, Peter Robinson on keyboards and Mick Underwood on drums.

They recorded one album (original copies are valued at about £40) which was released again in 1975 due to popular demand. In fact, the first ever CD release shifted 20,000 units, despite being released by a small German label.

So who are Quatermass II?

The new band consists of four musicians who have between them an awesome amount of musical experience:-

Nick Simper is the new bassist. In 1966, he was a member of the final line-up of

Johnny Kidd And The Pirates. This was in the post Spence/Farley/Green era. Kidd had been going through some tough times and enjoyed a new lease of life with his New Pirates (as they became known). In so much as Simper shared in Kidd's joy, he was also present at the very end of his career. On 7th October 1966, Nick and Johnny were passengers in a car that was taking them back from a gig. The vehicle was in a collision, tragically killing Johnny Kidd. Nick suffered torn muscles and lacerations. Thankfully he recovered, founding the band Deep Purple and playing on their first three albums, before joining Warhorse (featured close to the end of this book) and Fandango (featured earlier).

Mick Underwood is the only survivor from the original line-up of Quatermass. He has worked with Richie Blackmore, Gene Vincent, Jet Harris, Johnny Cash and Gillan to name but a few.

Bart, an Irish-born session singer, has a distinctive voice which has ensured that he has remained much in demand throughout his career. He has worked with Geezer Butler (Black Sabbath), Adrian Smith (Iron Maiden) and has carved out a solo career, releasing music under his own name.

Gary Davis is a popular lead guitarist who has played with Raw Glory and North-Star.

Don Airey (Rainbow and The Strawbs) guests on keyboards.

The Quatermass II album, *Long Road,* is a worthy follow-up to the original 1970 release.

Reviews for *Long Road*: SJPCD033

"...The songs on *Long Road* are perfect in every conceivable way, from their loving construction straight on through to the final studio performances...This is a very upbeat album and, dare I say, danceable! It is melody and rhythm in complete synchronicity...

There is a power here that is uncontrived and intangible and no other song on this record is a better example than, 'River'...beautiful, powerful and moving...grab this disc..."

"*On The Record*", Music America Magazine

"This is an absolute cracker of an album and should ensure that Quatermass II makes more of an impact than the original band..."

Terry Craven, *Wondrous Stories* (May 1999)

See also Warhorse, Fandango, Gillan.

RABBIT

"Loaded with good, grinding funk heavy pounding rock, solos a-go-go and so much more, it's a dynamic showcase for one of rock's most vaunted sidemen…"

Goldmine (March 2002)

John 'Rabbit' Bundrick will be almost as familiar to millions of Who fans as the names Daltrey, Townsend and Entwistle. He has been ever-present whenever the band has toured, helping to create the on-stage sound of arguably the greatest live rock band of all time.

Aside from The Who, John has become one of the most sought-after keyboardists in the music business. His versatility has been his strength, working with the likes of Bob Marley, Duncan Browne, Ralph McTell, Richard and Linda Thompson, Paul Kossoff, Free, Mick Jagger, Jethro Tull, Sandy Denny and of course, Crawler (featured earlier).

John 'Rabbit' Bundrick was born in Texas on 21st November 1948. His father was a major musical influence, holding regular Country and Western sessions in the home.

When John was just six years old, his mother bought him a piano from some neighbours. John took to it like a duck to water. Initially, he would jam with his father and the various visitors to the home and partake in recording sessions at the local studios. It was only when he heard rock 'n' roll for the first time that he knew where his musical destiny lay.

John joined a band called The The, who changed their name to Blackwell and released one album, in 1970. Blackwell were a 'house' band who were regularly hired out by a local studio. Visiting musician Johnny Nash used them and was immediately taken by Bundrick's keyboard skills, offering him a job scoring a movie in Sweden. The young pianist accepted, promising his band mates that he would return…a promise that was ultimately broken.

The aforesaid film, *Northscene* was a commercial disaster but Nash had assembled together a strong team of musicians who stuck with him. They even numbered Bob Marley at one stage. Nash's career underwent a renaissance and he scored a number of major U.K. chart hits.

In 1971, John recorded an album with former members of Free and on the strength of these recordings, was offered a two album solo deal. He recorded *Broken Arrows* and *Dark Saloon.* However, his popularity as a session musician meant that he never properly promoted either release.

John teamed up with Free to play on their final album, *Heartbreaker* and later joined Paul Kossoff in his new band, Back Street Crawler.

Kossoff's tragic death in 1976 left the band in confusion until they found a new guitarist and launched themselves as Crawler.

In 1978, John announced to a wave of disbelief that he was leaving Crawler to join The Who. He joined in time for the *Who Are You* sessions. However, a drunken evening with Keith Moon resulted in John tumbling out of a cab and breaking his wrist! Rod Argent stood in for him. John has been on call with The Who ever since.

As for John's solo work, he has been quietly building up a catalogue of material and saving it all for release. Angel Air's *Welcome to America* is an excellent collection of 'Rabbit' songs featuring the talents of Terry Wilson-Slesser (Back Street Crawler and Crawler) and Geoff Whitehorn (Maggie Bell and Paul Rodgers).

Reviews for *Welcome To America*: SJPCD096

"...There's an awful lot to chew on in Rabbit's music, so I'm going to single out a few songs that capture his sound 'in a nutshell' so to speak. 'Madrid', to me is the finest song on the disc, is a groovy number that has an absolutely hypnotic melody. There aren't too many lyrics in the song, just a moving bass line, rock-solid drumming and Rabbit chanting melody...

...what appeals to me most about this CD are the bonus tracks. There are four of them and the first three are from several Native American projects in which Rabbit has been engaged over the years...the final bonus track is a Crawler song...

Welcome To America represents only one facet of a many faceted musician...Unsung session players, such as Rabbit have an awful lot to say and I'm glad Angel Air is giving them a forum in which they can pursue and present their musical ideas."

Ben Likens, *BeatBoss* (November 2001)

"...class and slick sophistication."
Hartlepool Mail, (November 2002)

With thanks to David Clayton.
www.thewho-rabbit.com

See also Crawler.

RACING CARS

Welsh band Racing Cars came to prominence in the spring of 1977 when their single, 'They Shoot Horses Don't They?' climbed to number 14 in the U.K. singles chart. The song was inspired by the movie of the same name and composed by vocalist Gareth Mortimer (known as Morty), who has admitted that he feels nothing but indifference towards the composition.

Prior to the formation of Racing Cars in the mid-Seventies, Morty was singing with a band called Good Habit, who performed many of his compositions.

A re-union with old friend Graham Williams saw Good Habit transform into Racing Cars. The name change came about as a consequence of a hilarious interview they saw on television. A rather plump Yorkshireman was being interviewed by a journalist about a new band he planned to form. As he puffed on a fat cigar, he waxed lyrical about how he was going to make a success of the band, which he was going to call Racing Cars.

When Morty and Graham had stopped laughing, it was agreed that they HAD to call themselves Racing Cars…and the rest as they say is history.

In 1976, Racing Cars (comprising Morty and Graham, bassist David Land, guitarist Ray 'Alice' Ennis and drummer Robert James Wilding) relocated from Wales to London. This proved to be a shrewd move at the time because the pub rock movement was vibrant and in full swing. They had a ready-made market.

Racing Cars secured a deal with Chrysalis Records and their debut album, *Downtown Tonight* made the top forty. 'They Shoot Horses Don't They?' was a hit at this time and they made an appearance on Top Of The Pops.

Two further albums, *Weekend Rendezvous* and *Bring On The Night* (featuring Timothy B. Schmit on vocals) followed, prior to the band splitting in 1980.

Racing Cars reformed in 1988 and have toured regularly since then.

The line-up changed a number of times with Colin Griffin joining on drums and Simon Davies on keyboards.

In 2000, they released an album called *Bolt From The Blue* and played a sell-out show at St. David's Hall in Cardiff.

In 2006, Racing Cars celebrated their 30th anniversary. Angel Air marked the occasion with the release of a live DVD (NJPDVD626) and album. The former is laden with interviews, acoustic tracks and a band history.

A new studio album is planned for later in 2007.

With thanks to Racing Cars www.racing-cars.uk.com

See also Gary Pickford-Hopkins.

MICK RALPHS

"Ralphs remains a tasteful song writer and scintillating guitarist…"

Jo-Anne Greene, *Goldmine* (May 2003)

Mick Ralphs has rightfully earned his place in the music business as one of the great guitarists of his generation, much in the mould of Joe Walsh and the late Mick Ronson.

Mick Ralphs was born in Herefordshire, the same neck of the woods which brought us Mott The Hoople. Unlike many of the musicians profiled in this book, he did not pick up a guitar until he was in his late teens. His early influences included Chuck Berry, Eddie Cochran and Buddy Holly.

Mick progressed through a number of Sixties bands including The Mighty Atom Dance Band, The Melody Makers and The Buddies. The Buddies had a line-up that included Stan Tippins (vocals), Peter Watts (bass) and later, Dale 'Buffin' Griffin on drums. The group played under a number of other names, including The Silence, The

Doc Thomas Group and Silence. In 1966, The Doc Thomas Group recorded an album in Milan and made a number of television appearances. Mick also worked with Verden Allen in The Shakedown Sound.

The Doc Thomas Group/Silence became Mott The Hoople, whose story has been told in some detail earlier in this book but it is fair to say that Mick contributed an enormous amount to the band's sound with his song writing and distinctive guitar work.

He left in 1973, forming the super group Bad Company with Paul Rodgers and Simon Kirke of Free. Boz Burrell of King Crimson made up the quartet.

Again, their story has been told earlier in the book.

Over a period of ten years, the band notched up a feast of top twenty albums, repeatedly toured America and produced a string of classic singles, including 'Can't Get Enough', a Ralphs composition. Paul Rodgers left in 1983, when the band folded.

In 1984, Mick released a solo album; *Take This*, which received little promotion at the time.

By 1986, Bad Company had reformed with a new line-up. They released a total of seven album over the following decade, including *Fame And Fortune* (1987), *Here Comes Trouble* (1992) and *Company Of Strangers* (1995). But by the early Nineties, Mick was the only remaining original member and in 1996 he brought the project to an end.

In 1999, the four original members of the band re-united, recording four tracks which appeared on *The Original Bad Company Anthology*. They also completed an enormously successful tour, rekindling the glory days of the Seventies

Mick has always been in demand as a guitarist, working with The Who, Lonnie Donegan, Jon Lord, Maggie Bell, David Gilmour (a neighbour and close friend) and George Harrison.

He continues to write a prolific number of songs and in recent years has recorded two solo albums, *It's All Good* and *That's Life – Can't Get Enough*.

All of the aforementioned solo works have been re-released by Angel Air with bonus material.

Reviews for *Take This*: SJPCD037

"Mick Ralphs, guitarist with Mott The Hoople and Bad Company originally released *Take This* in 1984 and this re-issue by Angel Air contains ten bonus tracks of previously unreleased material and working mix/demos of the original album...

...he is one hell of a guitarist and his album highlights his controlled but restrained style to perfection...

Ostensibly a rock album but with some blues roots showing this album is as valid today as it was in 1984 and is another excellent release by Angel Air. Interesting sleeve notes and an extensive discography make worthwhile reading."

Terry Craven, *Wondrous Stories*
"...showcases Mick's talent as a writer of songs and not just a riff merchant...but the guitar playing on the album shows that Mick is still one of rock's most tasteful players...As usual with Angel Air releases the packaging is great with the CD accompanied by a twelve page booklet with unreleased pictures and extensive liner notes..."
Keith Smith, *Two Miles From Heaven* (May 1999)

Reviews for *It's All Good*: SJPCD052

"Rich in ideas and full of the most flavoursome playing this is a delightful album…"
Peter French, *Hartlepool Mail* 6 July 2002

"This is nice; in fact this is very nice…The way it has been put together is nothing short of inspirational, I just love it…It's a joy to listen to, laid back with a beer; it's the way life should be. There is a passion flowing from the instruments which were all played by Mick (except the Bad Company song) and he even did the artwork for the cover. I have to say this is a sensational instrumental album."
Modern Dance #39 (August 2002)

Reviews for *That's Life - Can't Get Enough*: SJPCD136

"Track 13 is the original 1970 demo for 'Can't Get Enough' with loads of fat distortion and Mick himself providing all the instruments and vocals. It is quite different to the final version and well worth hearing."
Feedback (March 2003)

"...it's magnificent...In style its like Keith Richard's solo albums and some of the latter stuff that Ronnie Wood is putting out, it's a real 'groover' (if you can't move to this, then you've got no moving parts).
I can't praise this enough, it's an imperative album for Mott/Bad Company fans plus anyone who has good musical tastes."
Modern Dance, Issue 43 (March 2003)

With thanks to Mick Ralphs and http://www.mickralphs.co.uk.
See also Verden Allen, Mott The Hoople, Crawler, Overend Watts, The Doc Thomas Group, Midnight Flyer, Bad Company.

THE RATS

"Ronson's guitar work is stamped all over the album which sees The Rats playing a style of British blues/R&B which bears comparison with the Yardbirds work of the same period."

Steve Ward, *Classic Rock Society* (May 2004)

The Rats are perhaps most well known for their famous guitarist, Mick Ronson, who later carved out a name for himself as Bowie's sideman. However, there is far more to this Hull band than meets the eye.

The forerunners to The Rats were a local band called Rocky Stone And The Stereotones, who could be found gigging around the locality in the early Sixties. Fronted by the aforesaid Rocky Stone, the band featured Frank Ince (lead guitar), Joe Donnelly (rhythm guitar), Brian Buttle (bass) and David Barron (drums). Unfortunately for Mr Stone, he found himself fired from his own band for apparently singing and talking in a cod-American accent! Donnelly and Barron soon followed him out of the band.

The band went through a new incarnation as Peter King And The Majestics. Peter was in fact local boy Benny Marshall. Jim Simpson took over on drums. They played the chart hits of the time in local pubs.

In 1964, a local manager by the name of Barry Paterson approached Peter King And The Majestics with a view to securing them dates on the lucrative ballroom circuit. He in turn introduced them to an agent called Martin Yale who suggested a name change to River Rats. This perhaps reflected the rawer, bluesier sound that the band was now pursuing. They liked the suggestion and shortened it to The Rats.

Yale took over as manager and proved to be a great publicist. Using his connections, The Rats travelled to London and recorded a number of tracks and secured their first record deal, with the Laurie label. Their debut single was released in the U.K. and America. The Music Echo gave the single a number 67 chart placing based upon 15,000 record sales. The follow up single, 'New Orleans', featured a new member, keyboardist Robin Lecore.

By 1966, a number of departures saw The Rats reduced to just Jim Simpson and Benny Marshall. However, by co-incidence, a young Hull guitarist by the name of Mick Ronson was without a band, following a disappointing attempt to launch his musical career in London. He teamed up with Marshall and Simpson and brought a world of fresh influences into the band, which he had picked up on the London music scene. Geoff Appleby completed the line-up, on bass.

In 1967, local agent Joe Wilkinson played an influential role in securing The Rats a month long residency in a Parisian club. Jim was unable to make the trip and left the band, to be replaced by John Cambridge on drums. It was an exciting trip, punctuated by unreliable transport and a venue run by local mobsters. They returned home broke but full of wonderful stories.

Beyond the trip to France, The Rats found themselves frustratingly locked into a regional music scene that offered little room for expansion or progress. They decided to try their luck in London but after a miserable week spent living in the back of their van, headed home. They stopped in Grantham and secured a booking which led to a support slot with Jeff Beck.

Later that year, The Rats were presented with the opportunity to record a new track and cut 'The Rise And Fall Of Bernie Gripplestone' at Keith Herd's new Hull studio.

An extraordinary period followed in 1968, when under the 'guidance' of manager Don Lill, the band changed their name to Treacle. Lill offered plenty but delivered very little and the band dispensed with his services and reverted back to being The Rats.

In 1969, The Rats returned to Herd's Fairview Studios and recorded three new tracks but with new bassist, Keith Cheeseman. Geoff had got married and was taking a break from the band. John Cambridge also departed, joining Junior Eyes. He was replaced by Mick 'Woody' Woodmansey. History was already in the making with two thirds of David Bowie's future band assembled!

Whilst The Rats had recorded a number of original songs, their live set consisted of cover versions, including Hendrix, Cream and Led Zeppelin.

In late 1969 (or early 1970) Geoff Appleby returned to the fold, replacing Keith Cheeseman and the band cut two further tracks – their final recording session.

In 1970, Mick Ronson had the opportunity to return to London and have another crack at the big time – this time in David Bowie's band. Bowie was pulling together a new band and on the recommendation of John Cambridge, he was recruited on guitar. In turn, Mick Woodmansey was to join him, strangely enough as a replacement for Cambridge.

Mick Ronson is sadly no longer with us but The Rats still are, having played at Mick's memorial concert. Three tracks from this show, together with a host of original recordings can be found on Angel Air's *The Fall And Rise - A Rats Tale*.

Reviews for *The Fall and Rise - A Rat's Tale*: SJPCD166

"The pre-Ronson R&B (he joined in '66) is decent, the brief foray into psychedelia the most successful...1969 saw a return to The Rats moniker and with it came the layered guitar sounds Ronson would bring to *The Man Who Sold The World* session...
...even at this stage it was apparent that Ronson was something special."
Jon Mills, *Record Collector* (July 2004)

"The disc contains some insistent and chugging gems that are just draped in Sixties imagery...Any collector of the British R&B boom sound or archivists and Bowie fanatics alike - should be pleased to add this to their collection. Ronson was such a sad loss to the world and it's great to see him honoured in this way. Angel Air has played a blinder here."
Jim Tones, *Modern Dance* (August 2004)

With thanks to Keith Smith.
www.mickronson.com

See also Mott The Hoople.

THE RECORDS

"I looks, harmonies, steady tempos and melodic guitar fills. Flash without trash...The liner notes (written by John Wicks) are a hilarious, odd and fascinating insight into the apparent chaos and underachievement that was The Records...pure pop splendour."

Colin Bryce, *Mohair Sweets* (July 2001)

The Records emerged from the remnants of a Southend band called The Kursaal Flyers (see the section on Paul Shuttleworth, their lead singer). In the final days, the band became known simply as Kursaal and featured Will Birch, John Wicks, Paul Shuttleworth, Barry Martin and Richie Bull.

Following the demise of Kursaal, John and Will continued to work together, writing new songs and formulating a plan for a brand new band.

An advert was placed in Melody Maker and Phil Brown was recruited on bass guitar and Brian Alterman (ex-Shanghai with Mick Green) on lead guitar. After a few weeks, Brian had to leave due to family commitments and was replaced by Huw Gower. John played rhythm guitar with Will on drums. The Records were born!

1978 saw the band get off to a flying start. Dave Edmunds recorded the song 'A1 On The Jukebox' for which Will had penned the lyrics, The Searchers recorded the Birch/Wicks composition 'Hearts In Her Eyes' and Stiff Records' young American singer Rachel Sweet, recorded another of their compositions, 'Pin A Medal On Mary'. John and Will were on a roll!

Indeed, it was Dave Robinson at Stiff who asked The Records to back Rachel on the 'Be Stiff Route '78' package tour of the U.K. and Ireland (and later, America). The Records agreed to this request in return for their own slot on the tour.

For Stiff, the tour was enormously expensive, with the artists and crew travelling everywhere by train. Mercifully this unique road show was captured for all time by a documentary team.

The Records found time to record and privately press their debut single, 'Starry Eyes', which they took to America during the final leg of the aforesaid tour.

However, they received a massive break when they signed to Virgin Records, recording the album *Shades In Bed* (1979). This featured a re-recording of 'Starry Eyes'. The album was sold with a bonus 12" EP of cover versions.

In May 1979, The Records went on a U.K. tour as support to The Jam, which was followed by an eight week tour of America, both as a headlining act and as support to the likes of The Cars.

Atlantic (to whom the debut album had been licensed) pushed the album mercilessly and The Records were rewarded with a placing in the U.S. album chart. They had become stars on the other side of the Atlantic, although had yet to make a big impact at home.

In July 1980, a second album was released, called *Crashes*. The Records concentrated their efforts in Europe on this occasion, supporting Robert Palmer.

At about this time, Huw left the band. Jude Cole was recruited in his place, fitting into the line-up comfortably.

A second tour of America was arranged but something was remiss this time around. There were no limousines, interviews and publicity that accompanied the first visit. They even had to carry their own equipment on public transport! It was puzzling in the extreme…it was as if they had been abandoned by their record label after so much fuss and adulation first time around.

Will, John and Phil returned home to the U.K. but Jude remained in America. The inevitable management fall-out followed along with an unwelcome court case.

Aided and abetted by the barrister, Gordon Bennett (!), The Records won their case. However, down to a three piece, they were on the brink of meltdown.

Remarkably, Virgin picked up the option for a third album. Auditions were held, securing the services of a new lead singer, Chris Gent and guitarist, Dave Whelan. In fact, Will happily handed over drumming on the new album to Bob Irwin and took over as the album's producer.

The end result seemed to lack the magic of the earlier albums and Virgin took a year to release the end result, *Music On Both Sides*.

The Records played two final concerts in London before splitting in 1982.

Reviews for *Paying For The Summer Of Love*: SJPCD078

"The material here is a clever mixture of power pop, Jam-type mod and a little punk all combined into guitar-led short and sharp sing-alongs…The sleeve notes are

incredibly detailed and almost approach novel proportions but this is only what is expected with Angel Air ."
Terry Craven, *Wondrous Stories*, (April 2001)

"...an effervescent, unstoppable Byrds for the blank generation. This album is *Shades In Bed*, plus four extra tracks, recorded in cheap, punk fashion...and it's fab. Birch/Wicks classics like *Starry Eyes* and *Teenarama* and more, all sing-along with perfect harmonies, neat guitar fills and a solid backbeat."
Country Music International, (May 2001)

With thanks to John Wicks and Will Birch.
www.therecords.com; www.willbirch.com
See also Paul Shuttleworth.

GREG RIDLEY

"This enjoyable new CD explores the musical legacy bequeathed by former Humble Pie bassist Ridley...a fitting tribute to one of the forgotten men of British rock."

Kevin Bryan, (April 2005)

The death of Greg Ridley in 2003 robbed the music community of one of its most accomplished and seasoned bass players.

Greg was born in Carlisle, Cumbria on 23 October, 1947. He took up the bass guitar from an early age and was blessed with a strong voice. His teenage years were spent fronting a number of bands including Dino And The Danubes and The Dakotas. He also played for The V.I.Ps who signed to RCA, releasing the single 'Don't Keep Shouting At Me' (now worth in excess of £40 for a mint copy).

The V.I.Ps moved to London in 1964 and played the club scene as well as undertaking a stint at The Star Club in Hamburg (where The Beatles spent their early years).

A short contract with CBS yielded one single, 'Wintertime' before they moved on to Island Records, releasing two singles, 'I Wanna Be Free' and 'Straight Down To The Bottom' (each now fetch about £25 a piece).

A line-up change resulted in a name change and V.I.Ps became Art, releasing 'Supernatural Fairy Tales' in 1967 or 1968 (depending upon which source you rely upon).

So far, commercial success had eluded Greg.

Another line-up change saw American keyboardist Gary Wright join Art and the band underwent another re-branding, becoming Spooky Tooth. Still with Island Records, they released their first album, *It's All About A Roundabout* (1968). 'Sunshine Help Me' was released as a single but it failed to chart.

In support of the album, Spooky Tooth gigged constantly, earning a reputation not only within their fan base but throughout the music community as consummate musicians.

During one particular gig, they were sharing the bill with The Small Faces. Front man Steve Marriott was reportedly aggravated with his band's inability to re-produce their classic album, *Ogden's Nut Gone Flake* as a live show. In frustration, Marriott walked off stage and quit the band. The story goes that he approached Greg backstage and recruited him to his new venture, a super group called Humble Pie, which also featured drummer Jerry Shirley and guitarist Peter Frampton.

The new band wrote fresh material (enough for two albums) and rehearsed before signing to Andrew Loog Oldham's Immediate label. Indeed, two albums were released in 1969, *As Safe Is Yesterday Is* (a U.K. top forty hit) and *Town and Country*. They also scored a massive hit (number 4) with the (now) classic song, 'Natural Born Woman'.

The band undertook a series of shows, which combined an acoustic set in the first half and a rhythm & blues set in the second half.

The financial collapse of Immediate caused untold problems for Oldham's signings, including Humble Pie who went through a period of uncertainty until A&M picked up their contract. A change of management also saw the group embrace more of a rock and blues sound, which can be heard on the 1970 album, *Humble Pie*.

Humble Pie then had America within their sights and embarked upon a series of U.S. tours. Frampton left the band at about this time. 'Clem' Clempson (ex-Colosseum) took his place.

The release of the album *Rockin' The Fillmore* (1972) bore witness to one of the greatest live albums of the era which was followed by their biggest seller, *Smokin'* (1972).

In 1973, they released *Eat It*, a double album jammed with rhythm and blues, backed by The Blackberries, three former Ike-ettes. Humble Pie continued to tour the globe and wild antics were often reported on the road!

The album *Thunderbox* followed in 1974 but by this time band members had started to pursue solo projects. A&M released a final album, *Street Rats* (1975) and Humble Pie embarked on a farewell tour, bringing the curtain down on a phenomenal band.

Greg continued to work with Steve Marriott but the material was never released. He went on to join 'Clem' Clempson and Cozy Powell in the band Strange Brew and picked up again with Marriott in Steve Marriott's All Stars, recording an album and touring the U.K. and America.

At the age of thirty, Greg retired from the music business.

In 1991, Marriott tragically died in a fire. Ten years later, Greg played at the Steve's Memorial Concert in London.

Once again acquiring a taste for the limelight, Greg took part in the Humble Pie reformation and the album, *Back on Track* (2002) was released. A tour of Europe followed.

Tragically, Greg passed away in November 2003 from pneumonia and related complications. He is survived by his wife Patricia, two daughters, two sons and his sister.

Angel Air's Greg Ridley Anthology is a fitting footnote to a great career. The music here is drawn predominantly from his solo work and Humble Pie years. It features Steve Marriott, Peter Frampton, Dave Colwell and Iron Maiden's Adrian Smith.

Reviews for *Anthology*: SJPCD194

"...the music here is timelessly attractive and the main attraction here is the more recent material by Ridley, which proves the man was capable of delivering powerful, bluesy hard rock, with his low vocals that grew thicker with time."
Avi Shaked, *www.maelstrom.nu* (April 2005)

"...'All I Ever Needed' stands as a beautiful tribute to a much missed musician and even packs its own tribute, in the form of 'Live To Learn', an uncompleted Ridley composition that was completed, and recorded, by Dave Colwell and Dean Rease. Ridley himself is not on the track, but the song belongs here regardless."
Jo-Ann Greene, *Goldmine* (March 2005)

See www.gregridley.com

ROCK WORKSHOP

"...a stylish effort...it's the musicians that carry the day. Powered by a five-piece horn section, Russell's strafing lead, busy congas and some earth-moving fuzz bass..."

Chas Chandler, *Record Collector* (August 2004)

Rock Workshop was an astonishing project borne out of an incredible era.

The founders were Ray Russell and Scotsman, Alex Harvey. The two musicians had met during the run of the Musical, *Hair*.

The philosophy behind Rock Workshop was to create a 'leftfield' jazz-orientated sound based upon experimentation in the studio. Ray pulled together a host of musicians (including a brass section) and took them to Kingsway Recorder Studios. Despite there being a dozen musicians involved, Ray recalls that the recording process was seamless:-

"The idea of the band at the time was to make it punchy, raw and as organic as possible. I went in with a chart for the brass arrangement and the spirit and strengths of the band then worked around that. I wrote some of the lyrics but Alex wrote most of them."

Their debut album (titled *Rock Workshop*) was original, innovative and supremely creative but suffered from lack of promotion. The band were in competition with stable mates, Blood Sweat and Tears, so little in the way of resources were spared, despite Alex Harvey's fame in the U.K.

The group played a number of gigs at the Marquee and at local balls where they were well received. However, with a dozen members, touring was impractical in the extreme. Besides, Rock Workshop was never meant to be a touring band but a studio indulgence. That said it was Ray's hope that they would achieve some level of commercial success.

The second album, *The Very Last Time*, lacked the raw and spontaneous edge of its predecessor and the band found themselves at odds with the record label over how the album should sound. Alex had also left the line-up to tour with his own group and the writing was consequently on the wall. With the project heading in the wrong direction, *The Very Last Time* was indeed just that.

Reviews for *Rock Workshop*: SJPCD132

"Among other things that make this release interesting is that it contains 'Hole In Her Stocking' which also made its appearance on Sensational Alex Harvey Band's debut album *Framed*...Musically, this is an album of its time, with loads of brass and good honest rock but for me, it is the vocals that lift it out of the ordinary and for SAHB fans this is essential."
Feedback (November 2002)

"Alex Harvey's voice, against such a fulsome backdrop, is nothing less than a sheer pleasure...it's one of the most enjoyable packages of its ilk in a good while."
Record Collector (December 2002)

Review for *The Very Last Time*: SJPCD171

"...another obscure early Seventies U.K release catches Rock Workshop performing tight, funky material, along with expansive instrumental passages."
Joseph Tortelli (June 2005)

With thanks to Ray Russell. www.rayrussell.co.uk

See Ray Russell, RMS, Running Man, Mouse.

RMS

"...it's an extravagant vehicle for all three men's talent, and justification for the high esteem in which all three are held."

Jo-Ann Greene, *Goldmine*, (December 12, 2003)

It is fair to say that the three musicians that came together as RMS have more pedigree between them than the current champion of Crufts!

'R' stands for Ray - Ray Russell. Ray is a consummate musician who has built up a formidable reputation as a composer for television and theatre.

'M' stands for Mo – Mo Foster. It seems that Mo has played bass for pretty much most of the music business as well as ploughing a happy furrow as a solo performer.

Both Ray and Mo crop up regularly throughout this book.

'S' is for Simon – Simon Phillips. Simon (affectionately known as 'King Cannon') is quite possibly the greatest drummer of his generation. Currently with Toto, he has drummed on more hit records than this book has room to list.

From time to time, session work would bring these three talented souls together. Often, a group of session musicians will gain a reputation as a coherent and sought-after unit and this was indeed the case with Ray, Mo and Simon.

Ray and Mo started writing some material with a view to making an album - it was just a matter of finding the time to get together between busy schedules to record the songs.

Luck would have it that the three musicians finished a session for an artist at Trident Studios a day earlier than planned. With a paid studio and engineer on hand, on 1st February 1982, they embarked upon a mammoth fourteen hour marathon to record a whole album. The end result (plus some bonus live tracks and demos) is the excellent *Centennial Park*.

Later that year, RMS performed their first ever live show. Any nerves the band may have felt prior to the show soon evaporated when the audience displayed their warmth and enthusiasm. This landmark performance has at long last been released for the first time on compact disc as *RMS Live At The Venue 1982*.

However, perhaps the icing on the cake is the Angel Air DVD release of RMS and Gil Evans live at the Montreux Jazz Festival, filmed in 1983. It catches the band at the peak of their powers, playing songs from *Centennial Park* as well as Evans 'Gone' and two terrific Hendrix numbers – truly a feast of jazz lovers.

Reviews for *Centennial Park*: SJPCD148

"1982's *Centennial Park* is firmly in jazz-rock-funk fusion mode but what lifts it from the usual fare is strong and melodic composition. Russell plays superbly with a wonderful tone and equal in technicality to many of his jazz-rock peers who perhaps get feted more widely...

This CD with bonus live and demo tracks is superbly remastered and an excellent companion to the simultaneous DVD release recorded in Montreux and the two together are worthwhile reissues. Another gem from Angel Air who specialise in mining a rich vein of material that - ordinarily - would have festered in some vinyl store undiscovered or - like this one - gathered dust in someone's tape library."
David Randall, _getreadytorock!_ (Nov 2003)

"...it's an extravagant vehicle for all three men's talents and justification for the high esteem in which all three are held."
Jo-Ann Greene, *Goldmine*, (December 12, 2003)

Review for *Live At The Venue*: SJPCD174

"When you have a rhythm section of Mo Foster and Simon Phillips, topped by the likes of Neil Innes and Ray Russell, you know you're in for some fine playing..."
Record Collector (December 2004)

www.rayrussell.co.uk www.mofoster.com

See Ray Russell, Running Man, Rock Workshop, Mouse, Mo Foster.

ROUTE 66

"Taking a lead from the likes of Joe Jackson and Elvis Costello, tracks such as 'I Know It's Not True' and 'I'm Not A Punk' have a certain garage-band rawness and engaging energy delivered with some aplomb...Route 66 should tickle a few mod and ska fancies."

Rich Wilson, *Record Collector* (November 2001)

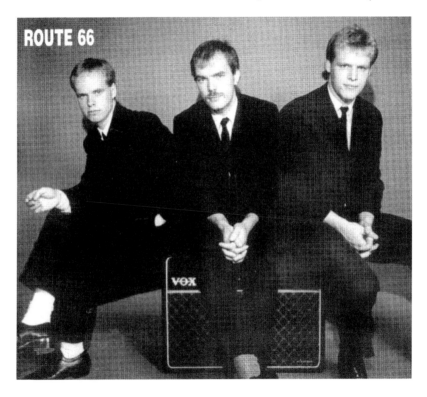

Albertslund (about ten miles west of Copenhagen, Denmark) is not a place that springs to mind when considering the various Mod revivals that have occurred over the years. However, this was the home of singer and keyboardist Claes Johansen, who is perhaps better known to readers as the author of many of the excellent sleeve notes produced by Angel Air over the previous decade.

Claes spent the early part of his musical career in a band called The Squad, who released an album in 1980 called *Born In The Concrete*.

When the band split in 1982, Claes seized the opportunity to form a band with his younger brother, Kasper Johansen, who played bass. They were joined by Mons Olesen on drums.

266

The three musicians called themselves Route 66 and performed a mix of cover versions and original material. They cut a few demo recordings and made a four track E.P. called *Back To The Garage*, which they financed themselves.

During this time, Claes was also writing as a music journalist. Through his journalistic work, he became friends with Matthew Fisher (ex-Procol Harum) who allowed Route 66 to use his Old Barn Studios to record an album. The songs (all original) were inspired by the likes of Joe Jackson, Squeeze and Elvis Costello. Much to the joy of Claes, Matthew took over the producer's chair, sang on the album and played keyboards too.

The album (called *Route 66*) was released in 1984. In a stroke of appalling luck, the record company closed down their Danish branch the same week as the album came out! Only five hundred copies were pressed and Claes bought a hundred of those and distributed them by hand to various shops in London, mainly in Carnaby Street.

Upon their return to Denmark, Mons left Route 66 and was replaced by Carsten Jorgensen. The band reverted to playing mainly Mod covers again for the next couple of years. Claes reflected that, "it was as if the album had never happened."

In 1987, Route 66 recorded five tracks in Copenhagen with a view to releasing a mini album. They were remixed by Matthew Fisher but it was impossible to drum up interest, although two of the tracks made it on to a single some eight years later.

Route 66 finally disbanded in early 1988.

At long last, the Mods from Albertslund have received the recognition they deserve with the release of the *Route 66* album on Angel Air, along with ten bonus tracks.

Reviews for *Route 66*: SJPCD005

"Route 66 are a Danish band who came over here in 1984 and recorded this album at Matthew Fisher's studio. It was also produced by the former Procol Harum keyboard player and he even helped out on backing vocals. That is rather a surprise when you hear the CD, as this music is mostly 60's R 'n' B/soul...Musically, the first thing that struck me was that the vocals were a dead ringer for Joe Jackson (remember him?)...All of the songs are originals, apart from Bo Diddley's 'I Can Tell' and all are pleasant pop in an R 'n' B style, with possibly 'It's Over' and 'Give Or Fake' having a good stab at the charts should they ever come out as singles."
Feedback

"They clearly modelled their sound on Joe Jackson...It's not all Joe Jackson comparisons though as 'I Know It's True' is straight from the Elvis Costello school of song writing and the CD's best track 'I Can Tell', which lurks amongst the bonus cuts, stays faithful to the better known Dr. Feelgood cover..."
Steve Ward, *Wondrous Stories* (October 2001)

RUNNING MAN

"...emerges deliberately unfocused, defiantly experimental and, in its own dizzying way, a grandiloquent excursion into the deepest recesses of early Seventies rock."

Goldmine (July 2005)

The Seventies was a busy decade for guitarist Ray Russell.

In between an assortment of session engagements and recording various soundtracks for John Barry, he still found time for his own projects - The Ray Russell Quartet, Chopyn and Running Man. The latter featured Alan Greed, Alan Rushton, Harry Becket and Gary Windo.

Ray's influence is stamped all over the sound of Running Man, which fuses jazz with progressive rock. Indeed, it was Ray who shared the writing credits throughout the project.

They made just the one album, *The Running Man*, which was recorded in 1972 at Trident Studios in Soho. The band toured the country and were greatly entertaining as Ray recalls:-

"The late Gary Windo was a superb player whose imagination was endless and extreme. He would march around the hall like the Pied Piper of the sax getting everyone into a conga line. Gary would be playing with one hand at this time so he could direct the crowd with the other."

A mint copy of the original 1972 RCA vinyl release now costs in excess of £120. Angel Air has re-released the album, with an added bonus track for good measure!

Reviews for *The Running Man*: SJPCD199

"...offers a rather interesting take on progressive rock, extending blues-rock into jazz regions...The recording is driven by a truly hard rocking section..."
www.maelstrom.nu (June 2005)

"...the music is raw and superb, a crossover between rock and jazz in the finest traditions of Brian Auger, Patto or If...Don't miss this one!"
Phil Jackson, *Acid Dragon* # 49

See Ray Russell, RMS, Rock Workshop, Mouse.
www.rayrussell.co.uk

RAY RUSSELL

"If you are looking for some nice guitar, then look no further...Ray's 'guitaring' is a pleasure to listen to...there are 24 musicians in all contributing to this splendid music...Music to time travel to!"

Zaphod, *Modern Dance* (August 2004)

We are now coming to the end of 'R' which takes us nicely back once again to one of the world's finest guitarists, Ray Russell.

We have already encountered the talents of Ray through the sights and sounds of jazz trio RMS, Rock Workshop, progressive rock band Mouse and, of course, The Running Man.

Ray's career started at the age of fifteen, when he auditioned for the John Barry

Seven. His guitar work can be found on the soundtracks to *Dr No, Goldfinger* and *Diamonds Are Forever*.

Earning a reputation as a purveyor of cool music on the London music scene, the young guitarist soon found himself appearing in The Graham Bond Organisation and with Georgie Fame.

Ray was soon much in demand and worked with dozens of prolific and celebrated musicians, including Cat Stevens, Jack Bruce, Phil Collins and Alex Harvey to name but a few. However, his love of jazz has regularly shone through in his work and this is best represented in his collaborations with Gil Evans.

Ray has released three solo albums through Angel Air, each one offering a different window on his career. The first, *Ready Or Not,* was originally released in 1977 and includes the talents of Simon Phillips (drums) Mo Foster (bass), Tony Hymas (piano and synthesiser) and a plethora of other accomplished individuals. Long-haired, youthful and bearded, Ray's talents as a rock guitarist are showcased in all their glory. The second offering, *Why Not Now* catches an older and more reflective Ray exploring sounds and textures with great success – again featuring the aforementioned musicians and the legendary Gil Evans. The third album is a surprise offering of Ray's compositions for television, including a string of high profile productions for the BBC and ITV.

Reviews for *Ready Or Not*: SJPCD155

"It is a remarkably good piece of work. It's definitely rock but with a very soulful and funky edge...The mixture of original material and covers is just about right...all in all this is a fine album well worth further investigation."
Steve Ward, *Classic Rock Society* (March 2004)

"...a dynamite set whose contents wander through a clutch of tight Russell originals and onto visionary covers of 'The Clapping Song' and Stevie Wonder's 'Living For The City'. Five bonus tracks, meanwhile, include two distinctly alternate versions of 'The Clapping Song', and a terrific 'groove mix' of the album's 'Sweet Surrender'.
Jo-Anne Greene, *Goldmine* (March 2004)

Review for *Why Not Now*: SJPCD178

"...comprises mood pieces, arranged with meticulous attention to texture and featuring exquisite playing from musicians of the calibre of former Miles Davis arranger/keyboard player Gil Evans, Van Morrison's trumpeter Mark Isham, Grease Band keyboard player Tommy Eyre and Jeff Beck drummer Simon Phillips."
Trevor Hodgett *Blues in Britain* (November 2004)

Reviews for *The Composer's Cut*: SJPCD214

"Largely orchestrated, or with keyboards, while others are more jazzy or blues; the tracks are often moody and atmospheric. Music appears here from shows including *Frost, Plain Jane, Diamond Geezer, A Bit Of A Do, My Wonderful Life, Remembering 911, The Quest* and others...Well packaged and annotated." ***

Joe Geesin, *www.getreadytorock.com* (April 2006)

"...marvellous tracks, the majority of which combines classical music and jazz influences into subtle, gentle movements; one is plainly witty ('*A Bit of a Do*'); and a few others, such as the bluesy 'The Blue Room', provide a wider glance into Russell's all-round musical territories."

Maelstrom (June 2006)

www.rayrussell.co.uk
See RMS, Running Man, Rock Workshop, Mouse.

SAILOR

"All the excitement of old-pros rocking out and having a good time is here."

Preview, October 2002

The mid-Seventies saw Sailor fill a musical void before the dawning of the punk movement, which they happily plugged with their own unique European brand of music.

Formed in 1973, the band featured Georg Kajanus (vocals and twelve string guitar), Henry Marsh (harmonies and treble Nickelodeon), Phil Pickett (harmonies and bass Nickelodeon) and Grant Serpell (harmonies and drums). Like Atomic Rooster, they were one of the only bands to use a bass keyboard sound in lieu of a bass guitar.

Signing to CBS, Sailor took the Dutch charts by storm with their debut album, *Sailor* (1974), a concept piece about sailors on shore leave based around Kajanus's Red Light District Review. They had scored four consecutive Dutch top ten hit singles by 1975.

The following year, they released their most commercially successful album, *Trouble,* which contained the hits 'Girls Girls Girls' and 'A Glass of Champagne' (No. 1 on the NME top forty). Both songs conquered almost every chart around the globe and were simultaneously in the German top ten, the first band to achieve this feat since The Beatles.

In 1976, Sailor released *The Third Step*. This spawned a minor hit in the U.K. with 'One Drink Too Many'. However, they continued to ride high in the European charts with the single 'Stiletto Heels' capitalising on earlier successes.

By the time they released *Checkpoint* in 1977 (produced by Bruce Johnston of The Beach Boys) the U.K. market had all but disappeared. However, Sailor scored a top thirty hit in Germany with the disco-driven 'Down By The Docks'.

The fifth and final album of the era, *Hideaway* (1978) was released in Scandinavia and produced a massive Danish hit, 'Stay The Night'.

Kajanus moved on to form Data, with Phil and Frankie Boulter.

Phil and Henry reformed Sailor (with Gavin and Ginny David), securing a lucrative deal with Jimmy Guercio (ex-Chicago manager). They recorded two albums, *Dressed For Drowning* (1980) and *TV Land* featuring Carl Wilson (1981). The former failed to make a commercial impact and the latter was disappointingly shelved due to a record company re-structure.

Sailor then split for the best part of a decade, during which time Phil went on to work with Culture Club, co-writing some of their biggest hits, including Karma Chameleon.

The original line-up came back together in 1988/89 and released two albums, *Sailor* (1989) and *Streetlamp* (1992). Amazingly, they charted throughout Europe with 'La Cumbia' and 'The Secretary', winning a 'Comeback Of The Year' award in the process.

Georg left in the mid-Nineties, forming Noir with Tim Dry. Peter Lincoln was recruited as Sailor's new front man.

Angel Air's release of *Sailor – Live In Berlin* caught this new incarnation of Sailor in full swing during gigs in and around Europe during the mid-Nineties. It was not uncommon for the band to play to audiences in excess of 20,000 as part of the celebrated Oldie Nacht circuit.

In November 2002, Angel Air filmed Sailor performing a live concert at the Wycombe Swan Theatre in front of an enthusiastic and loyal audience. Henry Marsh had departed at this stage to pursue an award winning career in theatre (picking up a coveted Jefferson Award) and had been replaced by Rob Alderton, who designed the elaborate stage set for the show (resplendent with treasure chest and anchor!)

The evening was a triumphant success and cemented the band's reputation as first rate entertainers. In 2006, highlights from the concert were released by Angel Air as a double CD.

In 2007, Sailor are still going strong. Henry Marsh is back in the fold and his son Ollie has taken over from Peter Lincoln as lead singer. Peter now fronts Andy Scott's Sweet.

An opera-trained singer, Ollie made his British debut on 8th December 2006.

Reviews for *Live In Berlin*: SJPCD122

"...Quirky, catchy and, hell, different from what was going on...back in the Seventies!...Cracking production for a live album...A fun album."
Modern Dance, (Issue 41 November 2002)

"...lovely smart pop, Latino, swing and rock elements...An entertaining CD with songs that help to cheer you up on the long dark winter nights..."

Good Times (Germany) June 2002

Review for *A Glass of Champagne-Live 2CD Set*: SJPCD222

"Definitely a must for fans of the band and lovers of Seventies soft rock, which is on the rise due to all the coverage of the Guilty Pleasures club and CD's." ***1/2
Jason Ritchie, *www.getreadytorock.com* (August 2006)

www.sailortheband.com; www.sailor-marinero.com; www.henrymarsh.co.uk
www.kajanus.com

See also Affinity, Ice, Culture Club, Mike d'Abo.

SAMSON &
PAUL SAMSON

"Mixing live and studio tracks it showcases the sparkling diamond-edged sound that made Samson so popular with heavy metal fans."

Peter French, *Hartlepool Mail* (May 2006)

The name Samson is synonymous with rock and The New Wave of British Heavy Metal.

Paul was born in the industrial town of Dartford in 1953. He spent the early part of his career touring the London circuit with bands such as Refugee and Kelly.

His first break came when he replaced guitarist Bernie Tormé in the band Scrapyard. He found himself rubbing shoulders with bear-like bassist John McCoy and ex-Kelly drummer, Roger Hunt. The band became the original version of McCoy.

275

When John left the band (teaming up with John Du Cann) Paul took over the existing bookings with Chris Aylmer on bass and Clive Burr on drums. At the suggestion of Chris, the band was renamed Samson.

Samson gigged regularly throughout 1978 and released two singles, making an impact on the Indie chart and the Sounds Magazine Heavy Metal chart.

The band briefly expanded to a four piece with the addition of Mark Newman but this arrangement didn't work out.

In the first fifteen months of Samson's existence, they had played an awesome 231 gigs and built up a considerable following as support act to Gillan.

In January 1979, Clive left the band and was replaced by Barry Purkis, who had enjoyed a brief stint with another up and coming young band, Iron Maiden. At around this time, Samson were offered a management deal and recording contract, but Chris was initially reluctant to sign the former. Consequently, he was temporarily replaced by John McCoy on the recording of Samson's debut album. He did however eventually commit to the deal and it was 'business as usual' thereafter.

Samson went on to share the bill on the Metal Crusade Tour, which featured Saxon, Iron Maiden, Angelwitch and The Nicky Moore Band, all leading lights in The New Wave of British Heavy Metal.

During this period, Paul received a very tempting offer from John McCoy to join Gillan as a replacement for Bernie Tormé who had since moved on. Paul declined, choosing to concentrate on his own project.

The Samson line-up was expanded after the Metal Crusade Tour when the band was joined by vocalist Paul Bruce Dickinson, or 'Bruce Bruce' as he was commonly known. They cut an album for Laser Records called *Survivors* (1979). Samson then embarked upon a headlining tour, followed by support slots for Robin Trower and Rainbow. The press were getting excited about Samson and the Daily Mirror tipped the band to be one of 'the' bands of the Eighties.

However, all was not well. Despite recording a new album (*Head On*) and releasing a promising single ('Vice Versa', which charted at number 75), the band was starting to lose ground on its nearest rivals who were now playing bigger venues and gaining greater momentum.

Out of frustration, Samson sacked their management, who embroiled the band in lengthy legal wrangles. In the melee, they lost the rights to their back catalogue and lost ground on their competitors.

Samson returned to the studio and recorded the album *Shock Tactics* (1980) which was designed to bolster the band's credibility. Indeed, they were all set for a European tour with Iron Maiden when their record label (Gem) went into liquidation. RCA picked up the album and a subsequent single, 'Riding With The Angels', charted at number 63.

Samson went on the road again and said goodbye to Barry Purkis, who left with his entertaining alter-ego, Thunderstick, who would be housed in his own special cage during gigs. Funk drummer Mel Gaynor was brought in as his replacement.

Things started looking up when Samson stormed the Reading Rock Festival. This was coupled with the offer of two five-year record deals...which were immediately withdrawn when 'Bruce Bruce' left to join Iron Maiden.

Paul was determined that Samson should not lose momentum and brought in Nicky Moore (later of Mammoth) who improved the dynamics of the band no end. Following rehearsals, they went on tour.

Mel Gaynor also left due to conflicting commitments and went on to achieve worldwide success with Simple Minds.

Pete Jupp came in on drums and the band played their first major U.K. tour together, supporting American giants, Blackfoot. Another single was released, 'Losing My Grip', which reached the lower reaches of the chart.

In 1982, Samson recorded their fourth album, *Before The Storm* and embarked upon some European dates supporting Uli Jon Roth and Barbara Schenker's Viva. The new album shifted 12,000 copies in the first week and was supported by a tour with Whitesnake. They also played to 30,000 people in Yugoslavia with Girlschool.

The much anticipated first single of 1983, 'Red Skies', peaked at number 65 in the U.K. singles chart, assisted by no less than 10,000 advanced orders. During this time, the record label was trying to push Paul in to a highly commercial direction which he was somewhat reluctant to follow. To prove the point, he wrote the song 'Are You Ready', with tongue firmly in cheek.

Samson went on to tour Germany with the band Accept and Holland with Vandenberg. Paul also took time out to contribute to John McCoy's solo album.

A new album was recorded and a tour secured with Gary Moore. However, the record company wanted Paul to sack Chris Aylmer as they felt he failed to suit the band's image. Paul had little time for image but reluctantly gave in for the survival of the project. Mervyn Goldsworthy (ex-Diamond Head) joined on guitar but Paul felt that the band had lost a great deal of their power as a consequence. A second guitarist was hired, Dave 'Bucket' Colwell, to bolster the sound.

The tour with Gary Moore was a success and the album *Don't Get Mad Get Even* was released. However, once again all was not well in the Samson camp. Polydor wanted Paul to employ a younger lead singer but he felt that the spirit of Samson had died. Consequently, he disbanded the band on 4th May 1984.

Paul went on to join up with John McCoy and appeared on his *Think Hard* album (the first ever Angel Air release). He also produced an album for Rock Goddess.

In 1986, Paul took to the road with a new band called Paul Samson's Empire, featuring Kevin Riddles, Mark Brabbs and Sam Bluitt (later to be replaced by Mick White). They went on tour supporting Iron Maiden. However, it was not long before Paul disbanded Empire and re-launched Samson with Mick White, Dave Boyce, Toby Sadler and Charlie Mack. This line-up headlined a festival in Belgrade in front of a staggering 66,000 people.

There was a hiatus before the release of the next Samson album when Paul broke his hand practising martial arts with Barry Purkis. However, the resultant release, *Refugee*, came out in 1990 on the Communique label.

Samson gradually fell by the wayside and Paul turned to record production for a while, as well as appearing on television as a member of Far Corporation.

In 1993, Samson returned as a power trio and released a new album. Thereafter, Paul spent some time restoring his back catalogue and playing with a string of eclectic musicians, including Ric Lee and Chris Farlowe.

In 1999, Samson made a triumphant return at The New Wave of British Heavy Metal 20th anniversary festival, with Chris Aylmer and 'Thunderstick'. To Paul's delight, Nicky Moore rejoined the band, restoring them to a four piece.

In 2000, Paul built his own studio in Norwich but sadly died two years later.

As a tribute to Paul's talent and legacy, Angel Air has released two albums. *Tomorrow and Yesterday* is a comprehensive Samson retrospective.

The second, titled *P.S...,* was originally planned as a Samson album. However, it was decided that the songs should be put out as a Paul Samson solo album, a fitting 'post script' to a wonderful career. The project was finished in 2006 by a big man with a big heart...John McCoy.

Reviews for *Yesterday & Tomorrow*: SJPCD219

"Throughout the Eighties (including a solo album and recording as Samson's Empire) Paul produced some decent metal, and into the Nineties there's some classic stuff too; check out 'Room 109' for an excellent and catchy riff.

The excellent 'Mr Rock 'n' Roll' and the new 'Brand New Day', both recorded at the 2000 reunion show with Moore, bassist Chris Aylmer and drummer 'Thunderstick', prove how good the band were.

Sadly, no unreleased material but it's a good set, and the sleeve notes cover the complex history well. It's worth your money for the history lesson alone." ****
www.getreadytorock.com (April 2006)

"This is hardly the definitive Samson collection, since the all-important Bruce Dickinson years are completely absent. Still, it gives a very good idea of what Paul Samson and his band stood for after that era. As can be expected from Angel Air Records, this release features a very nice 20-page booklet, with an informative, extensive biography (by Rob Grain of the official Paul Samson website) and lots of photographs."
Metal Nose (April 2006)

Reviews for *P.S...*: SJPCD220

"Paul's guitars shine, the same goes for Nicky's voice in an otherwise uneven sound. Apparently there was a good deal of material that was recorded on two track that must have caused John a lot of work. The song material shows that Paul still had a lot of

music in him; 'Do Right', 'Shooting for the Moon' and 'It's Going Wrong' are really good tracks. Blues-based riff dominated (hard) rock dominated this disc and all in all the experience is clearly audible."
http://www.spray.se/bredbandsvalet

"This CD is filled with the last recordings of Paul, so probably the most interesting CD release of Paul Samson. The man was a legend, which can be heard on these last couple of recordings. Paul died during the recordings and so guitarist John McCoy finished the final guitar parts, so this CD can be seen as a tribute to Paul. The included music is high quality Eighties inspired British melodic hard rock/heavy blues rock meets New Wave of British Heavy Metal melodic heavy rock/metal and surprisingly sounds very strong, just listen to the fast opener 'No Way Out'.

What a sad day it was in August 2002 as one of Britain's most underrated guitarists died. This CD shows the man had a lot more sensational to offer. Fans of classic British hard rock, like Whitesnake, Bad Company, Paul Shortino and the old Samson records will have to buy this CD ASAP. The sound is a bit raw but the recordings are rare and very interesting, especially for fans of Paul." (Points: 8.1 out of 10)
http://www.strutter.co.nr

With thanks to Rob Grain, Joe Geesin and John McCoy.
www.paulsamson.co.uk

See also McCoy, Bernie Tormé, Gillan, Mammoth, Atomic Rooster, John Du Cann, Sun Red Sun.

SAXON

"...you can almost smell the mud, hot dogs and tobacco as well as feel the pure magic of the day."

Nuclear Submarine (February 2000)

Saxon made their name as the leaders of the New Wave of British Heavy Metal. The band originated in the mid Seventies from two local gigging bands in the North of England, SOB and Coast.

Steve Dawson (bass) and Graham Oliver (guitar) toured and performed with the former and Peter 'Biff' Byford (vocals) and Paul Quinn (guitar) with the latter. They joined together (with Peter Gill on drums), as Son Of A Bitch.

Both bands at the time had a sizeable following due to incessant touring and it was inevitable that the record industry would soon take notice. In 1979, Son Of A Bitch signed to the French label, Carrere.

The band toured America but the name of the band was causing problems and met with some dissent from their distributors, Warner Brothers. As a result, Saxon was born.

In 1980, Saxon played the first ever Monsters Of Rock Festival at Donnington, supporting such giants as Rainbow, Judas Priest and Scorpions. They released their debut album, *Saxon*, which was followed by their breakthrough album, *Wheels of Steel*. It spent over half a year on the U.K. charts and peaked at number 8. It also spawned two smash hit singles, including the classic '747 (Strangers In The Night)'.

In November of the same year, Saxon released a third album, *Strong Arm Of The Law,* which re-enforced their position as the greatest rock band of the era.

By 1982, Peter Gill had left the band and was replaced by Toyah's drummer, Nigel Glockler, who soon became a firm favourite with the fans.

1983's *Power and the Glory* saw Saxon make headway in America, shifting fifteen thousand units in Los Angeles alone in the first week of sale.

Saxon went on to make four more albums between 1984 and 1988 but found that they were starting to lose their way creatively, often giving in to producers and abandoning the original formula that had produced such fruitful results in the early Eighties.

To compound matters, a key component of the band was forced out of the line-up in 1986. Steve Dawson had been bassist since the days of Son Of A Bitch and his departure changed the shape of the band.

Byford and Quinn kept Saxon on the road but also lost Graham Oliver on the way, leaving them as the only founding members.

Oliver and Dawson decided to form their own version of Saxon, a story told earlier in this book.

Angel Air has released two albums by the original, definitive Saxon line-up. *Live at Donnington 1980* is taken from that first ever Monsters Of Rock show. The tapes remained undiscovered until 1994 when they were dusted off and eventually released in 1997.

The second is *Diamonds and Nuggets*, a collection of live tracks and studio outtakes from the early Saxon days.

Reviews for *Live At Donnington*: SJPCD045

"Musically, we are treated to a band at the peak of their powers...At times, particularly on the first CD the interplay between the band is brilliant...a good well packaged release giving more than just a snapshot of a short lived band on fire.

...for a time in the early Eighties, they moved the metallic hordes, Donnington 1980...was their performance peak and twenty years on, *Wheels Of Steel* remains a lost AC/DC creaming classic."

Q, January 2000

"...'Still Fit To Boogie' and 'Backs To The Wall' are delivered with typical bare-knuckled bluster, while 'Wheels Of Steel' and '747 (Strangers In The Night') are simply colossal tunes..."

Dave Ling, *Classic Rock*, January 2000

Review for *Diamonds And Nuggets*: SJPCD070

"Never was so much spandex donned so badly for so long by so few. But if you can ignore Saxon's piss-poor dress sense, they did actually produce some fine old-school hard rocking, and this collection of nineteen tracks covering their earlier incarnations reveals that the Oliver/Dawson and Byford-led mob had what it took from the word go...Numerous unreleased session recordings...contain excellent, melodic licks and distinctive vocals...A thoroughly worthwhile archival trawl."

Record Collector (January 2001)

See also Graham Oliver, Steve Dawson, Oliver Dawson Saxon, Son Of A Bitch.

THE SHARKS

"Anyone looking for a REAL rock record should look no further. Snips has a voice most rock singers would die for and Spedding is a master of the simple, understated big guitar sound and riff. Couple that with Thomas' pulsing backbeat, a sensuous production, and you have a winner."

Colin Bryce, *Mohair Sweets (*May 2001)

The early career and history of Seventies band The Sharks can be described at best as a fracas.

The Sharks witnessed the coming together of seasoned pros Andy Fraser (ex-John Mayall and Free), Chris Spedding (ex-Jack Bruce, Nucleus and Pete Brown) and Canadian drummer Marty Simon (ex-Allen Toussaint). They were joined by relative newcomer, Steve 'Snips' Parsons.

The story goes that The Sharks were talent spotted and subsequently managed by Chris Blackwell, owner of Island Records. Chris subsequently vanished to Jamaica leaving the band rudderless for over a year.

Upon his return, Blackwell was loaded with fresh ideas and decreed that Spedding's Pontiac Le Mans should be adapted and re-sprayed to promote the band. A shark fin was fixed to the roof and huge gleaming teeth tacked to the grille. The transformation was complete!

A recently bereaved Andy Fraser hated the vehicle and decreed that the band should change its name to Mutha in honour of his late mum. The other band members disagreed and the inevitable split occurred within the ranks.

The making of the debut album was consequently an unhappy affair and during their tour in support of Roxy Music, the Pontiac 'shark' skidded off the road, breaking Andy's hand in the process! Seizing his chance, Andy left the band.

While the soap opera was being played out this side of the Atlantic, in America, the debut album had broken into the Billboard Top One Hundred!

Auditions to replace Andy led to the hiring of a six foot black man called Busta Cherry Jones. An American, Busta had worked with the likes of Albert King and Isaac Hayes but he now wanted to play 'white rock'. The Sharks were an answer to his prayers…and vice versa!

Nick Judd was also recruited on keyboards thereby completing the new line-up.

The 'new' Sharks signed to MCA Records, who took the band to the States where they toured for four months, receiving standing ovations and winning friends as they supported a string of top names including Mountain, Blue Öyster Cult and Aerosmith.

Upon their return to the U.K., Judd left the band to work with ex-Shark Andy Fraser. Spedding and Parsons fired Marty Simon, who in turn persuaded Busta to leave. It was a disaster! Chris Spedding and Steve Parsons attempted to record a third album but the moment was lost.

Fast forward some twenty years:-

In the mid Nineties, a die-hard Sharks fan paid to bring the group back together again. Spedding and Parsons were joined by Pete Thomas on drums and Jackie Badger shared bass duties with Chris. Alas, Busta could not be traced, a major disappointment to all concerned. The result, *Like A Black Van Parked On A Dark Curve* is the end result, recapturing the energy of the original band.

Reviews for *Like A Black Van Parked On A Dark Curve*: SJPCD090

"The album kicks off in fine style with a superb synth/pop/rocker called 'Perfect Days'. Reminiscent of Aussie act Midnight Oil it's impossible to ignore the quality oozing from this song…'Gone To The Dogs' is more of what I was expecting from a Chris Spedding composition, featuring his trademark guitar sound…'Wake Me Up When It's Time To Dance' is a great rocker with a Joe Walsh type guitar playing that works well…A worthy (re) release."
Jilly's Rock World (May 2001)

"…classy rock on this gem of an album…An entertaining and exciting collection."
Hartlepool Mail, 31 December 2001

SHEV AND THE BRAKES

"Good to see such quality music finally get the release it deserves but you can only wonder at how well it could have done back in 1989 when this style of rock music was very much in vogue."

Jason Ritchie, _getreadytorock_ (September 2003)

It is now time to introduce the 'Baby Spice' of the Angel Air catalogue. Shev And The Brakes are a band that were firmly rooted in the Eighties and therefore only just qualify for release on the label.So who was Shev and what were his Brakes?

Tony 'Shev' Shevlin had a plan to conquer the music industry, which involved poaching some of the best musicians on the London music scene. He pulled together Andy Williams (guitar), Mark Walker (drums) and Nigel Pierce (bass). Jules (Shev's sister) provided vocal harmonies.

The band gigged relentlessly, honing their style and receiving superb reviews. They caught the eye of record producer Colin Fairley who saw the potential in Shev and his band. Fairley (who trained as an engineer under George Martin) knew what was required to bring out the best in his protégés. He encouraged the band to toughen up their sound, turning them from a pop act into a rock act. He also brought out the best in Shev's song writing.

Colin approached his friend Robin Millar who signed the band to his fledgling Scarlet record label. In turn, Robin secured a production deal with a major American record label and at last it looked like Shev And The Brakes were destined for the top. They had the talent, the right sound and financial backing behind them. Everything was set!

As is always the way, things did not go entirely to plan. A top American record producer made some unfavourable comments about the band's rhythm section. Mark and Nigel were dropped from the session but remained a part of the line up. Instead, their places were taken in the studio by two thirds of Elvis Costello's Attractions – Pete Thomas and Bruce Thomas.

Recording started in 1988 and a frenzy of photo shoots and meetings followed. Everyone was gearing up for a major release and the first wave of success.

Then in 1989, the American backers were taken over by a Japanese company and the band was dropped. The unthinkable had happened.

A lengthy battle followed in the New York courts as Shev endeavoured to escape his contract but by then it was all too late. With dreams dashed, Shev And The Brakes split.

All the musicians involved with the project have since found plenty of work in the music business and despite the views of the unnamed American producer; Mark and Nigel have gone from strength to strength. Andy plays in Geno Washington's band and Shev is a music writer and director.

At last, Shev And The Brakes debut/farewell album has been given an airing, much to the delight of today's critics.

Reviews for *Shev And The Brakes*: SJPCD142

"This is music caught in a time warp - and all the better for it...and yes, the sound is fifteen years out of date. But those old enough to remember the great days of live rock, before sampling, drum 'n' bass and all that other artificial stuff took over, will only see that as a recommendation...There's plenty of range here, from the full-on rocker 'That's OK' to the wistful solo 'When Friends Let You Down', to the whimsical 'Story Of Robert The Bunny'..."
Golden Oldie, *East Anglian Magazine* (September 2003)

"...All power to Angel Air for digging this up...it is very enjoyable indeed and deserves to be heard...While there are some rockers in here, it is mostly pop based rock with a strong emphasis on the vocals...This is definitely one of Angel Air's releases where the album is as fun to listen to (if not more so) than it's importance historically. And anyone who writes a song called 'The Story Of Robert The Bunny' deserves our support..."
Feedback (Nov 2003)

PAUL SHUTTLEWORTH

For anyone who has encountered Paul Shuttleworth or his legendary Southend band, The Kursaal Flyers, the image of the 'Spiv' front man will be indelibly engraved on their memory, like a modern day version of Arthur English, complete with co-respondent shoes!

Paul was born in Southend in 1947 and learned the ropes playing in local progressive rock band Surly Bird alongside Will Birch and Graeme Douglas. Surly Bird came close to receiving their big break when they were spotted by the manager of The Who, Peter Meaden. Peter endeavoured to secure a record deal for Surly Bird but was unsuccessful and the band split up.

Paul's next venture was a country rock band called Cow Pie, which featured Vic Collins. Again, Paul found himself in a popular act, this time playing mainly American material by the likes of Gram Parsons and New Riders Of The Purple Sage.

In the winter of 1973/74, Paul came together once again with Will and Graeme from his Surly Bird days. They were joined by Vic from Cow Pie, Richie Bull and Dave Hatfield.

The band called themselves The Kursaal Flyers after a mocked-up train that appeared in the local carnival (surely the most original way to name a band?)

The band was a part time act, with members maintaining regular day jobs to pay the bills. However, through a leg-up from pub rockers Doctor Feelgood, they secured a regular booking at The Kensington and their success snowballed from thereon in.

Within six months, The Kursaal Flyers had signed to Jonathan King's UK label. It was at this stage that the group decided to turn professional and ditch the day jobs. The only person who decided not to make the leap was Dave (who came up with the band's name). He left at the end of 1974.

In early 1975, The Kursaal Flyers went on a tour of Europe, supporting the Flying Burrito Brothers. Upon their return, they recorded their debut album, *Chocs Away*. Two singles were lifted from the album, 'Speedway' and 'Hit Records'. Despite neither charting, they had received a fair amount of radio play and some excellent reviews, making for a promising start.

The follow up album, *Cruisin' For Love,* also failed to make a great impact and it was at this stage that they parted company with the UK label.

They did not have to wait long before securing a new deal, and they were snapped up by A & R man Dan Loggins (brother of Kenny) for the mighty CBS Empire.

The band was almost immediately thrust into the studio, recording an album called *The Golden Mile* (1976), with Mike Batt in the producer's chair. At last, they hit the big time with the single 'Little Does She Know' which climbed into the U.K. top twenty and led to a number of Christmas appearances on Top Of The Pops.

Graeme left at this time, reportedly unhappy with the commercial sound of the album. He linked up with Eddie And The Hot Rods and co-authored the classic song, 'Do Anything You Wanna Do'. He was replaced by Barry Martin.

The Kursaal Flyers continued to tour on the back of their new found success but soon their manager, Phil Conroy, departed for Stiff Records and guitarist Vic Collins decided to leave the band too.

Vic was replaced by John Wicks, just in time for the recording of a live album, *Five Live Kursaals* (1977). The Kursaal Flyers embarked upon what turned out to be their final tour that autumn, an entertaining extravaganza which saw each show climax with Paul demolishing a television set with an axe. However, it was Paul's wish to leave the band which saw the Kursaal Flyers grind to a halt.

Paul re-signed to CBS and embarked upon a solo career which turned out to be short lived. His first single, 'Mixed Up Shook Up Girl' was championed by local radio but failed to make the Radio One play list. Without the 'big one' behind it, the song had little chance of commercial success. The follow up, 'It Hurts To Be In Love' (produced by Mike Hurst) also failed to chart as indeed did the final single, recorded with a Southend band called Black Gold. These, together with a series of unreleased gems from the era make up Paul's solo album on Angel Air, *Mixed Up Shook Up Girl*, released in 2006.

The Kursaal Flyers were resurrected on a number of occasions during the Eighties and again in 2001, with Paul at the helm and featuring founder member Graeme Douglas.

See also Mike Hurst, The Records.

SNAFU

"...you'll find appearances are deceptive: the laidback country-rock groove sustained throughout has held up remarkably well in the quarter-century since its release...Had it come from an American band, *All Funked Up* would undoubtedly have done better..."

Michael Heatley, *Classic Rock* (April 2000)

'Snafu' is an an acronym for 'Situation Normal - All Fucked Up'. It is a phrase that was adopted by the military during either the First or Second World War (probably the latter) and was used by the Americans in Vietnam. The phrase is used to describe a confused or perilous situation.

Snafu could be described as an early super group, pulled together from the crème de la crème of musicians around during the mid-Seventies.

The band was founded by Bobby Harrison (featured earlier in this book). Bobby had just left the group Freedom and embarked upon a solo album with the help of ex-Jucy Lucy front man Micky Moody. Such was the success of the collaboration that they decided to form a band with an R and B/funk slant.

Bobby and Micky recruited drummer Terry Popple (ex-Tramline), bass player Colin Gibson (ex-Ginger Baker's Air Force) and keyboard wizard and fiddle player, Pete

Solley. So began the career of one of the funkiest, finest and most soulful British acts of the era.

The chemistry between the musicians was very special and they ploughed a creative but un-commercial furrow, much in the vein of Little Feat and The Allman Brothers.

They recorded their debut album, *Snafu,* at Richard Branson's Manor Studio and took their show on the road, supporting The Doobie Brothers in Europe and The Eagles in America. They were adored by both audiences and critics alike.

The band reconvened for a second album, *Situation Normal.* They knew that touring was the key to their success and were paired up with Emerson Lake and Palmer for an American tour. It was a mismatch and did not further their cause.

Snafu's third and final album, *All Funked Up,* was recorded without Pete Solley who left to join Procol Harum (a band which had previously featured Bobby Harrison). Solley was replaced by Brian Chatton (and later by Tim Hinkley).

Sadly, this line-up was short lived and Micky Moody left to join David Coverdale. Snafu had run its course and disbanded.

Angel Air has paired the first two albums as a double CD release. The release of *All Funked Up* is the first time the album has been made available in this format.

A review of *Snafu/Situation Normal*: SJPCD030

"This double album features two albums recorded by the band in the early Seventies. I can remember catching the band at Reading Festival and with a line-up including Micky Moody on guitar and Bobby Harrison on vocals and a sound similar to Lynyrd Skynyrd, success seemed just around the corner. However, all the members of Snafu moved on eventually to bigger things and Snafu were just another part of rock 'n' roll history. Maybe, but they were one of only a couple of bands from the U.K. to challenge that southern States style - and sound convincing. Moody's use of mandolin on *Snafu* enhanced the idea of such a U.K. based band challenging the mighty Americans and on 'Monday Morning' they achieved just that. Hearing Moody and Snafu play in this style would convince even the biggest non-believer that rock was really great fun in the Seventies.

...*Situation Normal*...is my favourite with The Allman Brothers and Little Feat becoming heavier influences, those being favourite bands of Harrison. The debut album was actually recorded at the famous Manor at the same time as *Tubular Bells* and (Pete) Solley actually plays on that album briefly. Meanwhile, the band toured with The Doobie Brothers and The Eagles; no surprise there, as that was their stage. Solley's control and country influence becomes more apparent the more you listen to *Situation Normal* and as the sleeve notes say, "It makes you either love it or hate it". Songs like 'Brown Eyed Beauty' and 'The Blue Assed Fly' helped me to love it.

The hit single though never came and they had to support ELP in the States which turned out to be a total mistake; they simply weren't that sort of band. By the third album, again recorded at The Manor, Solley was missing and for several reasons the band diminished which was a damned shame. Harrison has attempted to form Snafu more recently but found it impossible as the original band was a unique combination. Never mind, there's always these greats."

Martin Hudson, *Classic Rock Society*

Review of *All Funked Up*: SJPCD032

"*All Funked Up* is Snafu's elusive third album reissued on CD for the first time. The blues debt is evident...while the Billy Gibbons-like overdriven slide adds a touch of Southern boogie to the mixture..."

Joel McIver, *Record Collector* (April 2000)

See also Bobby Harrison, Freedom.

SON OF A BITCH

Long before the days of the New Wave of British Heavy Metal, a band called SOB were carving out a living in the Barnsley area.

SOB were formed in 1974 by guitarist Graham Oliver and bassist, Steve Dawson. They toured the local clubs and scraped a crust during difficult economic times. Singers came and went until the line-up received some continuity when Peter 'Biff' Byford, the lead singer of another local band, Coast, was invited to join the group.

Peter brought with him guitarist Paul Quinn and Peter Gill joined on drums. The group became Son Of A Bitch and built up a large local following.

In 1979, they secured a record deal with French label Carrere, who insisted that the band should choose a less controversial name. They settled upon Saxon, achieving fame and adulation on a scale they could never have imagined (see earlier chapters).

Steve Dawson left Saxon in the mid-Eighties and Graham Oliver left a decade later.

Together, they reformed Son Of A Bitch, with Peter Gill on drums. It was an exciting time with the group signing to the Hengest label and releasing a brand new album, *Victim You* (1996).

The album was under-promoted by the label and after a series of gigs, the band folded. They re-emerged with a new line-up as Oliver Dawson Saxon.

Oliver Dawson Saxon began a heavy touring schedule, joined by Nigel Durham on drums (a former member of Saxon), Haydn Conway (ex-Saracen) and John Ward on lead vocals (ex-Shy). They recorded the album, *re://Landed.*

In 2003, Angel Air released *It's Alive,* a superb DVD which caught Oliver Dawson Saxon in storming form at a night club in Bradford, playing to a large and appreciative audience. The band played a mix of old and new material, including a feast of Saxon classics. The result was electric and can be found on both the aforesaid DVD and on CD.

Angel Air has also re-released the Son Of A Bitch album *Victim You* with four additional live tracks recorded at the Isle Of Man.

See also Graham Oliver, Steve Dawson, Oliver Dawson Saxon

THE SPENCER DAVIS GROUP

"..the album is a fine reflection of the tour and is a great collection of blues and R & B standards...all performed with aplomb by a seasoned band of musicians...Quality stuff ."

Classic Rock Society (November 2004)

The Spencer Davis Group have by their own admission never been a pop band, steadfastly ploughing a furrow as a leading rhythm and blues outfit since the early Sixties. Yet such is their enduring appeal that between 1964 and 1968 they clocked up ten top fifty hits, including two consecutive chart toppers.

Spencer and his band undertook their apprenticeship supporting some of the greatest blues musicians on the planet, including Sonny Boy Williamson and Jimmy Witherspoon. Williamson once asked Spencer what his ambitions in life were. Spencer takes up the story:-

"I told him that I wanted to become a rich and famous musician. And why not? He frowned and said 'Listen, you live in a nice place [it was a listed ruin], you got a fine little car [it was a clapped out Morris Minor], you make good bread [fifteen shillings and a bottle of brown ale], some day the right girl will come along [given all the above I doubted it], be happy with what you've got' [try telling that to the tax man!]"

In a climate dominated by The Beatles and The Rolling Stones, The Spencer Davis Group secured a solid fan base and assured themselves of a place in music history. Indeed, 'Gimme Some Lovin' has recently been voted as one of the top 100 singles of all time. Yet in 1967, Spencer found himself bereft of a full band when Muff and Steve Winwood left to pursue other ventures. Eddie Hardin was drafted in to fill the void on keyboards and the group carried on, still at the peak of their fame.

Over the years, the line-up has changed and diversed. In 2002, Angel Air caught the latest incarnation of the group in full swing, playing to a large and enthusiastic Mancunian audience. The result was filmed and has been released on DVD, which includes a selection of interviews and a fascinating and historically important German documentary catching the group in the late Sixties.

The DVD is supported by a CD release of highlights from the same show. Spencer is still ably supported by Eddie Hardin, original drummer Peter York (see Hardin and York chapter) with 'new' members Miller Anderson and Colin Hodgkinson.

Angel Air has also released *Funky*, an album that failed to receive a proper release back in 1969.

Reviews for *Live In Manchester 2002*: SJPCD131

"It may not be a recording from their heyday but they seemed to be having plenty of fun that night and sometimes it is nice to be nostalgic."
Feedback (November 2004)

"*Live In Manchester 2002* finds the same nine songs that appear on the DVD counterpart, yet this CD plays very well as a stand-alone. In fact, without the video presentation to distract, the listener gets a sense of how great a pop/blues unit Spencer Davis Group is even without the talents of a Steve Winwood.

Opening with 'Keep On Running', this Angel Air release delivers solid musical performances that provide clear evidence why 'Davis' deserves more credit for his contributions than he receives in America and elsewhere around the globe."
www.allmusic.com/cg/amg

With thanks to Pete York and Spencer Davis.
http://www.spencer-davis-group.com/index.html
See also Eddie Hardin, Hardin and York, Peter York's New York.

SPRINGWATER

"It's the Springwater album that demanded to see the light of day once again. One will keep going back to it time and time again…"

Jo-Anne-Greene, *Goldmine* (November 2002)

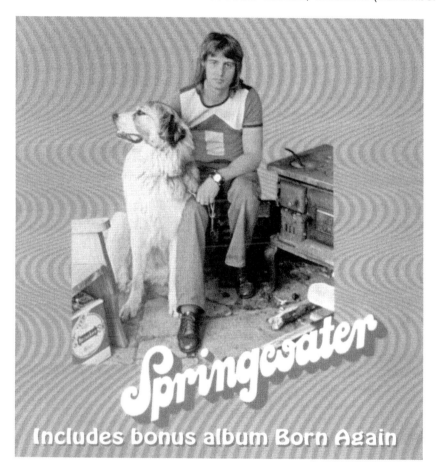

The next instalment in the Angel Air story is the band Springwater. Or to be precise, a one man band …Phil Cordell.

Phil released an album under the name Springwater on the back of the hit instrumental, 'I Will Return'.

'I Will Return' was a tremendous achievement. Recorded on a Revox A77 recorder, the song went on to sell a million copies, peaking at number 5 on the hit parade (number 2 on the rival NME chart).

Phil recorded a whole album of instrumentals, mainly original compositions which were unlike anything that was around at the time. The sound was based upon the drone tuning of a guitar (where the chords feature notes an octave apart) and was a remarkably clever piece of work. The album sold 150,000 copies.

A second Springwater album emerged in 1974 called *Dan The Banjo Man* on the back of the single of the same name, which was a number 1 hit in Germany. Phil took the sound off in a different direction, using the wah wah peddle in quick succession to give his guitar a banjo sound – hence the album title.

When it came to re-releasing the album on Angel Air, it was found that no one appeared to own a copy of the original vinyl release or indeed the master tapes. Indeed, such was its rarity that a copy was eventually tracked down in South America via an advert on the internet.

Both album releases come with extra tracks, the original album including *Born Again* from 1977, a Phil Cordell album which sold some 40,000 copies at the time.

Reviews for *Springwater*: SJPCD105

"…Angel Air has done their usual first class job with the release...
There's no doubting the quality on display...Although the hit is on here, the best track is actually a very good acoustic piece called 'Country Life'. Cordell really did know how to play!
A fine collection of eclectic Seventies pop."
Bernard Law, *Classic Rock Society* (August 2002)

"The album sold well at the time, despite being totally instrumental and eclectic in tone. The melodies are a typical mix of Seventies pop and folk…"
Joe Geesin, *Record Collector* (September 2002)

With thanks to Joe Geesin and Rich Wilson.
See also Dan The Banjo Man.

STACKRIDGE

"No longer quite as eccentric as old, the members have mellowed with age, although their love of pastoral styling, Beatles' chord progressions and a very English sound is as passionate as ever."

Jo-Ann Greene, *Goldmine* (July 2005)

Hundreds of bands and artists have graced the stages of Glastonbury Rock Festival since its inaugural year in 1970…all of them following the first ever opening act, a West Country band by the name of Stackridge (originally called Stackridge Lemon).

Stackridge comprised James Warren (guitar, vocals), Andy Davis (keyboards, vocals), Mutter Slater (flute), Mike Evans (violin), 'Crun' Walter (bass) and Bill Bent (drums). No other band at this time was producing music that could compare with the original Stackridge sound. It seemed to have a splash of everything – folk, psychedelia, progressive rock – you name it, it was in the melting pot. James Warren takes up the story:-

"Stackridge had three ingredients going for it; eccentricity, Englishness and an incredible stylistic diversity. We were flying in the face of Frees, Zeppelins and Sabbaths, undoubtedly; but none of us were out and out rockers at heart, so we just stuck to ploughing our own idiosyncratic furrow."

The band built up a phenomenal following and found themselves playing Wembley Stadium alongside the likes of Elton John, The Eagles and The Beach Boys.

With five albums under their belt (*Stackridge* (1971), *Friendliness* (1972), *The Man In The Bowler Hat* (1973), *Do The Stanley* (1976) and *Mr. Mick* (1976)), Stackridge came to a natural end in 1976, clearing the way for Warren and Davis to form The

Korgis (see elsewhere in this book).

Stackridge dramatically reformed at the end of the Nineties and again in 2003 much to the delight of their fans. Despite the passing of time, they had managed to retain their quirky Englishness and knack for a good tune. The tracks from these two sessions have been combined to create the 2005 album *Sex And Flags*.

As this book goes to press, Angel Air will be midway through re-releasing the bulk of the Stackridge back catalogue, commencing with the new compilation, *Purple Spaceships Over Yatton* (2006) (the title comes from a line in one of their earlier songs), followed by the five aforementioned Seventies albums.

So what does the future hold for Stackridge? James Warren still harbours one or two ambitions:-

"Nothing is definitely organised but one day soon I'd love to see us on stage again. I'm sure we'd do well on the festival circuit. Recording-wise? Certainly! Is there a finer way to spend one's twilight years?"

Plans are also afoot to put Stackridge back on the road again…keep an eye on your local concert halls!

Reviews for *Sex And Flags*: SJPCD205

"…draws its material from 1999's *Something For The Weekend* and the whole of the 2003 website only album *Lemon* with some previously unreleased material thrown in for good measure...will undoubtedly please the legions of Stackridge fans."
Classic Rock Society (July 2005)

"It all makes for an incredibly eclectic mixture of music, ranging from the epic 'Beating A Path', into the bright lights of the music hall-esque 'Grooving Along The Highway On A Monday Morning Once', then 'Sliding Down The Razorblade Of Love' into blues… a splendidly entertaining set all round."
Jo-Ann Greene, *Goldmine* (July 2005)

Reviews for *Purple Spaceships Over Yatton - The Best Of*: SJPCD228

"They really do cover all musical bases from the sublime folk-tinged instrumental 'Lummy Days' through to harmony soft rock of 'Friendliness' – very CSNY. Then you have 'Do The Stanley' which sounds like a Monty Python musical number! 'Coniston Water' with its sax verges into jazz rock territory. The title track was re-recorded especially for this compilation making it an enticement for fans of the band getting this release. One for collectors of quirky English rock/folk bands of the 70's and the good news for fans is that Angel Air will be releasing their back catalogue."
Jason Ritchie, *www.getreadytorock.com* (September 2006)

With thanks to James Warren and Michael Heatley. http://www.stackridge.net
See also The Korgis, James Warren, Andy Davis.

TONY STEVENS

"The musicianship is superb, and the unassuming Stevens, who co-arranged and co-produced the set, never highlights himself but prefers to showcase everyone's efforts."

www.allmusic.com (October 2006)

Tony was born in post war London during the late Forties.

By the age of eight, he had taken up the guitar and just three years later, formed his first band, The Invaders. The band evolved into The Down And Outs, who proved to be popular in the Willesden area, playing weddings, birthdays and the clubs.

In October 1967, Tony joined Savoy Brown on bass and featured on four of their albums.

By 1970, Tony (together with Roger Earl (drums) and Dave Peverett (guitar/vocals)) left Savoy Brown to form Foghat, with Rod Price (guitar/vocals). They came to be recognised as an extremely hard working band and made a name for themselves in America, though their impact at home was limited.

Tony left Foghat in 1975 to pursue a career in acting. He was given a part in the successful television series *Rock Follies* and played on the two best selling spin-off albums (which also featured Ray Russell).

Tony played on The Who's soundtrack album to the Rock Opera, *Tommy,* which also featured Mick Ralphs. He also played on Andy Mackay's 1978 solo album along with Ray Russell, Mo Foster and Chris Parren.

Between 1978 and 1979, Tony formed a band with Bobby Harrison (Snafu and Freedom) called Nobody's Business. They released one album (of the same name) that received a Japanese-only release.

Tony went on to join Midnight Flyer with Maggie Bell, releasing one album and touring extensively (detailed more thoroughly under 'M').

In 1984, Tony was invited to join Roger Chapman (Family), who was enjoying considerable success in Europe. He toured with Roger and played on three of his albums.

Tony then returned to acting, securing a number of small parts on prime time television before releasing his solo album on Angel Air, the amusingly titled *Don't Blame Me…I Just Play Bass.*

The following is an interview Joe Geesin conducted with Tony for Record Collector Magazine, featured in their September 2006 edition (number 327):-

JG: Tell me how your new album came about:
TS: Angel Air reissued the Midnight Flyer album I did with Maggie Bell on Swan Song and they asked me if I had any material. They loved the solo set and I started it in 1988, when I came off the road with Roger Chapman. Then I went into acting and did the Comic Strip, the Bill, East Enders. So it got backburnered 'til '98, when Dave Peverett (of Foghat) fell ill and I decided to finish it.
JG: You've left twice. Why?
TS: In 1975 I had differences with the manager – a typical New Yorker who shouted a lot; and we were always on the road. We were getting Oldhat! I was tired and I didn't want to live in the U.S. The second time, I was kicked out, so I went out as my own Foghat. There's a court case now over the name.
JG: Is there any unreleased material in the vaults?
TS: Not a lot. Dave would have some solo but not much Foghat. I also played on The Who's film version of Tommy and the original version of Evita.
JG: What are your interests outside of the music world?
TS: Tennis and skeet shooting. And from 1975, I took up property renovation and restoration, which I did for seven years – good fun. Oh, and drinking and laughing!
JG: Which bassists do you admire?
TS: My first influences were the simple bassists who played with the likes of Freddie King and BB King – steady stuff. But I loved Stanley Clarke and Jaco Pastorius and John Entwistle was a good friend. Most modern bassists are all technique but have no soul. Mark King is great, fast, but has soul.
JG: What are your future plans?
TS: To carry on playing and, when the legal battles are over, I'll tour, either as Foghat or Slowride. We'll be back!

Reviews for *Don't Blame Me...I Just Play Bass*: SJPCD223

"Good rock that doesn't tax you too much and has some decent tunes too. Issued outside the USA here for the first time and welcome too.

'Good Night The Sun' is a perfect summer evening song with a great bass line and the saxophone on 'In My Eyes' is a nice touch.

'Run The River' is more up-tempo and with the horns is catchy with a big band pop feel to the smooth rock.

Extensive sleeve notes and a discography too - he's done a lot of session work outside of Foghat." 4/5

www.getreadytorock.com (June 2006)

"...the emphasis firmly on the quality of the song writing and the uniformly excellent musicianship and the end result is a fine piece of work which proves that Tony Stevens has much more in his locker than blues rock."

Classic Rock Society (September 2006)

With thanks to Tony Stevens, Joe Geesin and Record Collector.
www.foghat.com www.slowriderocks.com www.recordcollectormag.com

See also Mick Ralphs, Mo Foster, Ray Russell, Maggie Bell, Midnight Flyer, Bobby Harrison, Freedom, Snafu.

THE STIFFS

Lancashire is not renowned for being a Mecca for the music business. However, it is known for being the home of the incomparable Stiffs, a Punk band with a hat full of great melodies and beautiful riffs.

The band was formed by school chums Phil Hendriks, Ian 'Strang' Barnes, Tommy O'Kane and John McVittie.

In 1977, they created their own record company, the amusingly named Dork Records, then released their debut single, 'Standard English'. Such was The Stiffs disappointment with the end result; they could have been forgiven for sacking themselves from their own label!

Their second release, 'Inside Out', was a hit with 'Uncle' John Peel who pronounced it "the greatest record in the entire history of the universe". The song sold five thousand copies, was a hit on the Independent Chart and was also licensed to EMI subsidiary, Zonophone.

The Stiffs subsequently signed to Zonophone but there was trouble ahead. The A & R man who signed them left his job and the band found themselves out of favour.

In 1981, a single was eventually released called 'Volume Control'. It was popular with Radio One and the music press, though it failed to chart.

The Stiffs eventually escaped their music contract with Zonophone and released a single through appropriately enough …Stiff Records. Despite having a wealth of their own material to choose from, they were instructed to record a cover version of The Glitter Band's 'Goodbye My Love'.

Sick and tired of the music business, The Stiffs split up.

In 1982, Phil Hendriks and Ian 'Strang' Barnes resurrected the band, with new boys John 'Juice' Mayor and Nick Alderson (better known as 'Billy Rumour' Bass). The band recorded a John Peel session with Mott The Hoople's Dale Griffin standing in on drums.

The Stiffs Mark II were short lived and evolved into Idol Rich, fronted by Phil. They proved to be a popular act and released two singles, 'Blaze of Love' and 'Skye Boat Song'.

In December 1984, the original Stiffs line-up reformed for a one-off gig. Such was the size and enthusiasm of the audience that it had to be re-scheduled for February of the following year. Later that year, Phil, Ian and John were joined by Mark Hurlbutt to record a new single, 'The Young Guitars'. They also recorded a 12" single called 'Look, Don't Touch' with Bob Ramsey on lead vocals (Bob is now 'playing' Noddy Holder in Bootleg Slade).

Between 1986 and 1988, Phil and Ian formed a glam punk outfit, playing over 250 gigs and touring the length and breadth of Europe.

It was over ten years before The Stiffs played together again. The original line-up reconvened for a live album and the 'Holidays In The Sun' punk-fest in Morecambe.

The Angel Air album *The Stiffs 1981-1988* pulls together a rake of glorious singles, lost gems and demo tracks from the archives.

Review for *The Stiffs 1981-1988*: SJPCD062

"Blackburn`s finest are back with a new collection of rarities, recorded between 1981 and 1988. 18 tracks never before available on CD! Angel Air Records have done their usual fine job of presentation, with impeccable sound quality and an informative and colourful 16 page booklet. [The album] makes an ideal companion set to the 1999 *Stiffs - The Punk Collection* release on Captain Oi! Records. Includes the 4 tracks recorded with Mott The Hoople`s Dale 'Buffin' Griffin on the drum stool. Dale Griffin also provides entertaining sleeve notes in the lavish booklet. Essential for Stiffs collectors."

With thanks to Dale Griffin ('Buffin').

STONE THE CROWS

"...the vibe that emanates from these brain-scorching fifty-plus minutes provides enough joy for any fan of mind-expanding, psychedelic blues-rock fever."

Jeff Monk, *Mohair Sweets* (June 2002)

Stone The Crows emerged from the tough Glasgow music scene of the Sixties. Originally called Power, they lived up to their name by producing commanding blues-based rock.

The nucleus of the band was a remarkable vocalist by the name of Maggie Bell and a talented guitarist called Leslie Harvey (brother of Alex), augmented by Colin Allen, Jimmy Dewar and John McGuiness.

Power soon caught the attention of Peter Grant (Led Zeppelin's manager) who signed them up and suggested a name change, adopting the Australian expression, "Stone the Crows".

Under Grant's guiding hand, the band recorded a total of four albums for Polydor (*Stone The Crows, Ode To John Law, Teenage Licks* and *Continuous Performance* (a top forty hit)). They had little trouble finding an audience, having built up a formidable following on the university circuit. Stone The Crows also attributed much of their success to John Peel, who regularly featured the band in his sessions.

The adventure came to a tragic end when Leslie Harvey was electrocuted during a sound check at the Swanage Top Rank Ballroom. His sad death was a massive loss to the music world. Maggie recalls the mood at the time:

"He put his hand on the mike, and he was gone. It was just as quick as that. It knocked the heart out of us and you just think 'what is the point? Why'?'"

The band recruited Jimmy McCulloch to replace Leslie but despite his best efforts, Stone The Crows disbanded soon after. Despite this miserable ending, Maggie's career blossomed throughout the decade and is told in more detail earlier in the book.

Angel Air has released a live album from this era together with a historically important DVD.

Reviews for *Live In Montreux 1972*: SJPCD116

"This live recording, taken from the personal archives of vocalist Maggie Bell, catches Stone The Crows at the height of their powers...This phenomenal band were one of the best British blues rock groups of the era and this wonderful live recording captures them in all their glory and is an indispensable piece of Rock history..."
Steve Ward, *Classic Rock Society* (June 2002)

"Progressive rock rules OK, well it did back when this album came out and this is a shining example of the art...I have to say this is an exceptional piece of work, a lot of it sounds like jamming, especially on the twenty-one minute cover of Bob Dylan's 'Hollis Brown'. Leslie (Harvey) was a master of what he did and was a sad loss but I am elated that this album has finally seen the light of day, it's outstanding."
Modern Dance, Issue 43 (January 2003)

With thanks to Rich Wilson.

See also Maggie Bell, Midnight Flyer, Tony Stevens.

SUMMER WINE

"The music is principally a tribute to those vocal bands of the Sixties who employed dense harmonies, especially The Beach Boys. That is the highlight of this release really, the vocal harmonies are quite superb…The package is well presented by Angel Air, with informative booklets and lots of photos."

Bernard Law, *Classic Rock Society* (March 2003)

In 1972, Mike Hurst's career was in what he describes as "a funny place". He had secured major success in the Sixties with The Springfields, released a couple of solo albums and was now working with Phonogram as an independent producer.

Part of his Phonogram brief was to come up with ideas for the label and it was with this in mind that he suggested to his friend and mentor, Roland Rennie, that he form a harmony group. Mike had a number of people in mind to join him.

First he recruited Ray Fenwick, an old friend and a talented and versatile guitarist. Tony Rivers was also an obvious choice to Mike due to his talents as a vocal arranger. Finally, John Perry made up the quartet – a man with an incredible falsetto and tremendous vocal range.

Grant Serpell was brought in on drums, though not as a named member of the line-up (he too was in a funny place, since this was post-Affinity and Mike d'Abo but pre-Sailor).

'Why Do Fools Fall In Love' was recorded as the first single and it climbed to number 88 in the American Billboard, no mean feat for a new band without a track record or tour experience.

The Summer Wine album (*The Fabulous Summer Wine* (1973)) was soaked in beautiful harmonies and boasted an inspired selection of cover versions, including 'Take A Load off Your Feet', 'Do You Wanna Dance', 'Sherry', 'Living Next Door To An Angel' and 'Shenandoah'.

By the end of 1973, the group had quietly disbanded, leaving a charming legacy. Angel Air has picked up the album, dusted it off and added six studio outtakes for good measure.

Reviews for *The Fabulous Summer Wine*: SJPCD126

"…the album mixes upbeat Seventies pop with a strong Beach Boys influence, giving a very eclectic and summery sound…a very enjoyable mixture…"
Record Collector (April 2003)

"…lush vocals and bubblegum pop songs…This is an album that only those of a certain age will want to buy…but the vocal harmonies are very good indeed…"
Classic Rock Society, May 2003

See also Mike Hurst, Ray Fenwick, Fancy, The Favourite Sons.

SUNDANCE

"...much of their material, a mixture of originals and covers, is very much in the Nicks era Fleetwood Mac vein although lighter and poppier in a Bucks Fizz sort of way...pleasant and inoffensive."

Steve Ward, *Classic Rock Society* (June 2002)

We are now well into 'S' and consequently the next instalment in Mike Hurst's story – Sundance. Mike, you will recall, was in The Springfields, Summer Wine and Fancy. He has released four discs on Angel Air under his own name.

In the early Eighties, Mike had the idea of creating a new band, much in the image of The Springfields. He recruited a local bass player, Michael de Alberquerque (of ELO fame) and Mary Hopkin, who was to be the sole female vocalist.

The three musicians found that their voices combined and gelled perfectly.

Knowing how difficult it was to find a footing in the music business, Mike paid for the initial recording sessions. Old friend Ray Fenwick was hired on guitar, Steve Price on bass and Steve Dimitri on drums. The sessions were a success.

Sundance were signed by Gerry Bron to his Bronze record label. They were now stable mates with Mötorhead and The Damned!

A prolific period followed with the recording of an album and the release of a single, 'What's Love' (a massive hit in South Africa). The trio toured with Dr. Hook and had plenty of television exposure.

All was not well in 'the Sundance family'. Mary started to experience fainting fits as Mike explains:-

"The first one was during the sound check at Newcastle Guildhall. In the middle of the first number, she went out like a light. Hook's soundman rushed forward shouting 'stand back, I was a medic in 'Nam', he ripped open Mary's top and exclaimed 'My God, what a chest!'"

Eventually, Mary left the band and was replaced by singer Catherine Howe. The new line up of Sundance went on tour in support of Buck Fizz but Catherine eventually decided to move on. A third female singer joined briefly, recording the old classic 'Walk Right In' which became the final single.

The story ended when Bronze folded.

Angel Air, in time-honoured tradition, has re-released the original album with added bonus tracks (from the television show *The Entertainers*).

Reviews of *Sundance*: SJPCD133

"Producing a sound that was packed with laid-back guitars and vocal harmonies, this, their only release, is surprisingly well-honed...

Sundance were at their finest when they veered away from the ballad and concentrated on a light-rock sound, as demonstrated here on 'A Good Old Song', 'Never Going Back' and the country edge of 'What's It Doing To You And Me'."

Rich Wilson, *Record Collector* (August 2002)

"With Michael's voice in beautiful harmony with the wonderful voice of Mary's it just seemed so perfect...Here we have the original nine songs plus four superb bonus tracks...this is an important part of music history...good album with a historic value of 10."

Modern Dance, Issue 43 (January 2003)

With thanks to Mike Hurst.
See also Mike Hurst, Summer Wine, Fancy, The Favourite Sons, Carmen.

SUN RED SUN

Sun Red Sun have achieved notoriety in the heavy metal fraternity for their quality of music and remarkable line-up.

In every sense of the word, the band is a super group, pulling together musicians who have featured in bands as diverse as Black Sabbath, Rainbow, Gillan and Alice In Chains to name but a few. The story of this short-lived band is a tale of woe which is best told by John McCoy. So sit up, pay attention and listen carefully:-

"When Al Romano, I and Mike Sciotto joined forces with Joey Belladonna from Anthrax to rehearse and record an album as Belladonna, things went seriously wrong.

Joey sacked Al and then Mike. I became confused and disillusioned, so returned to England to visit my mother who was in hospital. Shortly afterward, I was told not to return to continue the project as it had been finished!

After all the work Al and I had put in there was an idea mooted that Al, myself, drummer Bobby Rondinelli and singer Ray Gillen should join forces and complete an album together using some of the tracks we had already recorded. The idea was to add Ray Gillen's vocal as well as some new tracks.

Ray and Al called me from America (I was home in England at this time) and I discussed tracks with Ray.

They began working on 'Outrageous' and 'I Know A Place' from the McCoy sessions. Unfortunately, this was to be the last song Ray would ever record. His health deteriorated rapidly and he died of cancer shortly afterward.

I had had enough of America and Americans and withdrew from the world of music for a while. Al finished more tracks, doing the vocals himself and recruiting Mike Starr for bass duties. Other musicians/singers finished the album and released it in America as Sun Red Sun. We eventually reached an agreement for Angel Air to release the album worldwide and it's still selling well, due mostly I think to the sad circumstances surrounding it."

The album has been respectfully dedicated to Ray Gillen. The dramatic cover, arguably one of the best in Angel Air's catalogue, is neither staged nor posed. It catches Al Romano throwing one of his treasured Gibson Modernes into the sea following the death of Ray Gillen. John has nothing but praise for Al during this difficult time:-

"He did all anyone could do for Ray and should be commended for his work and patience in an impossible situation."

A proportion of the royalties from the sale of this album are donated towards research in to finding a cure for AIDS (SJPCD018).

See also Gillan, Samson/Paul Samson, Mammoth, McCoy, John Du Cann.

SURVIVORS

"Sophisticated yet accessible. Sky fans will know what to expect and Shadows fans prepared to step outside their favourite style should not fear to tread: it's musical rather than muso-indulgent."

Pipetalk, November 2002

The nucleus of Survivors can be traced back to the mid-Seventies when drummer Brian Bennett and keyboardist Steve Gray worked together under the banner of Wasp (also known as Das Funf).

Wasp (Das Funf) was created by Kevin Phillips (of the KPM Music Library) with a view to forming a group of composers who could record music for film, television jingles, radio and corporate presentations. Other members included Dave Richmond, Duncan Lamont and Clive Hicks. The project was an immense success.

During the Eighties, Brian recorded no less than ten albums with The Shadows whilst Steve embarked upon a successful career with John Williams, Tristan Fry and Herbie Flowers in Sky.

In the early Nineties, Steve approached Brian about forming a band. He had one condition as Steve explains:-

"The one absolute imperative was that Brian and Paul [Paul Hart – keyboards and violin] would be in it and if either of them had said 'no' that would have been that. Happily they both agreed and the next question was 'who else'?"

The choice was obvious. Mo Foster was drafted in on bass (five string and fretless) with Clem Clempson on electric guitar, acoustic guitar and Dobro.

Between the 13th - 17th January 1992 and 23rd - 27th June 1992, the five musicians recorded a total of eleven instrumental tracks. Democratically, everyone had the opportunity to contribute at least one original composition. The musicians chose the name Survivors for their band.

Survivors failed to secure a record deal, despite the pedigree in the band and an overwhelming urge to tour.

Ten years later, Mo Foster took the tapes to Angel Air and the songs were at long last given the release they so richly deserved.

Reviews for *Survivors*: SJPCD113

"Sophisticated yet accessible. Sky fans will know what to expect and Shadows fans prepared to step outside their favourite style should not fear to tread: it's musical rather than muso-indulgent."
Pipetalk, November 2002

"…this very nice album was locked away in a dungeon for ten years, until one day a shining knight from Angel Air came and rescued it…I hope this sells many copies before this story comes to an end."
Modern Dance, Issue 43 (January 2003)

With thanks to Mo Foster, Brian Bennett, Steve Gray, Clem Clempson and Paul Hart. www.brianbennettmusic.co.uk, www.mofoster.com

See also Ray Russell, RMS, Survivors, Fancy, Affinity, Mike d'Abo, Mo Foster, RJ Wagsmith, Colosseum.

TEE SET

"Tee Set are a Dutch band who can trace their origins back to 1962 and enjoyed their first chart success in 1966 with "Early In The Morning". This album traces the band's career from 1966 to 1983 during which time they sold fifteen million units."

Feedback

Tee Set are arguably the biggest band ever to emerge from Holland.

The group's founder and guiding light was Peter Tetteroo, a hero in his motherland who took the band on an orgy of chart success across the globe, aided and abetted over the years by a string of talented musicians including at one time or another, Polle Eduard and Englishman, Ray Fenwick (Ray and Polle broke away from Tee Set in 1967 and formed After Tea, another successful act).

During the course of a long and varied history, Tee Set managed to rack up twenty top twenty Dutch hits. Their success was not limited to their home shores.

With worldwide sales of fifteen million albums and singles, a fifth of these were attributable to America, two million to Italy and a million to Germany. They scored number one hits in Italy, Switzerland and France. They also conquered Canada, South America, New Zealand and Australia.

Angel Air's Tee Set compilation can best be described as definitive. It includes a total of twenty-four tracks and every single one has had a chart placing.

Sadly, Peter Tetteroo died in 2002.

Reviews for *24 Carat*: SJPCD014

"...there's a bluesy feel but generally the pop bubbles over in generous portions. Definitely not rock but music tastes vary so much collectors of historical pieces might find a space on the shelf for it."
Classic Rock Society

"Not including their homeland Holland...Tee Set will best be remembered for the multi-million selling single 'Ma Belle Amie' -which has ensured them a place in rock 'n' pop history. Well there was more - nicely presented via this 24 track CD selection.

Their earlier material was along the lines of Stevie Winwood/Spencer Davis Group certainly in vocals...pumping brass – R & B inspired - nothing staggering but competent. . 'Believe What I Say' is great - while 'Don't You Leave' plods.

Ex-Spencer Davis Group member Ray Fenwick was also involved with Tee Set and the last track is titled 'A Tribute To The Spencer Davis Group'. As always with Angel Air, there is an excellent CD booklet featuring discography/family tree/absorbing liner notes. Pleasurable listen."
Zabadak magazine

With thanks to Ray Fenwick.

See also Minute By Minute, Ray Fenwick, Fancy, Summer Wine, Ian Gillan Band, Guitar Orchestra, The Spencer Davis Group.

THIRD EAR BAND

"An atmospheric and ambient album, this is the point where electronic music, classical music and ambient music meet in an otherworldly journey through music...a superb album."

Classic Rock Society (November 2004)

The strangely named Third Ear Band emerged from the alternative music scene that burgeoned in the mid-Sixties. They came about as a fusion between two bands – The Giant Sun Trolley and The People Band.

They were renowned for their spontaneity and experimentation, working with Eastern raga sounds, folk and classical as well as medieval influences.

They recorded a series of notable albums for the Harvest label including *Alchemy* (1969), *Elements* (1970) and *Music From Macbeth* (1972).

Third Ear Band lasted into the Nineties, going through various incarnations.

In 2004, Angel Air pulled off an amazing feat with the release of the long-missing album, *Magus*.

The release came about due to the diligence of band member Ron Kort.

After the featured sessions were completed in 1972, he carefully saved and stored the tapes. The release of the album became a personal quest and he was involved in the project up until the final stages before he sadly died. Had it not been for Ron, the album would never have come to fruition.

The line-up on *Magus* (meaning master magician) includes Glen Sweeney (drums), Mike Marchant (guitars and vocals), Simon House (violin, sitar and piano), Paul Minns (oboe, recorders and Hammond) and Dave Tomlin (bass guitar).

Review for *Magus*: SJPCD173

Overall an adventurous and sometimes intimidating piece of work, but interesting nonetheless."

Feedback (November 2004)

STEVE PEREGRINE TOOK

"...should appeal to T-Rex historians and fans. As usual with Angel Air releases, there's a pretty good booklet too."

Bernard Law, *Classic Rock Society* (August 2002)

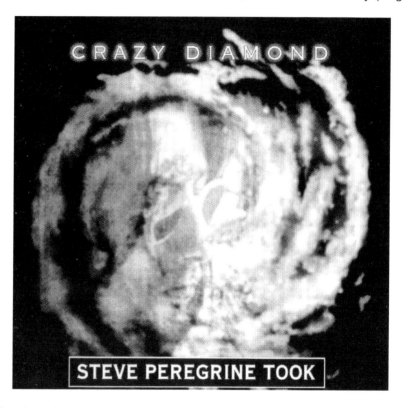

Marc Bolan is quite possibly one of the most famous names to emerge from the Seventies music scene. He enjoyed tremendous commercial success between 1970 and 1973 with T-Rex, scoring a succession of major hits with Mickey Finn as his sideman (see earlier in this book).

Prior to this, Marc had scored a number of minor successes in the late Sixties with Tyrannosaurus Rex, a partnership with the enigmatic Steve Peregrine Took.

Steve (born Stephen Porter) had answered an advert placed in Melody Maker by Marc in 1967 for 'good looking musicians'. What started as a band was soon reduced to a duo. Marc and Steve were a striking pair, both elphine in appearance and exceptionally talented. However, their outlook on life and ethos differed tremendously.

Marc was a steady and 'homely' individual who had settled down with his partner, June. Steve on the other hand was heavily into the drug scene and hung out with similar minded people.

Although this is a simplistic view of their relationship, it was in essence what led to Marc sacking Steve in 1969, following the release of three albums and a number of moderately successful singles.

Initially, Steve drifted from one project to another. He had no shortage of friends, but eventually, the money ran out and he found himself living in a seedy squat in Ladbroke Grove.

With the success of Marc's new partnership with Finn, there was a renewed interest in the Tyrannosaurus Rex back catalogue and the royalty cheques flowed again.

Tony Secunda, Steve and Marc's manager during this period, turned his attention to Steve's career.

Tony secured studio time for Steve but the errant musician seemed incapable of seeing anything through to its natural conclusion. The late Mick Wayne, who worked with him at the time, could see what was happening to Steve:-

"The trouble with all that dope-induced thinking was that he was always questioning the results. Nothing ever got finished."

Refusing to admit defeat, Tony moved Steve (and his pet rat) into the basement flat below his offices and set him up with a tape machine.

This was a prolific period for Steve, who recorded hours of tape, with visitors to the flat guesting as and when they turned up, including Twink from The Pretty Things and Syd Barrett.

The recordings from this period can be found on Angel Air's release *Crazy Diamond*. The results are charming, bizarre, crazy but ultimately very listenable. They were rescued by Tony Secunda who salvaged the tapes from a box marked 'Steve Took Ramblings'. The recordings received a warm reception from press and fans alike.

Steve's relationship with drugs continued until his premature death in 1980. Tragically, he choked to death on a cherry, having blown a royalty cheque on morphine and magic mushrooms.

Reviews for *Crazy Diamond*: SJPCD118

"Took's vocals are buried in a sonic pillow of some kind and in the end this album actually has a kind of catatonic charm not unlike the effect derived from the very drugs used to create the thing."
Jeff Monks, *Mohair Sweets* (November 2002)

With thanks to Dave Thompson.
www.steve-took.co.uk.
Steve Took Appreciation Society: 10 Spring Grove, Loughton Essex. IG10 4QB. England.

BERNIE TORMÉ

"Bernie Tormé does not actually play the guitar, he tames it, the way a fakir charms a cobra."

Classic Rock Magazine (April 2007)

It has been said of Irish guitarist Bernie Tormé that he plays his vintage Fender Stratocaster through a Marshall Amplifier as though he knew them both in a previous life.

Bernie played in a number of Dublin bands in the early Seventies, including The Urge, prior to relocating to England in 1974.

Upon his arrival in London, he joined pub rock band Scrapyard before forming a punk outfit called The Bernie Tormé Band, which toured extensively with The Boomtown Rats and Generation X.

In 1979, Bernie's career took an interesting twist when he joined Gillan, playing on a succession of albums and hit singles (some of these have been re-released on Angel Air).

Following his departure from Gillan, he played guitar for Ozzy Osbourne, standing in for Randy Rhodes, who was tragically killed in an air crash.

Bernie also joined forces with ex-Girl and current LA Guns front man Philip Lewis in Tormé during the mid-Eighties, as well as playing with Vincent Crane and Paul Hammond in a post-Du Cann era Atomic Rooster.

Bernie also played with Twisted Sister's Dee Snider and Iron Maiden's drummer Clive Burr in Desperado, writing with Snider and recording the album *Ace*, which until recently remained unreleased.

Bernie is currently working with John McCoy and drummer Robin Guy under the band name Guy McCoy Tormé - G.M.T. for short. Their debut album, *Bitter And Twisted* (2006) has been well received.

Angel Air has released an album and DVD of Bernie's work. Bernie explained to Billy Ifintis of Skylightzine how the DVD release came about:-

"Well I mentioned to Peter Purnell at Angel Air, who I've known for many years, that I had some old video footage, and he was instantly very keen to put it out as a DVD. Being a musician and having my own little label (Retrowrek records), it's a funny thing but I've never had much interest in video, so I definitely didn't want to try to do it on Retrowrek.

Following that conversation I really tried to forget about it but at regular intervals Peter kept calling me and asking if I'd got it together yet, of course I hadn't! So I finally gave up and realised that he'd never stop hassling me until I actually did it!

I did the basic choice of tracks and mixing the audio to 5.1 at my studios, Barnroom Studios. That was a real battle because the audio varied from 24 track analogue on 'Ghost Walking' and 'Shoorah Shoorah' to eight track on 'Star', 'Frontline', 'Turn Out The Lights', and 'Hardcore' from the Clarendon Ballroom right down to a crappy mono microphone at the back of the Marquee Club for 'Boney Maroney' and 'Getting There'. The twenty-four track stuff was fun. The mono stuff was distinctly not! Its also really weird watching yourself again and again from so long ago, remembering what was going on and the shit you were going through. A bit like therapy really!"

Reviews for *Live Sheffield 1983*: SJPCD115

"The highlight for me is the superb version of 'No Easy Way'. Bernie plays the guitar flat out, not only maintaining the melody but also utilising feedback, fills and any other form of improvisation that he can come up with…While he has obviously been influenced by Hendrix, Bernie really is a showstopper in his own right and has a truly distinctive sound…if you love rock guitar then you have to get this."
Feedback (June 2002)

"Good music, with a powerful edge and above average sound mixing to it. Over seventy full minutes of 'as-you-were-there' hard driving rock that will leave no true HR fan disappointed…Play this CD…..L-O-U-D!!"
Mike Reed, *Banzai* (February 2003)

Reviews for *Stratocaster Gypsy*: NJPDVD621

"The recording quality suffers in places but that's to be expected. And with a decent running time and extras, it's a great insight and good value too. One of Ireland's best if not best known exports." ****1/2
Joe Geesin, *www.getreadytorock.com* (May 2005)

"…I found this incredible, a trawl through his past and showing what a great showman he is. There is also a wonderful interview with Bernie where he talks about his life in music…"
Feedback (August 2005)

www.gmtrocks.com; www.bernietorme.com.

See also Desperado, Gillan, McCoy.

TROGGS

In 2002, Angel Air signed one of the finest bands of the Sixties to its roster – The Troggs.

Between 1966 and 1967, the Troggs succeeded in conquering the hit parade with a run of memorable top forty hits. Their first and perhaps most famous chart hit was with a Chip Taylor song called 'Wild Thing' (later also a hit for Angel Air signing, Fancy). The song had been spotted by their manager, Larry Page, who suggested that they give it a make-over. This was followed by 'With A Girl Like You', penned by lead singer, Reg Presley.

Reg recalled that he was encouraged to write his own songs, much like the other major acts of the time. This proved daunting, particularly as he had only recently given up his trade as a 'brickie'. However, he proved more than capable of writing superb slices of pop and this, coupled with his immense sex appeal (at the time!), proved to be a winning formula for the band. Reg-penned hits included 'Love Is All Around' (later successfully covered by Wet Wet Wet), 'With A Girl Like You' (number 1), 'I Can't Control Myself', 'Anyway That You Want Me', 'Give it To Me' and 'Night Of The Long Grass'.

The Troggs continued to record beyond the Sixties, producing a succession of high quality singles (in the region of forty) and albums culminating in *Athens Andover* in 1992, a superb collaboration with self-confessed Troggs fans, R.E.M.

In March 2002, Angel Air seized the opportunity to film The Troggs in concert. In front of a full house, they performed a total of ten songs (including all the above hits), interspersed with some customary dry and witty banter from Presley. The sound quality is superb and the musicianship from Chris Britton (co-founder), Peter Lucas and Dave Maggs is (as ever) polished.

The resultant 2003 DVD release also included the added treat of an interview with Reg, who talks openly about everything from song writing to aliens and crop circles, subjects which continue to fascinate him. A band history is also included as part of the package.

Long may they reign!

www.my-generation.org.uk/Troggs

TYGERS OF PAN TANG

"...New Wave of British Heavy Metal at its crustiest and finest..."

Classic Rock (August 2005)

The Tygers Of Pan Tang hail from Whitley Bay, Tyne and Wear. The band was formed in 1978 by guitarist Robb Weir who decided that a career as a jeweller perhaps wasn't for him after all.

Bob advertised in the local polytechnic and received responses from a drummer, Brian Dick and a bassist by the name of Rocky.

A gentleman known to Bob as Reverend Zack allowed the trio to rehearse in a local church hall. Placing an advert in the local paper, they set out to recruit a lead singer. Two candidates applied and the vocalist with the PA system got the job – Jess Cox.

Jess seems to recall that they had a singer of sorts who was wholly unsuitable:-

"They didn't have a vocalist. Well, they did but apparently he used to stick his dick in a vacuum cleaner and press 'suck', so they got rid of him!"

Rocky came up with the name of the band, which he found in a Michael Moorcroft book called Stormbringer. Pan Tang was an evil city and the Tygers were creatures that the warriors of Pan Tang took to war.

The Tygers Of Pan Tang progressed from playing cover versions to their own material and were spotted by Dave Wood, owner of local record label, Neat Records, who signed them up.

Their debut single, 'Don't Touch Me There' swiftly sold out and attracted the attention of the major labels. They eventually signed with MCA and went on tour, supporting Magnum. It was a tour punctuated by cramped guest houses and copious tins of Irish stew. It is fair to say that The Tygers worked their way into the music business the hard way!

A second tour followed, with Def Leppard, The Scorpions, Saxon and Iron Maiden.

In August 1980, The Tygers released their debut album, *Wild Cat*, which they recorded in just eleven days. The album reached number 18 in the U.K. album chart.

Guitarist John Sykes was brought in to broaden the sound of the band but the line-up was far from stable. Jess left the band (the true reason remains a closely guarded secret) but he went on to join Lionheart, featuring Dennis Stratton of Iron Maiden.

Jon Deverill was Jess's successor (even sharing a flat with him for a time) and The Tygers returned to the studio in 1981 to record *Spellbound*. They went on tour again, this time with Magnum in support!

However, the second album failed to make the level of impact the record company were expecting (reaching number 33 in the album chart). Consequently, The Tygers were told to come up with a new album in three weeks flat!

The end result, *Crazy Nights* was deeply disappointing and fared poorly.

In early 1982, John Sykes left the band and was replaced by Fred Purser, who had just four days to learn a whole set before the band toured France. Interestingly, when the tour culminated at La Theatre in Paris, they broke the attendance record, which they still hold.

A fourth album followed, *The Cage*, which proved to be their biggest success (both commercially and creatively) and boasted strong harmonies. The album had been produced to suit the American market but ironically, The Tygers never made it there; they were sent to Japan instead!

Upon their return, they found that their management had resigned.

To compound problems, MCA wanted The Tygers to become a pop band, which was met with dissent from within the ranks. The group fell apart.

In 1985, they briefly reformed. The line-up featured Jon Deverill, Brian Deck, Steve Lamb, Neil Shepherd and David Donaldon. They released two albums and lasted until 1987.

The Tygers story appeared to be over until 1999, when they were invited to reform for a German festival. Robb Weir and Jess Cox answered the call and the show was recorded and released as a live album. Following considerable interest, Robb took the band forward with a new line-up featuring vocalist Tony Liddle, guitarist Dean Robertson, Brian West on bass and drummer Craig Ellis. They recorded an album called *Mystical*.

Liddle moved on and was replaced by Richie Wicks. This new line-up recorded an album, *Live In The Roar* and a DVD, *Visions From The Cathouse*, both of which have been released by Angel Air. The latter includes nearly two hours of footage.

In 2005, Angel Air released a second live album from The Tygers, *Leg Of The Boot – Live In Holland*.

Robb Weir has secured the future of The Tygers Of Pan Tang for a new generation of fans:-

"As long as I draw breath, The Tygers will roar!"

Reviews for *Live In The Roar*:

"...some thirty years and many lost hair follicles later the group is back, in a form, and sounding damned impressive...a positively vicious live act that recalls those halcyon days of metal excess as perfectly as any ever could...passionately done Metal that will have balding accountants, lawyers, and line workers joining a new generation of kids in some of the most injurious head-banging there ever was. Class A work!"

David L.Wilson, www.electricbasement.com

"...The question is whether the power, energy and sheer exhilaration come over when transferred to disc and the answer is a resounding yes!

A fantastic performance by the band is equalled by crystal clear sound quality and superb production and ensures this is an essential souvenir of a memorable tour."

Classic Rock Society (August 2003)

Reviews for *Leg Of The Boot*: SPJCD206

"...finds the band in ebullient mood...the Tygers are very much a band for today and still a force to be reckoned with as this great live album proves."

Classic Rock Society (July 2005)

"...You can find 'most wanted' songs like 'Suzie Smiled', 'Euthanasia', 'Don't Touch Me There' and as bonus three different studio versions of the songs:- 'High-speed Highway Superman', 'Slave To Freedom', 'Don't Touch Me There'."

Skylight e-zine (July 2005)

VARIOUS ARTISTS

"I never thought it possible to create thirty years of Mod on one CD but the guys at Angel Air have come up trumps with this spectacular trek through the world of Mod through the eyes of one man, Ray Fenwick..."

www.modradiouk.com (March 2004)

During Angel Air's first ten years, there have only been three 'various artists' compilations (excluding the Mott The Hoople family collective).

The first, a CD compilation called *Air Sampler* from 1997, pulled together a selection of tracks from the very early releases on the label. This budget priced collection was a showcase for their first year in business and contains some interesting tracks. The majority of the songs featured are from albums that have long since been deleted so it is well worth checking out for those elusive rarities. The tracks are as follows:

'The Demon Rose' - McCoy, 'Live Wire' – Guitar Orchestra, 'Restless 1' – Gillan, 'Give or Fake (2nd version) – Route 66, 'Always and Forever' – Mammoth, 'Clear Air Turbulence' – Ian Gillan Band, 'Poem About A Gnome' – John Gustafson, 'Here I Go Again' – Mike d'Abo, 'In My Room' – Musicians Union Band, 'It's Over' – Bobby Harrison, 'I Won't Be There' – Mick Grabham, 'Back USA' – Ray Fenwick, 'Ma Belle Amie' – Tee Set, 'Lonely' – Steve Hyams.

The second compilation came courtesy of recordings from Ray Fenwick. Throughout his career, he found himself drifting in and out of (and producing) a series of top-notch Mod bands. *Mod City* was released in 2001 and featured tracks from Tich Turner's Escalator, Rupert And The Red Devils, Teenbeats and The South Coast Ska Stars.

The third 'various artists' compilation is a DVD called *Hits And Angels*, pulling together performances from Angel Air's first selection of DVD releases (up to 2004). These were either especially commissioned by the label or licensed from other companies. The track listing pulls together the best from the catalogue:-

'Karma Chameleon' – Culture Club, 'King Of Wishful Thinking' - Go West, 'A Glass Of Champagne' – Sailor, 'My Friend The Sun' – Roger Chapman, 'Gimme Some Lovin' – The Spencer Davis Group, 'Smoke On The Water' - Ian Gillan Band, 'Spooky' – Mike Hurst All Star Band, 'Love Potion No. 9' – Tygers Of Pan Tang, 'Rising Sun' – Medicine Head, 'Stone Free' – RMS And Gil Evans, '747 (Strangers in the Night)' – Oliver Dawson Saxon, 'Stormy Monday Blues' – Colosseum, 'Wild Thing' – Troggs, 'Jeepster' – Mickey Finn's T-Rex, excerpt from 'Wind In The Willows Concert' – Hardin And York, 'Bringing On Back The Good Times/A Day Without Love' – Steve Ellis's Love Affair.

Reviews for *Air Sampler:* SJPSIN501

"As Angel Air are at pains to point out in their press release, most labels wait to become established until they plunder their back catalogue, but not them. With their first release coming out as long ago as February (97), they have now issued their first sampler, which should be retailing at £4.99 or less. There is a song taken from each album, with details of that release and a picture of the cover. Angel Air Records are reissuing some prime material, and the sampler shows just what a good job they are doing. Fifteen cuts for under a fiver can't be bad."
Feedback

"Angel Air shouldn't be a new name to one or two of the regular readers amongst you. Bands and artists such as Gillan, John Gustafson, Tee Set, Steve Hyams, Musicians Union Band, The Pirates, Route 66 and Ray Fenwick have all had more than the odd tasty album out on Angel Air and the label's only just kind of started. This sampler album (at a damn cheap price) contains at least one track from at least one of the above."
(Dave W) *The Modern Dance* Issue 24

Reviews for *Mod City:* SPJCD097

"...transports us stylishly back to the days when Lambrettas were the vehicle of choice, parkas were the height of fashion and an entire musical sub-section sat cross-legged at the feet of guru Paul Weller, blueprinting what we now know as the great Mod Revival."
Goldmine(March 2002)

RJ WAGSMITH BAND

"...The sleeve warns that 'this CD contains material of a flatulent and silly nature' and it does not lie."

Jo-Ann Greene, *Goldmine*, (December 12, 2003)

The vaults of Angel Air have for the last ten years been jammed to the rafters with lost musical gems, rediscovered masterpieces and worthy recording sessions that have been saved for the nation.

Then there is The RJ Wagsmith Band. This is the first comedy release from Angel Air and features the vocal talents of Mo Foster (who needs no further introduction) and comedy actor and writer Mike Walling.

Mike is probably best known for playing the character of Eric in the BBC comedy *Brush Strokes*. He has also written for *The Brittas Empire*, *Birds Of A Feather, A Prince Among Men* and many more.

Mike did most of the voices while Mo played most of the musical instruments and, with the help of guest musicians and actors, The Wagsmiths produced a string of novelty singles including the U.K. top twenty hit, 'Chalk Dust', which they credited to The Brat (with Roger Kitter posing as The Brat).

Amongst the memorable TV performances was 'The Papadum Song' which struck a chord with anyone (i.e. everyone) who had ever had a few drinks and gone out for an Indian meal.

For a giggle, Mo and Mike sang the song on Blue Peter, though they nearly had to hand back their Blue Peter badges when inadvertently singing "fuck" instead of "duck" during the rehearsal.

Fifteen tracks (plus five bonuses) provide for a good hour of laughter and gentle, witty humour.

Review for *Make Tea Not War*: SPJCD149

"Although it's not your conventional sort of album, it's great fun."
Lister, *Modern Dance* (August 2004)

See also Mo Foster, Ice, Mike d'Abo, RMS, Ray Russell, Survivors, Fancy.

WARHORSE

"In many ways the music is just as innovative and forward looking as other bands with a similar approach from that era, such as Purple and Black Sabbath...it is actually very pleasant listening and would appeal to fans who still enjoy those bands' music from that era..."

Bernard Law, *Wondrous Stories* (November 1999)

Ged Peck - *guitar*

Mac Poole - *drums*

Ashley Holt - *lead vocal*

Frank Wilson - *organ & piano*

Nick Simper - *bass guitar*

At the beginning of the Seventies, a number of bands were threatening to be the next big thing as progressive rock gave way to heavy rock. Warhorse was a front runner, boasting massive amounts of talent, terrific song writers and a phenomenally successful bassist!

The band was formed in 1969 by Nick Simper.

Prior to this, Nick had kicked off his career as a member of Johnny Kidd And The Pirates. This was in the post Spence/Farley/Green era.

Kidd had been going through some tough times and enjoyed a new lease of life with his New Pirates (as they became known). In so much as Simper shared in Kidd's joy, he was also present at the very end of his career. On 7th October 1966, Nick and Johnny were passengers in a car that was taking them back from a gig. The car was in a collision, tragically killing Johnny Kidd. Nick suffered torn muscles and lacerations.

Nick recovered and resurrected his career, co-founding Deep Purple. He played on the first three albums, toured America extensively and shared in the joy of having five consecutive releases in the American charts…at the same time. The members of Deep Purple were superstars and few bands were bigger at the time.

In 1969, Nick decided to form his own band. Recruiting Rick Wakeman on keyboards, Ged Peck on guitar, Mac Poole on drums and Ashley Holt (ex-Bad Wax and The Reasons) on lead vocals, they were set for a massive assault on the music scene.

Problems initially arose when Rick failed to turn up for rehearsals. He was eventually asked to leave by his band mates and was replaced by Frank Wilson of The Rumble. This became the definitive Warhorse line-up.

On the strength of a demo, 'Miss Jane', Warhorse secured a record deal with Vertigo, becoming stable mates with Affinity, Black Sabbath and Status Quo.

In November 1970, the band recorded their debut album on a budget of just £1,500. It took five days to make.

The album sold extremely well throughout Europe, particularly in Germany and as a consequence, Warhorse were very much in demand as a live act. But problems were developing within the ranks. Ged Peck was struggling to accept Nick as band leader and eventually left. A new guitarist was found – an unknown musician by the name of Peter Parks.

For the second album, a much larger budget was promised but part way through the recording process, they were advised that money was in fact tighter than first thought. They had to finish the album quickly and vacate the studio. The album, *Red Sea,* was released in 1972. It maintained the high standards set by the debut album and bore witness to a self assured and musically accomplished outfit. Disappointingly, it also proved to be their swansong.

Warhorse had fallen out with Vertigo and were touting around for a new label. Mac Poole had left to join Gong and was replaced by Barney James. The sound of the band was also changing, with heavy rock giving way to a more funky edge.

Hope came in the form of Warner Records who were keen to sign Warhorse. Had a handshake been enough, their future would have been secured. However, the dawning of the oil crisis in 1973 sent Warner into a tail spin and they withdrew from the deal before pen had been put to paper. Indeed, the crisis had major ramifications throughout the record industry which suffered horribly due to the lack of vinyl. It was a dark time for the labels, song writers, publishers and musicians, all of whom relied upon the sale of albums and singles for a living.

Warhorse managed to secure an offer of a deal from a subsidiary of Tamla Motown but by this time, it was all over. Ashley Holt and new boy Barney James joined Rick Wakeman's band.

Warhorse failed to fulfil their potential and this is regretted by band members. They were a prime example of an early Seventies heavy rock band and should have achieved so much more.

Angel Air has pulled the usual metaphorical rabbit out of the hat by releasing both albums with a stack of bonus tracks, all of which maintain the same high standards as the original albums.

At the turn of the Century, the four original members of Warhorse came together for a few low key shows, which, through word of mouth, were packed to the rafters. One such show was recorded and remains in the vaults awaiting a bit of love and attention (how about it Mr. Purnell?)

Nick Simper can still be seen on stage with The Good Old Boys. They play a variety of popular numbers and can often be found supporting charity events.

Reviews for *Warhorse*: SPJCD034

"Angel Air continues to release material by 'obscure' artists, all superbly packaged with extensive sleeve notes explaining what great contributions these acts have made to rock history...The surprising aspect of this release is that the music is rather good.

Warhorse's debut LP mixed lots of Hammond organ and drum rolls with both rough and operatic vocals. Five bonus tracks (four live) and copious sleeve notes from Simper complete the package. *Red Sea* continued the formula, with plenty of fuzz guitar and keys, plus a more melodic approach than some of their contemporaries. Yet more unreleased live and demo tracks are again included...it's easy to see why these original LPs have such a hefty price-tag."

Joe Gleesin, *Record Collector* (January 2000)

"...Not only for nostalgic value or family tree ties, these albums would, and should, sit next to your Purple collection, excellent stuff, and once again thanks to Angel Air."

SC Rocks(April 2000)

Reviews for *Red Sea*: SPJCD035

"...there is a certain freshness here that other progressive classics of the time have lost...Highly recommended."

Zabadak

"...an ultimate hard rock group...with exciting, vibrating instrumental-approach with lots of keyboards and full-hearted vocals."

Psychedelic, No.9 (December 2001)

With thanks to Philip S.Walker and Nick Simper. www.nicksimper.com

See also Fandango, Quatermass II.

JOHNNY WARMAN

"...a perfect document of synthesised future think, daydreaming of robots, Martians and lost radio signals...a must-find for fans of Gary Numan and Thomas Dolby."

John M. James, *Positively Yeah Yeah Yeah* (November 2002)

Johnny Warman was always destined to be a singer from an early age. As a young boy growing up in Bethnal Green, he took great joy listening to his mother singing to him and in turn, she encouraged him with his musical career. As a young lad, he was part of the school choir that sang alongside Maria Callas and Tito Gobbi at the Royal Opera House, Covent Garden.

Johnny's recruitment into the band Bearded Lady has been documented earlier in this book. They earned a reputation throughout the early Seventies as a great gigging band, but only released one single during that time.

During the history of Bearded Lady, Johnny held down a full time job so he could support his wife and two daughters, Zowie and Tammy.

Following the demise of the band, Johnny made a resolution that he would go solo. He recorded three tracks and took them to Arista Records, who passed on them. However, Ringo Starr's label, Ring'O Records liked them and signed him up. For Johnny, a huge Beatles fan, this was pure heaven. He was given £3,000 to record an album, another £3,000 for the publishing, a Christmas tree in a pot and two cases of lager!

Johnny recorded his debut album *Hour Glass* at Tittenhurst Park, Ringo's home (it was also where Midnight Flyer recorded their album). It was a very special experience for him. He could choose his own producer and was under no pressure. A cook ensured that everyone was well fed and the experience generated a host of happy and cherished memories for Johnny and his family.

Disappointingly, the album was not a great commercial success.

Johnny went on to form a band called Three Minutes, which imploded after a very short time. However, they managed to complete two tours, with XTC and The Vapors respectively.

He then signed a record deal with Elton John's Rocket Records. Using material written for Three Minutes, he pulled together an outstanding album, *Walking Into Mirrors,* reminiscent of early Ultravox and sported a futuristic theme.

The album failed to make any great impact in the U.K. but launched Johnny to stardom throughout Europe and Australia, selling 100,000 copies and hitting the top twenty in most European countries. The single, 'Screaming Jets' (which featured Peter Gabriel), sold 76,000 copies and reached number 9 in the Australian charts. Johnny fulfilled a string of television and performing engagements throughout Europe and was regularly mobbed by adoring fans. He was always given a reality check upon his return home, strolling off the plane and through the airport without being recognised!

Incidentally, the Australian band, Screaming Jets, lifted their band name from Johnny's song.

Johnny describes his third album, *From the Jungle To The New Horizons* "…as an audio picture plotting man's progress from 'Apeman to Spaceman' and beyond". It remains a work he is extremely proud of and features an original interpretation of Norman Greenbaum's 'Spirit In The Sky'.

The album failed to make the same impact as its predecessor.

All three albums have been re-released by Angel Air along with a Bearded Lady collection. Each release is jammed with extra tracks.

It is still possible to catch Johnny Warman live in concert, in various guises.

Reviews for *Hour Glass*: SPJCD183

"..this is a sterling piece of work that was criminally undervalued at the time, and deserves to be reappraised today...high quality songs to provide a sound with echoes of classic Small Faces and early Seventies Pretty Things, Tubeway Army and a touch of Steve Harley...A true lost gem."
Record Collector (August 2005)

"*Hour Glass,* while retaining the short, sharp, almost Jam influenced post punk feel, is somewhat more eclectic than your average New Wave effort; yet is best appreciated in that context of the time."
Pete Feenstra. *www.getreadytorock.com* (July 2005)

Reviews for *Walking Into Mirrors*: SPJCD127

"The music is very rich and deep with so much going on you can't take it all in by listening to it once, it just gets better and better the more times you hear it...Excellent album."
Modern Dance, Issue 43 (January 2003)

"…a vital slice of electro-rock history…Across eleven tracks, *Walking Into Mirrors* still stands as a brittle, vital reminder of the fears that were part and parcel of the early Ronald Regan/Margaret Thatcher years, built around a chromatic sonic landscape that is as electrifying as it is evocative…"
Dave Thompson, *Goldmine* 27.12.02

Reviews for *From The Jungle To The New Horizons*: SPJCD170

"Originally released in 1985...Stage theatricals were part of his performance and some of the songs could be likened to David Bowie too...seven bonus tracks with informative sleeve notes by Johnny Warman ."
Alistair Flynn, *Classic Rock Society* (August 2004)

"...exists within a distinctly Gabriel-esque world of shifting percussion, uncanny synths and bizarre vocal effects...a unique and brilliantly individual artist who really, truly, should never have spent the last twenty years in such obscurity."
All Music Guide

With thanks to Johnny Warman. *www.johnnywarman.com* *www.themodsband.com*.

See also Bearded Lady.

JAMES WARREN

"...a set of beautifully composed and delicately performed songs. The voice is sugar sweet and just as tasty, while the music is incredibly rich and diverse."

Hartlepool Mail (March 2006)

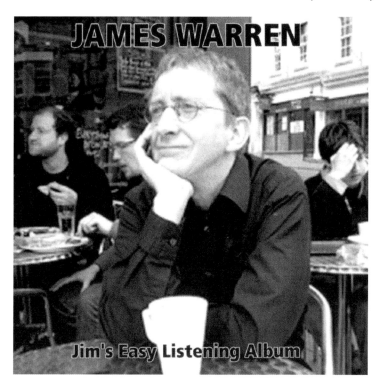

To fans of Seventies band Stackridge and its more commercially successful successor, The Korgis, James Warren needs little introduction. Indeed, if you have read this book chronologically, then you will be aware of his collaborative ventures and adventures in sound.

Aside from his two bands, James has been quietly ploughing a furrow as a solo artist.

In the mid-Eighties, he released an album on Sonet Records (the mother company of Mute Records) called *Burning Questions*. He was ably assisted by celebrated keyboardist, Nick Magnus (Steve Hackett's keyboard player). The album was not a commercial success and James admits to owning just the one scratchy old copy. However, Korgis and Stackridge fans will be thrilled to know that this has been re-released on Angel Air (SPJCD217).

By the mid Nineties, James was in the mood for writing more songs. Decanting to his Bath studio, he prepared a string of demo recordings, including a number of commercially appealing songs.

In 1995, he produced a limited album release for family and friends called *Jim's Special Edition Easy Listening Christmas Album*, which is now extremely sought after by his fan base. Through Angel Air, the album has received a make-over and re-release. The new version substitutes some of the original songs with more radio-friendly compositions and includes James' original demo to the smash hit 'Everybody's Got To Learn Sometime'. The album pays homage to his greatest influences – The Beach Boys, The Beatles and Paul Simon.

Sit back – listen – enjoy!

Review for *Jim's Special Edition Easy Listening Christmas*: SPJCD210

"It's a pleasant pop easy listening album...much more like his work with The Korgis than Stackridge."
Feedback (January 2006)

See also The Korgis, Stackridge.

OVEREND WATTS

The next section is the perfect opportunity to clear up a few myths.

We have met Overend Watts already as part of Mott The Hoople, Mott and British Lions.

So why Overend?

Did the young Mr Watts fall head first off a stage during a gig?

Or as American fans regularly surmise, did he earn the name through some sort of sexual prowess?

The answer is neither. Peter Overend Watts was christened just that…Peter Overend Watts. Overend is a family name which has been handed down over the generations and was once a family surname.

In the days when Peter performed as part of a band called The Silence in the mid-Sixties, he was simply known as Pete Watts. However, it was Guy Stevens, Mott The Hoople's legendary 'guru' who insisted that Pete should be known by his middle name, and it stuck. This is now his professional name.

So what about Overend's album?

When Peter Purnell heard that Overend had been working on an album, he allocated the release the prefix SJPCD050. So what has become of this elusive offering?

An explanation is in order:-

"I used to run a shop in Hereford with a friend and during quieter moments, I would write songs for the album and record them in my own studio. I no longer own the shop and five years have now passed, so many of the songs are no longer relevant to my life. I am also not happy with some of the vocals and musical parts. It is fair to say that the album is about sixty per cent complete."

Overend is also anxious that the album may actually be a success (though he is modestly doubtful!) He now leads a quiet life away from the glare of the limelight, going for walks and taking in the country air. He would not wish to lose the freedom that comes with anonymity.

Perhaps we can re-visit this chapter in 'Angel Air Is Twenty'!

DON WILLIAMS

In the spirit of Angel Air's philosophy that 'anything goes', the Purnells took the unusual step of licensing the Don Williams film *Into Africa – Live*.

Williams needs no introduction to fans of Country music. With 17 Country Music chart toppers under his belt; he is one of the most successful acts of his genre.

Don has also successfully crossed over into the U.K. mainstream, scoring hits with 'I Recall A Gypsy Woman' and 'You're My Best Friend'. His albums have repeatedly hit the top forty.

Don's career started in the Sixties with the Pozo Seco Singers. Since then, he has rarely looked back, striving to cover new ground and maintain an impeccable work ethic:

"What it is, is simple - I want the best songs possible. I don't look at songs as just singles or who the publisher is - I look at what it's trying to say, how it feels. Then when they're picked out, I want to treat them all the same. I want to make them as special as I can. Ideally, whether I'm in the studio or on stage, I'm totally into the story, or if there's no story, that emotion, that feel of what I'm doing at that moment is the only thing I want to experience. After a day in the studio or a show, the energy I've used just wears me out and if you're not 100% there, that's even worse. There's nothing more trying than not being completely there!"

In September 1997, Don realised a personal ambition by travelling to Africa. Through *Into Africa – Live* (NJPDVD618) he shares his impressions of Zimbabwe, from the breathtaking grandeur of the world famous Victoria Falls to the touching simplicity of local music students. Don's journey blends one of the most fascinating regions of the world (prior to the recent political troubles) with his first concerts performed in Africa.

Don has just completed a gruelling farewell tour, taking in arenas around the globe, marking five decades at the top of his field.

With thanks to www.don-williams.com.

337

WISHBONE ASH

"...If you never buy another Ash album, you should buy this one as it's truly spectacular."

Modern Dance, (Issue 41 November 2002)

Wishbone Ash have gone through a plethora of different incarnations over the years.

Hailing from Torquay, the band started life in the late Sixties as a three-piece called Empty Vessels.

In 1969, the definitive line-up was established and Wishbone Ash was born.

With Andy Powell (guitar and vocals), Steve Upton (drums), Martin Turner (bass and vocals) and Ted Turner (guitar and vocals), they recorded four studio albums together, all of which hit the top thirty and are generally acknowledged as classics.

Powell and Upton kept the band going throughout the Seventies and Eighties with an ever changing line-up. They continued to gig and record on an annual basis until the band went full circle in 1988, when Martin and Ted Turner rejoined.

By 1990, Steve Upton had hung up his drum sticks with Martin Turner leaving the following year.

In 1991, Andy and Ted were joined by Ray Weston (drums) and Andy Pyle (bass). This solid line-up lasted for three years and in 1992, they recorded *Live In Windy City*. The album was recorded on Easy Street, Glenview, Chicago on 24th and 25th January 1992.

Of the dozen or so live recordings that have emerged from Wishbone Ash over the years, this is regarded as the very best of the bunch.

Wishbone Ash are still going strong, fronted by Andy Powell who has been the one constant member of the band since the very beginning.

Reviews for *Live In Windy City*: SJPCD112

"This version of the band has no difficulty lifting the songs to the dizzying sonic heights expected by fans and the crowd that night in Chi-town were super-enthusiastic. The guitar wizardry of Turner and Powell – the requisite matched lead figures and awesome, uplifting crescendos – are still as tight as ever. For fans, this album will rank among the best of the group's past work."
Jeff Monk, *Mohair Sweets* (June 2002)

"The Seventies sound is mixed with AOR...But given the 'live album' appeal of such blues-rock bands, and with the classic *Argus* so well represented, this must please most fans."
Joe Geesin, *Record Collector* (July 2002)

With thanks to www.wishboneash.com (Andy Powell's Wishbone Ash). Go to www.wishboneash.co.uk for Martin Turner's Wishbone Ash.

PETER YORK'S NEW YORK

"...when these guys are cooking they are red hot...the result is a fine little jazz album."

Feedback (November 2005)

It is a testament to the versatility of drummer Peter York that he has three entries in this book, each covering a different style of music.

During the Sixties, Peter drummed for The Spencer Davis Group prior to teaming up with band mate Eddie Hardin in Hardin and York.

Peter moved on to The Chris Barber Band where he was happy to indulge his love of jazz. He learned a lot from Barber who was a magnificent band leader. Chris took good care of his musicians, ensuring they were paid a regular wage.

Peter went on to form his own band, called Peter York's New York. He vowed from the start to employ a similar ethos to Barber, ensuring that (where fiscally possible) he paid his musicians all year round.

He recruited three musicians - Saxophonist Mel Thorpe (a friend since the Sixties), keyboardist Roger Munns and bassist Steve Richardson. Peter was delighted with his ensemble:-

"The New York band was a nice situation as I had instrumentalists who were ready to do a bit of singing as well. The guys did a lot of writing and arranging, so playing with them was a lot easier than some of the rock groups I'd been in who couldn't read music. This way, people would come in to rehearsal with things written down – 'here's the chorus, here's the top line' and so forth – and would come up with an arrangement, which was a nice way to work."

They debuted with *Into the Furnace* in 1980 which was followed by *What's The Racket* and *Open Road*. The former has already been released by Angel Air, whilst the latter two releases are planned as a two in one package.

Peter York's New York were predominantly jazz orientated, yet refused to conform to the stereotypical jazz band. They were highly original and experimented with some beautiful harmonies and interesting lyrics, which ultimately caused promotional problems for the record label, Teldec as Peter explains:-

"At the time it was too jazzy for rock and too 'rocky' to go in the jazz slot...a crossover thing."

However, the three albums sold respectably well and the group regularly gigged, until they called it a day after four very busy years.

Peter York then teamed up once again with his old friend Eddie Hardin, released one further album before relocating to Germany with his family, where he still lives.

Reviews for *Into The Furnace*: SJPCD208

"This really is a jazz rock album and what really is surprising is just how fresh and vibrant it still feels...The liner notes are incisive and informative and the three bonus tracks sit comfortably with the material from the original release."
Classic Rock Society (September 2005)

"...The jazz is experimental in places, progressive in others but not too deep; it remains enjoyable. Touches of Focus in places. And as usual, there's a plethora of sleeve notes and extra tracks. Worth a listen." ***
Joe Geesin, *www.getreadytorock.com* (September 2005)

With thanks to Michael Heatley.
See also Hardin and York, The Spencer Davis Group, Ray Fenwick.

ZZEBRA

"Zzebra were at the forefront of mid Seventies progressive/afro/jazz rock/funk/folk…"

Feedback, (Sept 2001)

Well, we have now reached 'double zed' in our alphabetical exploration of the Angel Air catalogue. Since ZZ Top are not on the label, this can only mean that we have reached the end of our adventure.

Zzebra were one of the most astonishing bands to emerge from their era. Nothing like them existed either before or since. Merging an eclectic mix of jazz-rock, progressive rock and traditional Nigerian sounds, they were a joy to behold, both live (they had a regular residency at Ronnie Scotts') and on vinyl.

The group burst onto the music scene in 1973 and built up a formidable reputation as a gigging band. At the peak of their powers, they cut three albums on the Polydor record label – *Zzebra* (1974), *Panic* (1975) and *Take It Or Leave It* (1975).

Zzebra was fronted by Loughty Lassisi Amao, the driving force behind the band. He was joined by John McCoy, Liam Genockey (currently with Steeleye Span) and Tommy Eyre (also of Gillan and in the Nineties, Deep Purple).

Lost World is the fourth Zzebra album, which is dedicated to the memory of Loughty. It features a seven piece line-up, which (as well as the aforementioned musicians) included Dave Quincey, Alan Marshall and Steve Byrd.

341

These previously unreleased recordings salvaged from the vaults of John McCoy are a historical and valuable addition to the Zzebra catalogue. The musicianship is astonishing and the four live tracks included on the album are a testament to why Zzebra remained such a major draw across Europe.

In concluding this Angel Air A to Z, this album in many respects typifies the wonderful work Peter Purnell and his family are doing by offering such glorious recordings through their label, feeding our insatiable appetite for great music from a bygone era – preserving for all time these priceless recordings which in many cases, would have remained neglected and unloved, disintegrating in the back of cupboards or lost in dusty old attics.

Reviews for *Lost World*: SJPCD089

"...absolutely innovative, vibrating progressive hard (?) rock with lots of jazz, folk elements, extremely complex structures and brilliant musicianship...A very demanding, precious release, exclusively hot."
Psychedelic, No.9 (December 2001)

"...there is a sense of adventure the size of an interstate running through the band's musicianship...Eight studio recordings and four live cuts from a 1975 European tour catch Zzebra in audacious form, pushing *Lost World* up among the very best Angel Air releases of the year."
Jo-Ann Green, *Goldmine*, January 2002

See also McCoy, Gillan, Sun Red Sun, John Du Cann, Mammoth, Samson.

'TIL NEXT TIME...

I hope you have enjoyed trawling through *Angel Air Is Ten* as much as I have enjoyed writing and compiling it. I would like to thank the authors of the Angel Air sleeve notes for the consistently high standard of writing and research, which ultimately made my task so much easier than it may otherwise have been. I tip my hat to Keith Smith, Michael Heatley, Rich Wilson, Joe Geesin, Buffin et al. I have endeavoured to give you all credit where due.

Prior to writing this book, I was aware of many of the artists that made up the Angel Air 'family', although I was pleased to be introduced to some of the more rare and obscure gems that had passed me by (such as Springwater). I was also delighted to find myself listening to such innovative groups as Carmen, songs I had not heard since the early Seventies.

Rarely have such an eclectic and varied group of musicians been gathered together on one independent record label. This is due to the open minded approach of Peter Purnell who will give anything a fair hearing. Thus, we have progressive rock bands rubbing shoulders with electronica, rhythm and blues and punk rock. Hard rock and heavy rock bands stand shoulder to shoulder with the comparative 'new boys' who emerged during the New Wave of British Heavy Metal, which is admirably represented throughout the Angel Air catalogue.

Many of the albums re-issued by Peter failed to make a huge impact when they were originally released (for reasons explored in the book) but have since been embraced as lost gems by the music buying public. Take, for example, the re-release of Affinity's one and only album of the era, which has long since outsold the original vinyl pressing. Others were colossuses of their time, making a welcome comeback.

Peter will not shun a recording because it is likely to sell poorly. If he considers it is worth pressing, he will release it. This is a policy that few labels follow, tending to stick to the high earners or artists that are guaranteed to produce a reasonable return on their investment. By picking and choosing carefully, Peter can ensure that the big sellers (for example Mott The Hoople and Krokus) will always subsidise the more unusual and less universally popular releases, as Peter explains:-

"Some of our releases we know will be guaranteed good sellers. Others are real labours of love that we believe should be released and heard. Musicians by nature are talented and creative and we are fortunate to have so many satisfied partners that the word spreads and artists wish to work with us."

Perhaps the biggest public service provided by Angel Air is the release of material that would otherwise have rotted in attics or languished at the back of cupboards. As a consequence of Peter's infectious enthusiasm, worthy and much sought after recordings have been dusted off, cleaned up, remastered and released, saved for future generations. As you have probably read, these have included live recordings, shelved albums and original demos. It is often the latter that are especially prized, given the penchant for bands to suffer from 'demo-itus', where the final recordings sometimes fail to capture the spontaneity of the original concept or idea. He has also coaxed bands out of retirement, encouraged fresh recordings or exciting live outings, preserved 'for the record'.

Peter has an unwritten rule that the signing should be "over forty years of age" and you therefore have the unusual situation of bands being turned down "because they are too young" (enough to amuse any grumpy old man!)

This is in direct contrast to the major labels that seem to consider a musician washed up and out of date by the time they have passed through puberty! Indeed, as author and compiler of this humble tome, I only qualified by two months, having turned forty just before the presses rolled.

A good number of the Angel Air artists are now well into their late fifties and early to mid Sixties. Indeed, it is probably a reasonable assumption that the majority of them have given up touring.

One perennial musician (who recently celebrated his Sixtieth Birthday), explained the problem:-

"I am always trying to get friends together. Eventually we all synchronise diaries, which is never easy, and you KNOW that someone is going to cancel. And you KNOW that more often than not it is never for anything urgent - usually there will be something on television or they will want to walk the dog. It is terribly frustrating."

Make the most of these wonderful musicians – they won't be around forever. Some of them are still recording and gigging hard, like The Pirates, still with Mick Green at the helm. Bobby Harrison can still be found leading Freedom and Steve Ellis continues to front Love Affair. Maggie Bell and Chris Farlowe have recently toured with The Manfreds (featuring Mike d'Abo) and John 'Rabbit' Bundrick still cranks it up to eleven with The Who. The New Wave of British Heavy Metal is still ably represented by the likes of Jaguar, Graham Oliver and Steve Dawson.

Take time to explore the website links in this book and see what your favourite musicians are up to now – there will always be surprises in store.

Finally, take time to enjoy the Angel Air catalogue and savour the glorious treasures that have been unearthed by 'the Indiana Jones of the Music Business'!

www.angelair.co.uk

ALBUM RELEASES FROM ANGEL AIR

Cat Number	ARTIST	TITLE
SJPSIN501	V/A	Angel Air Sampler
RAJP901	Graham Oliver	Born To Rock'n'Roll (single)
RAJP902	Medicine Head	Only The Roses (single)
RAJP903	Korgis	Something About The Beatles (single)
SJPCD001	McCoy	Think Hard…Again
SJPCD002	Guitar Orchestra	Guitar Orchestra
SJPCD003	The Pirates	Home And Away
SJPCD004	Gillan	Gillan Tapes Volume 1
SJPCD005	Route 66	Route 66
SJPCD006	Mammoth	XXXL (reissued as SJPCD141)
SJPCD007	Ina Gillan Band	Rockfield Mixes (reissued as SJPCD166)
SJPCD008	John Gustafson	Goose Grease
SJPCD009	Eddie Hardin	Wizards Convention 2
SJPCD010	Musicians Union Band	Musicians Union Band
SJPCD011	Bobby Harrison	Solid Silver
SJPCD012	Mick Grabham	Mick The Lad
SJPCD013	Ray Fenwick	Keep America Beautiful
SJPCD014	Tee Set	24 Carat
SJPCD015	Steve Hyams	Mistaken Identities
SJPCD016	Hardin & York	Live In The 70's
SJPCD017	Ian Gillan Band	Live At The Rainbow
SJPCD018	Sun Red Sun	Sun Red Sun
SJPCD019	Eddie Hardin	Wind In the Willows Concert
SJPCD020	Doc Thomas Group	The Italian Job/Shotgun Eyes
SJPCD021	Spencer Davis Group	Funky
SJPCD022	The Rats	The Rise And Fall (reissued as SJPCD166)
SJPCD023	Gillan	Gillan Tapes Volume 2
SJPCD024	Eddie Hardin	Circumstantial Evidence
SJPCD025	MOTT	Live-Over Here And Over There (2CD set)
SJPCD026	McCoy	Brainstorm
SJPCD027	Freedom	At Last/Through The Years 2CD set (reissued as SJPCD175 and SJPCD177)
SJPCD028	Freedom	Black On White
SJPCD029	Mott The Hoople	All The Way From Stockholm To Philadelphia (2CD set)
SJPCD030	Snafu	Snafu/Situation Normal (2CD set)
SJPCD031	Krokus	Round 13
SJPCD032	Snafu	All Funked Up
SJPCD033	Quatermass 11	Long Road

SJPCD034	Warhorse	Warhorse
SJPCD035	Warhorse	Red Sea
SJPCD036	Verden Allen	Long Time No See
SJPCD037	Mick Ralphs	Take This
SJPCD038	Atomic Rooster	The First 10 Explosive Years
SJPCD039	Steve Hyams	Feather And A Tomahawk
SJPCD040	Verden Allen	For Each Other
SJPCD041	Fandango	Slipstreaming/Future Times (2CD set)
SJPCD042	Krokus	Stampede/To Rock Or Not To Be (2CD set)
SJPCD043	John Du Cann	The World's Not Big Enough
SJPCD044	British Lions	Live And Rare
SJPCD045	Saxon	Live Donnington 1980
SJPCD046	Blue Oyster Cult	Bad Channels
SJPCD047	Pirates	Land Of the Blind
SJPCD048	John Fiddler	The Big Buffalo
SJPCD049	Morgan	The Sleeper Wakes
SJPCD050	Overend Watts	**Not Yet Released (2010 maybe?)**
SJPCD051	Gillan	Gillan Tapes Volume 3 (plus free CD) 2 CD set)
SJPCD052	Mick Ralphs	It's All Good
SJPCD053	Andromeda	Definitive Collection (2CD set)
SJPCD054	MOTT	Gooseberry Sessions & Rarities
SJPCD055	Gillan	Live At The BBC 79/80 (2CD set)
SJPCD056	Bobby Harrison	Funkist
SJPCD057	Ray Majors	First Poison
SJPCD058	Mick Abrahams	Lies
SJPCD059	Five Day Week Straw People	Five Day week Straw People
SJPCD060	Atomic Rooster	Live And Raw 1970/71
SJPCD061	Mott The Hoople	Rock n Roll Circus-Wolverhampton April 72
SJPCD062	Stiffs	Stiffology
SJPCD063	Freedom	Freedom
SJPCD064	Igginbottom	Igginbottom's Wrench
SJPCD065	British Lions	British Lions
SJPCD066	Tommy Bolin	Snapshot
SJPCD067	Morgan	Nova Solis
SJPCD068	McCoy	Live Reading 1977
SJPCD069	Atomic Rooster	Rarities
SJPCD070	Saxon	Diamonds & Nuggets
SJPCD071	Love Affair	No Strings
SJPCD072	Morgan Fisher	Ivories
SJPCD073	Freedom	Is More Than A Word
SJPCD074	Mr Big	Seppuku
SJPCD075	British Lions	Trouble With Woman
SJPCD076	Ian Gillan Band	Live Yubin Chokin Hall, Hiroshima 1977
SJPCD077	Steve Ellis	Last Angry Man
SJPCD078	Records	Paying For The Summer Of Love
SJPCD079	Son Of A Bitch	Victim You WITHDRAWN

SJPCD080	Attack	Final Daze
SJPCD081	Mamas Boys	Relativity
SJPCD082	Gillan	Live Tokyo 1978
SJPCD083	Pirates	Rock Bottom
SJPCD084	Eric Bell	Live Tonite…Plus
SJPCD085	Graham Oliver	End Of An Era
SJPCD086	Atomic Rooster	First 10 Explosive Years Volume 2
SJPCD087	Love Affair	Live Edinburgh 95
SJPCD088	Luther Grosvenor	Floodgates Anthology
SJPCD089	Zzebra	Lost World
SJPCD090	Sharks	Like A Black Van Parked On A Dark Curve
SJPCD091	Medicine Head	Live At The Marquee 1975
SJPCD092	Canned Rock	Kinetic Energy/Machines
SJPCD093	Huw Lloyd Langton	On The Move…Plus
SJPCD094	Fancy	Wild Thing/Turns You On
SJPCD095	Medicine Head	Two Man Band
SJPCD096	Rabbit	Welcome To America
SJPCD097	V/A	Mod City
SJPCD098	Mike Hurst	Home/In My Time
SJPCD099	Mott The Hoople	Two Miles From Live Heaven (2CD set)
SJPCD100	Maggie Bell	Live At The Rainbow
SJPCD101	T-REX	Renaissance
SJPCD102	Steve Dawson	Pandemonium Circus
SJPCD103	Melanie	Solo Powered (2CD set)
SJPCD104	Atomic Rooster	Live At The Marquee 1980
SJPCD105	Springwater	Springwater
SJPCD106	Crawler	Live Agora Club 1978
SJPCD107	Buddy Miles	Hey Jimi-Tribute To Hendrix
SJPCD108	Minute By Minute	Long Hot Night
SJPCD109	Maria Muldaur	Live In London
SJPCD110	Verden Allen	20 Year Holiday
SJPCD111	Affinity	Affinity
SJPCD112	Wishbone Ash	Live In Windy City
SJPCD113	Sundance	Sundance
SJPCD114	Survivors	Survivors
SJPCD115	Bernie Torme	Live Sheffield 1973
SJPCD116	Stone The Crows	Live In Montreux 1972
SJPCD117	Linda Hoyle	Pieces Of Me
SJPCD118	Steve P Took	Crazy Diamond
SJPCD119	Gillan	On The Rocks
SJPCD120	Crybabys	Daily Misery
SJPCD121	Mott The Hoople	Hoopling – Best of Live
SJPCD122	Sailor	Live In Berlin
SJPCD123	Mike Hurst	Producers Archives Volume 1
SJPCD124	Crawler	Demo Anthology 1975 to 78

SJPCD125	Mike Hurst Orchestra	Drivetime
SJPCD126	Summer Wine	The Fabulous Summer Wine
SJPCD127	Johnny Warman	Walking Into Mirrors
SJPCD128	Maggie Bell	Live In Boston, USA 1975
SJPCD129	Broken Home	Broken Home
SJPCD130	Oliver Dawson Saxon	It's Alive
SJPCD131	Spencer Davis Group	Live Manchester 2002
SJPCD132	Rock Workshop	Rock Workshop
SJPCD133	Steve Holley	Reluctant Dog
SJPCD134	Ian Gillan Band	Rarities 1975-77
SJPCD135	Affinity	Live Instrumentals 1969
SJPCD136	Mick Ralphs	That's Life-Can't Get Enough
SJPCD137	Jay Aston	Alive And Well
SJPCD138	Gary Pickford Hopkins	GPH
SJPCD139	Favourite Sons	That Driving Beat
SJPCD140	Automatics	Walking With The Radio On
SJPCD141	Mammoth	Larger And Live
SJPCD142	Shev & The Brakes	Shev And The Brakes
SJPCD143	Crawler	Roots Chapter 1-A Pre History
SJPCD144	Honest John Plain	HJP & Amigos
SJPCD145	Affinity	1971-72
SJPCD146	Tygers Of Pan Tang	Live In the Roar
SJPCD147	Medicine Head	Fiddlers Anthology-Live
SJPCD148	RMS	Centennial Park
SJPCD149	RJ Wagsmith Band	Make Tea Not War
SJPCD150	Jaguar	Run Ragged
SJPCD151	Mo Foster	Bel Assis
SJPCD152	Gillan	Live Wembley 1982
SJPCD153	Bearded Lady	The Rise And Fall Of
SJPCD154	Desperado	Ace
SJPCD155	Ray Russell	Ready Or Not
SJPCD156	Mike d'Abo	Treasured Gems And Hidden Friends
SJPCD157	Mott The Hoople	Mott The Hoople
SJPCD158	Mott The Hoople	Mad Shadows
SJPCD159	Mott The Hoople	Wildlife
SJPCD160	Mott The Hoople	Brain Capers
SJPCD161	Mott The Hoople	Two Miles From Heaven
SJPCD162	Colosseum	Live Cologne 1994
SJPCD163	Mo Foster	Southern Reunion
SJPCD164	Greenslade	The Full Edition
SJPCD165	The Rats	The Fall And Rise-A Rats Tale
SJPCD166	Ian Gillan Band	Rockfield Mixes…Plus
SJPCD167	Affinity	Origins 1965-67
SJPCD168	Greenslade	Going South
SJPCD169	Broken Home	Life
SJPCD170	Johnny Warman	From The Jungle To The New Horizon

SJPCD171	Rock Workshop	The Very Last Time
SJPCD172	Mike Hurst	Producers Archives Volume 2
SJPCD173	Third Ear Band	The Magus
SJPCD174	RMS	Live At The Venue 1982
SJPCD175	Freedom	Freedom At Last
SJPCD176	Ice	Ice Man
SJPCD177	Freedom	Through The Years
SJPCD178	Ray Russell	Why Not Now
SJPCD179	Dave Davies	Bug
SJPCD180	Jan Akkerman	CU
SJPCD181	Mammoth	Left Overs
SJPCD182	Gary Husband	The Things I See
SJPCD183	Johnny Warman	Hour Glass
SJPCD184	Gillan	MAD-Glasgow 1982
SJPCD185	Medicine Head	Don't Stop The Dance
SJPCD186	Broken English	The Rough With The Smooth
SJPCD187	Andromeda	Originals
SJPCD188	Atomic Rooster	Atomic Rooster
SJPCD189	Mouse	Lady Killer
SJPCD190	After The Fire	Live At Greenbelt…Plus
SJPCD191	Dan The Banjo Man	Dan The Banjo Man
SJPCD192	The Look	Pop Yowlin'
SJPCD193	Roger Chapman	He Was She was You Was We Was (2CD set)
SJPCD194	Greg Ridley	Anthology
SJPCD195	McCoy	Unreal - Anthology 2CD
SJPCD196	Mott The Hoople	Family Anthology (2CD set)
SJPCD197	Deke Leonard	Freedom & Chains
SJPCD198	Midnight Flyer	Midnight Flyer
SJPCD199	Running Man	The Running Man
SJPCD200	Maggie Bell	Queen Of The Night
SJPCD201	Maggie Bell	Suicide Sal
SJPCD202	Chas Jankel	Chas Jankel
SJPCD203	Mike Hurst	Producers Archives Vol 3
SJPCD204	The Korgis	The Kollection
SJPCD205	Stackridge	Sex And Flags
SJPCD206	Tygers Of Pan Tang	Leg Of The Boot-Live In Holland
SJPCD207	Mo Foster	Live Blues West 14
SJPCD208	Pete York's New York	Into The Furnace
SJPCD210	James Warren	Jim's Easy Listening Album
SJPCD211	Andy Davis	Clevedon Pier
SJPCD212	Dave Davies	Transformation
SJPCD213	Korgis	Unplugged
SJPCD214	Ray Russell	The Composers Cut
SJPCD215	Chris Norman	One Acoustic Evening (2CD set)
SJPCD216	Consortium	Rebirth

SJPCD217   James Warren   Burning Questions
SJPCD218 After The Fire   ATF2
SJPCD219   Samson   Tomorrow And Yesterday
SJPCD220 Paul Samson   P.S…
SJPCD221   Bad Company   Live   Albuquerquc,   NM   USA   (2CD   set)-
WITHDRAWN
SJPCD222 Sailor   A Glass Of Champagne – Live (2CD set)
SJPCD223   Tony Stevens   Don't Blame Me-I Only Play Bass
SJPCD224   Big Boy Pete   The Perennial Enigma
SJPCD225   Carmen   The Gypsies/Widescreen (2 CD set)
SJPCD226   Mott The Hoople   Live Filmore West, San Francisco
SJPCD227   Paul Shuttleworth   Mixed Up Shook Up Girl-The Solo Years 1977-1980
SJPCD228   Stackridge   Purple Spaceships Over Yatton
SJPCD229   Carmen   Fandangos In Space/Dancing On A Cold Wind
SJPCD230   Stackridge   Stackridge
SJPCD231   Stackridge   Friendliness
SJPCD232   Stackridge   The Man In The Bowler Hat
SJPCD233   Stackridge   Extravaganza
SJPCD234   Stackridge   Mr Mick (2CD set)
SJPCD235   Stackridge   Something For The Weekend
SJPCD236   Racing Cars   76-06 30th Anniversary Concert/Love Blind (2CD set)
SJPCD237   Nobody's Business   Nobody's Business
SJPCD238   Affinity   Origins – The Baskervilles
SJPCD239   Phil Cordell   Heart Of Glass
SJPCD240   Diesel Park West   Damned Anthems
SJPCD241   Atomic Rooster   Oddities
SJPCD242   Slowride   Slowride
SJPCD243   Andromeda   Beginning
SJPCD244   Korgis   This World's For Everyone
SJPCD245   Racing Cars   Second Wind
SJPCD246   Maggie Bell/Midnight Flyer   Live Montreux '81
SJPCD247   Dicken   From Mr BigTo Broken Home And Back (2CD set)
SJPCD250   Mott The Hoople   Live Fairfield Hall 1970

DVD RELEASES FROM ANGEL AIR

Cat Number   **ARTIST and TITLE**

NJPDVD600   Mickey Finn's T-REX "Back In Business"
NJPDVD601   Hardin & York's "Wind In the Willows Rock Concert
NJPDVD602   Spencer Davis Group "Live In Manchester"
NJPDVD603   Oliver/Dawson Saxon "Rock Has Landed-It's Alive"
NJPDVD603N   Oliver/Dawson Saxon as above but NTSC version-all regions
NJPDVD604   Steve Ellis's Love Affair "Last Tango In Bradford"
NJPDVD605   Colosseum "Complete Reunion Concert 1994"

NJPDVD605N   Colosseum as above but NTSC version-all regions
NJPDVD606   Troggs "Live And Wild In Preston"
NJPDVD607   Culture Club "Live At The Royal Albert Hall-20th Anniversary Reunion Concert"
NJPDVD607N   Culture Club as above but NTSC version-all regions
NJPDVD608   Ian Gillan Band "Live At The Rainbow 1976"
NJPDVD608N   Ian Gillan Band-as above but NTSC all regions
NJPDVD609   Sailor "Live-Pirate Copy"
NJPDVD610   Hadley Norman & Keeble "An Evening Of Gold"
NJPDVD611   Roger Chapman "Family & Friends"
NJPDVD611N   Roger Chapman-as above but NTSC all regions
NJPDVD612   Mike Hurst & All Star Band "In Concert"
NJPDVD613   Go West "Kings Of Wishful Thinking-Live"
NJPDVD613N   Go West as above but NTSC version-all regions
NJPDVD614   McCoy "Large"
NJPDVD615   Tygers Of Pan Tang "Visions From The Cat House"
NJPDVD616   Medicine Head "Live In London"
NJPDVD617   RMS & Gil Evans" Live Montreaux"
NJPDVD617N   RMS as above but NTSC version –all regions
NJPDVD618   Don Williams "Into Africa Live" (NTSC only-all regions)
NJPDVD619   V/A "Hits And Angels-The Stowmarket Sound"
NJPDVD620   Chicken Shack "I'd Rather Go Live"
NJPDVD620N   Chicken Shack as above but NTSC version –all regions
NJPDVD 621   Bernie Tormé "Stratocaster Gypsy"
NJPDVD621N   Bernie Tormé - as above but NTSC all regions
NJPDVD622   Korgis "The DVD Kollection"
NJPDVD622N   Korgis as above but NTSC all regions
NJPDVD623   After The Fire" Live At Greenbelt"
NJPDVD623N   After The Fire-as above but NTSC all regions
NJPDVD624   Chris Norman "One Acoustic Evening"
NJPDVD625   Gillan "Live Edinburgh 1980"
NJPDVD625N   Gillan as above but NTSC all regions
NJPDVD626   Racing Cars "30th Anniversary Concert"
NJPDVD627   Stone The Crows "Live Germany 1973"
NJPDVD628   Diesel Park West "Damned Anthems"
NJPDVD629   Maggie Bell and Midnight Flyer "Live Montreux 1981"
NJPDVD630   Stackridge "The Forbidden City"
NJPDVD631   British Lions "One More Chance To Run – Live Germany 1978"

BIBLIOGRAPHY

Guinness Book Of Hit Albums And Singles.
Record Collector Rare Price Guide.

'WOTABLOKE' LIST
WE SALUTE AND THANK YOU

John McCoy, Ray Fenwick, Mick Grabham, Claes Johansson, Lawrence and Keith at L&K Graphics. Peter Taylor, Bobby Harrison, Eddie Hardin, John Gustafson, Peter Tetteroo, David Randall, Hans Vermeulen, Steve Hyams, Jennifer Banks, Pete York, Dale Griffin, Pete Watts, Mick Green, Karl Adams, Ken & Pauline Miller, Mark Nauseef, Benny Marshall, Morgan Fisher, Ray Majors, Roger Saunders, Trudi and Ian Hunter, Mick Ralphs, Verden Allen, Romek Parol, Keith Smith, Mike Lease, Steve Shirley, Stan Tippens, Micky Moody, Andy Gross, Nick Simper, Mick Underwood ,Bart Foley, Gary Davis, Don Airey, Lisa Bardsley, Thomas Fenn, Franco Ratti, Gunther Kutsch, Hans de Deugd, Dominic Plomer Roberts , Mac Poole, Nic and staff at SRT, Richard Ellen, Sally Hayes, Ashley Holt, Frank Wilson, Peter Parks, Campbell Devine, John Du Cann, John Fiddler, Nick Dalton, Graham Oliver, Steve Dawson, Sven Gusevik, Chris White, Tim Staffell, Bjorn Almquist, Joe Geesin, David Clayton, John Knowles, Neil Smith, Phil Hendriks, Vincent Ras, Steve Ellis, Tony Harris, Ian Crockett, Shaun Godfrey, Dicken, John Wicks, Hugh Gower, Jo Anne Green, Will Birch, Pete Barnacle, Martin Hudson, Spencer Davis, Eric Bell, Luther Grosvenor, Bob Laul, Don Maxwell, Mike Hurst, Mo Foster, Rabbit, Maggie Bell, Roger Chapman, Don McKay, Barry Newby, Rich Wilson, Tony Braunagel, Terry Slesser, Geoff Whitehorn, Andy Gray, Mike Gott, Barry Ryan, Terry Wilson, Polle Eduard, Anna Boogard, Maria Muldaur, Mike Jopp, Phil Cordell, Steve Donoghue, Brian Wakerley, Linda Hoyle, Kevin Mitchelson, Steve Johnson, Grant Serpell, Clem Clempson, Brian Bennett, Mikiya Okamoto, Reg Presley, Bernie Torme, Colin Towns, Steve Byrd, John Glover, Peter Cox, Richard Drummie, Chris and Jim at Alexander's, Darrell Bath, Honest John Plain, Bart Roos, Phil Pickett, Chris Furness, Johnny Warman, Justin Purrington, Ray Russell, Boy George, Jon Moss, Tony Gordon, Tom Hays, Steve Holley, Stan Webb, Tom Hays, Jay Aston, Gary Peet, Gary Pickford Hopkins, Bronwyn, Dave Philp, Tony Shevlin, Glenn Gibson, Ian Dennis, Rob Weir, Simon Phillips, Gary Pepperd, Joe Elliott, Jerry Bloom, Mark Wheatley, Mike d'Abo, Iestyn David, Jon Hiseman, Carl Palmer, Fabio Golfetti, Matthew Fisher, Dave Greenslade, Ron Kort, Thea Kort, Glenn Sweeney, Simon House, Dave Tomlin, Mike Marchant, Glyn James, Nic Pod, Tony Hadley, Dave Davies and Kate, Jan Akkerman, Gary Husband, Grahame Maclean, Peter Banks, James Devlin, Gus Goad, Mick Bass, Johnny Whetstone, Frank Rodgers, Pete Feenstra, Patti Ridley, Keith Stalibories, Alan Rushton, Deke Leonard, Ed Seaman, Michael Heatley, Nicolas Bouchard, Dave Dowle, Tony Stevens, Ant Glynne, Chas Jankell, Alan Robinson, Stephen Foster, James Warren, Andy Davis, John Baker, Sarah Brown, Gavin Robertson, Len Fico, Lars Olaf Erickson, Gavin Mulhoney, Richard and staff at SFH, Brian Parker, Rob Grain, Nicky Moore, Joe Sweetinburgh, Dee Snider, Marc Russell, Clive Burr, Paul Samson, Tony Morris, Glenn Tommey, Big Boy Pete, Paul Shuttleworth, Paul Fenton, David Allen, Simon Davies, Steve Elson, Joe Jammer, Jerry Franks, Michael Waidelich, Henry Marsh, Oliver Marsh, Peter Lincoln, Rob Alderton, Georg Kajanus, Dee Dee Wilde, Mich Serpell, Anne Pickett, Barbie Wilde, Peter Bryant, Chris Carter, Nick McCormick, Sarah Clark, Graham Head, Christine Head, Malcolm McCarraher, Richard Coombs, Lin Cordoray *and anyone else we may have omitted but not forgotten*!